Investing in the Technologies of Tomorrow

Discovering the Super Companies of the 21st Century

Gregory Georgiou

PROBUS PUBLISHING COMPANY
Chicago, Illinois
Cambridge, England

ISBN 1-55738-493-2

Printed in the United States of America

BB

1 2 3 4 5 6 7 8 9 0

TAQ/BJS

To my mother, Vaslea, better known as **Betty,**
a special person.

Also to the memory of my late father, **Pete,**
a Greek immigrant with his own small business
who always found time for family,
and somehow taught me to play baseball.

And to the memory of my late sister **Deanna**
(the way she wanted it spelled)—too beautiful,
too creatively talented, too smart,
too compassionate for here.
Thoughts of her outrageous sense of humor
can still make me laugh out loud.

Contents

A DAY IN THE LIFE

Oh, what a fight it was.

Their first. They screamed. It got ugly. She walked out. What was her last throwaway line? "Try virtual sex!"

Brother.

He'd been upset all day about the fight. First thing in the morning, the mini-diagnostic screen in his smart bathroom flashed that his blood pressure was way off the norm. His diagnostic system, hooked into the information highway, automatically transmitted the abnormal reading to his doctor's office and red-alerted the physician.

Later in the morning, the doctor called him on the multi-media, interactive, widescreen, high-definition television/computer/videophone and made a 21st century version of a housecall. After some comforting words, and setting up an appointment, the doctor's last words of advice were to stay away from the booze.

The man turned to his living room companion. "Mix me a drink," he said.

"The usual?"

"Yea . . . you're the only one who understands me, " the man muttered.

The service robot, endowed with artificial intelligence, deftly made his favorite, handed it to him, and said, "Alcohol is bad for you. You really should stop," and then continued to clean up the room the man trashed after the fight.

She must have programmed that last line into the robot.

He had a couple more stiff ones. "I'll show her," he said finally, and reached for the face-sucker.

He put on the head-mounted display unit of his home virtual reality system, and entered a 3D computer-generated alien cosmos of strange, sparkling minarets and towers illuminated by three moons. Screeching, bird-like creatures swooped out of the night sky and threatened him. Other humanoid aliens popped out of the extra-terrestrial structures and shot their light-beam weapons at him. He shot back. It did nothing for him today, and anyway he had to get to work.

He used the same virtual reality system to meet his colleagues from around the world in cyberspace. In the virtual meeting place they talked over, and walked through, life-like representations of their latest design projects so they could get a better feel for them than any exchange of blueprints could provide.

But artificial world or real world, at the moment he was cock-eyed. He excused himself.

Back in his living room, having never left it, he tried to contact her on the videophone. No answer. He tried tracking her down through the PCS (personal communications service) that assigned a personal number to each user. The phone number had nothing to do with location–it traveled with the user. No matter what area code they were in, you dialed the same number. Again, no answer. On the PCS unit, he faxed her a brief message of apology. He knew she was right, he'd have to make some changes.

But he also realized he'd have to talk to her personally. Soon. He knew where she was, but it was miles away and he hated to fly. But thanks to a recently constructed floating train network, he could get there by ground transportation almost as fast.

On the way to MagLev station, he ordered some genetically engineered, softly glowing, blue roses to send to her.

In the 20th century, the song called for red roses for a blue lady. In the 21st century, biotech-created blue roses may be the choice to try to help patch up an affair of the heart.

A genetically engineered blue rose will be propagated sometime in the 1990s, at least according to the companies involved. The blue rose may be a small footnote to the wonders of biotechnology, but it could still be a source of new profits in the new millennium.

Investing in the Technologies of Tomorrow means making money from floating trains, trash-talking robots, light-beams of information, and maybe even blue roses. While money is almost always on almost everyone's mind, the Third Millennium will increasingly be so. Amid the spectrum of expected scenarios for the new millennium — the utopias and dystopias — its best symbol may be new and emerging technologies.

In his 1993 inaugural address, President Clinton called technology "almost magical." Superconductivity and MagLevs, virtual reality, robotics and artificial intelligence, nano-technology, photonics, photovoltaics, electric cars, exotic materials, biotech, and utilization of space — those are just some of the almost magical industries and technologies that could dramatically change the way we live and do business in the 21st century.

According to the U.S. Government, *emerging technologies could generate global revenues of $1 trillion by the year 2000.* There are *publicly-held* companies working in those fields now. Many are small companies whose growth years lie ahead.

This book attempts to pick those technologies that could explode in the next 10 to 20 years, and names some of the companies that may be in the best position to become the next Microsofts, AT&Ts, or U.S. Surgicals. Whether you are interested in making a buck, or in the mysteries of the 21st century, this can be a guide to future wonders, and a brace against future shock.

Acknowledgment

Thanks to my colleagues Ted Bonnitt, Tony Chapelle, and Bill Tucker for their professional/publishing tips, and/or sometimes encouraging, often annoying, comments along the way. Special thanks to Stuart Varney — an early manuscript reader.

Thanks to Eleanor Sullivan of the New York Daily News who went out of her way to find out where certain cartoon syndicates were located.

My appreciation to Carol Anshaw, and to Kevin Commins, Kevin Thornton, and Probus Publishing Company.

Also thank you to everyone who sent me information, or granted me permissions, or allowed me to interview them.

MONEY, MADNESS, AND THE MILLENNIUM

"Take a look around ya boy, it's bound to scare ya boy,
and ya tell me over and over and over again, my friend,
you just don't believe we're on the eve of destruction."

— Barry McGuire, "Eve of Destruction" [1]

"The most beautiful thing we can experience is the mysterious.
It is the source of all true art and science."

— Albert Einstein

He shouted at the Devil.

Raging, carrying a naked sword and red crucifix, Middle Age millenarian prophet Thomas Muntzer incited his followers: "I tell you, if you will not suffer for God's sake, then you must be the Devil's martyrs!

"Don't be so disheartened, supine, don't fawn upon the perverse visionaries, the godless scoundrels! Start and fight, the Lord's fight, while the fire is hot ... don't let your sword get cold ... hammer cling, clang!

"At them! At them! And at them!"

Quoting Revelation, Muntzer attracted a rabid following of 16th century German peasants who believed it was apocalypse now, that the final battle between good and evil was soon to be fought, and they were willing to give up their possessions for the cause. [2]

Muntzer's words, so powerful, seem to have rippled from his forest glade down through the ages and exploded again out of the high-tech 20th century.

Compare the eloquence of Robert Tilton. Broadcast on KDFI-TV in Texas in 1991, the televangelist, gripping a Bible, raved, "The Devil would not be making a play for God's servants over the last couple, three, four, five years if there wasn't something God's trying to do ...

"But I want you to know something. I'm taking the sword of our television, bless God, and I'm telling you what God says ...

"Take that, Devil! Take that, Devil! Take that, Devil!" [3]

It had a twisted sales genius. With that type of thunderclap, countdown-to-doom delivery, Tilton apparently convinced his followers to send him $80 million annually.

Still, the Devil-Antichrist resurfaced later in the 1900s, again troubling some fundamentalists in Texas. It was then that the Oral Roberts Ministry allegedly made a desperate, written appeal to members. Apparently, the ministry was being threatened by "Satanic forces." The partial solution? Send money.

MONEY OFTEN IN MILLENNIUM'S SHADOW

Through the millennia, during periods of flux, economic and social chaos, when the "norm" was threatened and traditional values shattered, preachers, prophets and self-proclaimed messiahs often flourished, palms together, palms out. There has always been an evocative potency to millennial times, the specter of the Devil, cataclysms, and carnage, or the hope for a Golden Age, that has brought out the fanatical, the best, and the worst in people.

And money has often been the shadow figure accompanying doomsday times and thoughts, a lightning rod for millennial fervor. The Bible says, "In the last days ... men will be lovers of self, lovers of money."

If certain accounts are to be believed, as the year 999 A.D. winked out, Europe's night sky metamorphosized into a Poe-ish hell, "haunted by ill angels only," filled with celestial fire-whorls and blazing rapiers. Penitents saw the millennial signs, signs of the Antichrist, and listened for the final blast from Gabriel's trumpet. While churches swelled to their gargoyles with those seeking absolution, debts were wiped from the books, wealth was disavowed. In some regions, the masses became frenzied rabble and reportedly screamed for the death of rich men.[4]

Other modern historians say this is all a crock. There was no panic as the second millennium approached. No money-shunning, no rich-bashing. Which makes sense, as in those days there was no European consensus as to what day marked the New Year. Nor, in those days did numbers have much mystique. In fact, in Europe there were no numbers per se for recording years, only Roman numerals. So, 999 would be written DCCCXCIX or DCCCLXXXXVIIII or CMXCIX or something like that. It probably took all year just to get that right.

In any case, the year 1000 would be written 'M' — simple, but no countdown tension-builder, no number-magic. Nothing as millennium-inspiring as the zero-trifecta.

MILLENNIUM AND COLLECTIVE PSYCHE

But millenarianism often has less to do with dates and numbers and more to do with the collective psyche.

In the catastrophic 14th century, the shadow of millennium/apocalypse did fall on Europe. It was a time rife with fears of the Devil in the fold because of the Black Death, which killed 75 million, the Catholic Church's Great Schism, a 100 Years War, and "idolatrous" Saracens battering at Europe's door. It was also a time when money was non grata. Official Christian attitude stated that money was evil, the Antichrist's work. The Papacy condemned the new spirit of capitalism, calling it usury. The church quoted St. Augustine: "Business is in itself an evil." And St. Jerome: "A man who is a merchant can seldom, if ever, please God." [5]

Self-denying groups like the Beghards and the Flagellants, whose members literally whipped themselves into a frenzy, challenged the church's authority. The dancing mania struck many people, mostly the poor. Dancing themselves into a paroxysm for hours on end, they whirled and jumped and contorted and screamed out for release from the demons that possessed them.

The more average 14th century denizens did try to make amends with the millennium sensation via money. "When sudden death threatened everyone with the prospect of being carried off in a state of sin, the result was a flood of bequests to religious institutions," according to historian Barbara Tuchman.[6]

Money and the millennium. There has always been a historic convergence and psychic connection. Each ignites basic hopes and fears. Both have magnetic pulls, drawing out experts and eccentrics, the charismatic, charlatans and gurus. Both seem to touch raw nerves and perhaps even racial memories. Each has a mystique and mythos.

Money has links to Gods. The word money is derived from the Latin Moneta — originally a surname of the Roman goddess Juno, in whose temple coins were minted. Moneta also mean to admonish. To warn. Monster is derived from the same root. The Money/Monster. Something with great power. Something that comes with a warning sticker.

The millennium. It too is associated with gods, and looms with a warning, or as a beacon. A symbol for future shock, a turning point when the planet will either go down in flames, or rattle the bones and rise again to recast the scheme of things for the better.

Now, millennial times loom again. Many of us will have the chance to live through the one-in-one thousand chance social experiment as the new millennium already begins to tug on our peripheral consciousness.

A scan of the New York City phone book shows Millenial (sic) Entertainment, Millenium (sic) Financial Services Inc., Millenium (sic) Graphics Inc., Millennium Film Work Shop Inc., and Millennium III Real Estate Corp. The Hotel Millenium (sic) has opened in New York's financial district. Nearby, the play, "Angels in America: Millennium Approaches," is a hit. In late 1992, Fidelity Investments started the New Millennium Fund.

The millennium impact years 1999, 2000, and 2001 are obviously no longer a far-future inkling, metaphysical abstraction, or science fiction muse. They now stand before us, stark, as stark as the black monolith in "2001: A Space Odyssey" which provoked some sub-Sahara band of shambling proto-humans into semi-intelligence. Their little world of hunts and gatherings, food fights, turf and watering hole was disintegrated, changed forever by some product of alien intelligence and technology. In the 21st century, our little world may again be changed forever by technology — home-grown, but to some, seemingly alien nonetheless.

TECHNOLOGY OFFERS OWN WARNINGS

That very technology may add to the millennium furor. The rapid pace of technological change already causes some stress, confusion, and fear. It was, after all, $E=MC^2$ that lead to the A-bomb. Many of the technologies and markets mentioned in this book seem to provide their own built-in end-of-the-world scenarios. Genetic engineering loosing some mutant, molecular death merchant. Robots endowed with artificial intelligence plotting their carbon-based masters' downfall. Nano- or atomic-sized machines that self-replicate *ad infinitum* to ultimately form a world-suffocating "gray-goo."

"The Human Genome (gene mapping) Project may be nearing a conclusion by the 21st century ... and some of the more worrisome possibilities of biotech, combined with the millennium, and if the economy is in the doldrums, could create some increasing paranoia," said Dr. Maureen O'Hara, Founding Fellow of the San Francisco-based Meridian International Institute for Governance, Leadership & Learning.[7]

On the other end of the spectrum, some techno-weenies claim that interactive multimedia, virtual reality, and other human-computer interfaces will wire us into the 21st century equivalent of the black monolith, somehow sparking a leap in humanity's evolution and intellect.

The Third Millennium may indeed merit some special attention. There does seem to be a deadline, or maybe a bulls-eye, tagged on to the year 2000.

It's like a black hole, a portal that we may collectively be dragged through to a new birth or a near-death experience, into an unfamiliar elsewhere and, as Carl Sagan would say, elsewhen.

Some people suggest the year 2000 be pronounced twenty "uh-oh."

From the Fundamentalists, to New Agers, to Edgar Cayce's trance-prophecies, to some American Indian legends and calendars, the years around 1999/2000 are forecast to be history's finality. When, after centuries of dancing to some mad piper's music, of vicious give and take and wars to end all wars, humanity begins its final millennial march and chooses one path or the other — utopia or asphyxia, Golden Age or Final Days.

Certain prophecies suggest we watch the skies. Some New Agers expect the UFOnauts to save us. Some Andean Indians say the third age will start in the year 2000, and it will be the age of the "warp'ayog" — the winged people. History's Dr. Doom, Nostradamus, hints we should keep our heads up. He says:

In the year 1999, the seventh month,
A great king of Terror will come from the sky,
To bring back to life the great king of the Angoulmois,
Before and after, Mars (God of War) will reign unrestrained.

(Who in the hell the Angoulmois are is just about anybody's guess.)

In any case, July, 1999 — perhaps it's not too early to start planning that package summer vacation tour of the world's great caves.

WILL MILLENNIAL MADNESS STRIKE AGAIN?

Indeed, in November of 1999, one ancient herald of bad times will hit on schedule. The often resplendent Leonid meteor showers are due to blaze the skies. Against that background, sophisticated though we like to think ourselves, could some type of money or millennium madness happen again? With a snort,

From *Bloom County Babylon* by Berke Breathed. © 1986 by the Washington Post Company. By permission: Little, Brown and Company.

we think of a bhagwan, who told his followers to forsake their possessions while he kept a stable of Rolls-Royces. But in our minds are also burned the names of Koresh and Jones.

Of course, any millennium reaction could be magnified by the tenor of the times, the global social/economic conditions and geopolitical tensions. Also, many of the Baby Boomers will be about the age of 50, so you could have a lot of people running around facing mid-life crises as the century/millennium turns over. As for Generation X, if they're still called that, who knows what their reaction, or lack thereof, to anything might be.

Labels aside, certainly some segments in society, or individuals, may overreact. The con artist messiahs may multiply. The charismatic preachers are more and more likely to be at the fore, raising the specter of the Devil-Anti-christ, and the beginning of a literal Biblical millennium—a period of a thousand years, when Christ rules supreme. But not before a final, bloody, winner-take-all with Satan.

They will all have a mass market to play to. High-tech may have a part there too. By the year 2000, we face the possibility of 500 TV channels, some interactive and two-way, to choose from. Equally available, as the Rev. Billy Graham once noted, to religion and smut. A millennium proxy fight played out on multi-media, high definition television—the "sword", as our television evangelist Tilton called it. And there's nothing like a good fight to draw a crowd. Or hype. Or money. I can see an all-Fundamentalist channel, or all-New Age channel (a channel for channelers?), or perhaps even, since the last couple of years of the 20th century will probably generate a hype-o-rama—an all-millennium channel.

SPIRITUAL IMPACT

"For the average person, the millennium may have a spiritual impact—more reflection, celebration and soul searching. But the cultural attention on it could affect more strongly those individuals who are less "well" held together, and those who fix on symbolic things like numbers, or pattern repetitions," said Dr. O'Hara. "Also, you may have the same type of reaction found during the (1987) 'harmonic convergence' when planets supposedly were aligned, and many expected energies would be released, and psychic events were to take place. The millennium could galvanize, or be a punctuation mark to, that type of thinking ... and it's possible millennial-cults may appear."[8]

According to one forecast, in 1999, scientists, religious leaders, and governments "... may launch campaigns of education and appeasement to calm the general public, but psychologists predict that many people will complain of violent dreams depicting scenes of danger ... survivalism may reach its zenith

... residents demanding more and better fallout shelters from their city governments ... religious colonies may be established near the poles ..." [9]

Perhaps.

"The more the human environment presents itself as threatening and unpredictable, the more we begin to see a kind of catastrophic reaction in 'normal' people, the kind of reaction formerly seen mainly in certain schizophrenic and brain injured individuals," according to one psychologist. [10]

Perhaps.

Norman Cohn, in his *The Pursuit of the Millennium*, says "... the holocaust is to be an indispensable purification of the world on the eve of the Millennium. And one fact about the Millennium which emerges with great clarity is that it is to be strongly anti-capitalist." [11]

Again, perhaps.

But more than likely, from the hawking of "I SURVIVED THE 20th CENTURY" t-shirts and buttons, to survival-specialist companies selling get-you-through-the-disaster starter packs, to the planning, throwing, and catering of massive trans-world parties, the millennium will be strongly capitalist. For better or worse, that will probably be this generation's money/millennium madness.

As the Third Millennium creeps, then bursts, into the collective consciousness, it will offer itself up to a potentially huge market — religious, pseudo-religious, or otherwise.

Some of the millennium markets are a given, built-in.

Fundamentalists are already a multi-billion dollar market, including books, videos, gifts, and music.

The Late Great Planet Earth, written by the millenarian evangelist Hal Lindsey, was a best-seller of the 1970s. The book has a simple premise — based on Biblical prophecies, Lindsey concludes Armageddon will happen, if not in the years 1999/2000, "... within our generation ..."

For the fundamentalists, the millennium must come with a Day of Yahweh, a Day of Wrath, when the moon and the stars blacken, and the earth shakes, rattles, and rolls. The big sound and light show.

But a rival group, The New Age Movement, prefers to see the upcoming Third Millennium somewhat differently.

Whether they gather at the local New Age bookstore, California mountains, or Michael Jackson's specially-built UFO landing field, New Agers apparently expect, around the Third Millennium, some sort of vague transformation for the Earth, and for human potential — a "harmonic convergence" of man and universe.

NEW AGE PROPHETS (AND PROFITS)

Some New Agers may see the future through rose-colored crystals, as it were. But also with an eye on profits. New Age books, cassettes, videotapes for mind expansion, self-improvement and the like are a multi-million dollar a year business.

In alternative school catalogues, right alongside popular fitness video ads like "Buns of Steel," are offered entire pages of "New Thought" courses and cassettes, featuring titles like "Astral Adventure Guidebook," "Out of Body Adventures," "An Inner Journey Through Colors" (it's a beginners painting course), "Creative Visualization with Shakti Gawain," and "New Age Metaphysics & the Seth Material."

Channelers, their spirit name often trademarked, compete for new age dollars. For a hefty fee you can hear—actually hear—a space being, or a 35,000-year-old warrior-sage dispense sound bites of babble/wisdom through a contemporary medium called a channeler.

For example, Ramtha, Mafu, and Soltec have already been heard from. The last is a channeled space-being who once gave the following upbeat, cavalry-to-the-rescue assessment of the millennium: "Should you have a cycle closing out because of nuclear devices, don't you think for one moment that your air would not be filled with craft of all sizes … all of us … and I speak for every member of the substation platform … are all working on the exodus plan."[12]

Apparently, it's a philosophy difficult to resist. Channeling-related seminars, books, and the like, also add up to millions of dollars in annual sales. But the impending Third Millennium won't just mean a giant fire sale for a couple of specialty groups. Futurist and author Alvin Toffler reportedly once said he thought every major company will have millennium-related promotions, and whole new industries promoting the year 2000 may be born. Some companies and institutions are already gearing up.

- Twentieth Century Fox has reportedly already registered a new name—Twenty First Century Fox, of course.
- A new soap, Lever 2000, has hit the shelves.
- You can check your own phone book for the number of other companies whose name begins with 2000, or 2001, or 21st, or New Age.
- New York University has offered a course called "A.D. 2000 Plus—The Onset of the 21st Century."
- The Discovery Channel on cable shows 'Beyond 2000.'
- PBS broadcasted a multi-part series called 'Millennium.'

Along with TV and book publishers, expect Hollywood to cash in on the Millennium by going back to the future. There are films about Nostradamus and his predictions which could be big at the box office, or run over the airwaves. Expect theaters to run the Millennium equivalents of "It's a Wonderful Life" — science fiction visions of life in the new millennium, or further out in the future. But for the average working man and woman on the street, along with self-reflection, 1999/2000 will probably just be a never-ending search for the wildest, freakiest, party-to-end-all-parties of the year, century, and millennium.

MAKE YOUR RESERVATIONS NOW

You want a taste of the party-mania?

Many millennium hotel reservations for Times Square have reportedly already been made, and one young man made his reservation for New Year's Eve 1999 sometime in the early 1980s. For the Times Square-based Marriott Hotel. Which hadn't been built yet. He said he wanted to see the zeros flip over like an odometer, and he figured the neighborhood would get booked up quickly.

(Just to set the record straight — the Third Millenium officially, if not emotionally, begins with the year 2001, not 2000. This is not the place to really go into it, but in a nutshell — the Christian calendar begins with the year 1. There never was a year 0. So, the First Millennium — a period of a thousand years by definition — concluded at the end of the year 1000. The Second Millennium began with the year 1001. And so on.)

I already receive literature from an organization called the Millennium Society inviting me to join members at their December 31, 1999 bash — along with an invitation to subscribe to an investment newsletter. Another money/millennium connection. Times Square is just one potential party site. The society also plans to stage events at 23 other well-known places around the world, like the Great Pyramid and the Grand Canyon — one party for each of 24 international time zones. Some members may try to catch more than one party by using supersonic transportation.

So, on a larger scale, travel agencies should be salivating for the millennium. Madison Avenue will be in a tizzy. Survivalist-related companies, astrologers, and other soothsayer types should see banner 1999/2000 years. TV tabloids and talk shows, dating services, and liquor stores should get a short-term shot-in-the-arm. The list of businesses, organizations, and events that should benefit or take advantage of the millennium in one way or another is, of course, endless.

2000 is a U.S. presidential election year, and an Olympic year. Expect to hear millennium-related slogans, and much ado about new beginnings, transitions, and the future.

But other than an all-world hangover, what's in the Third Millennium for you?

Opportunity, perhaps, and riches.

We come full circle: "The coming millennium will usher in technologies that are already talked about with fanfare befitting the Second Coming," said one editorial.[13]

Blue roses. Robots smaller than the dot over this "i" that can enter your body and possibly rebuild damaged organs. Floating trains that move at a blur. The end of blindness. Clones. Bizarre alien planets whose crystalline and golden cities you can explore, see their dying red suns, and hold their last, tangled wild flowers—all in the comfort of your living room through virtual reality.

They, and much more, may all be possible in the 21st century because of new, emerging technologies. It may seem like Dark Age sorcery, but it's nuts and bolts science.

In a sense, with the late 20th century world-wide flourishing of democracy and capitalism, we are exploding out of another Dark Age into the millennium. Nanotechnology, superconductivity, virtual reality, optoelectronics and photonics, and other emerging technologies will literally re-light the pathways and networks of the new world order.

We may run into the ghost of old, hunched Diogenes on one of those luminous footpaths, still holding his dim candle, still searching for an honest

Reprinted courtesy *OMNI* magazine, © 1987.

man. Sadly, his search may be no easier or fruitful amid the high-tech glare. But we may be able to convince the old Cynic that 1984 came and went with just a clutched gasp, and perhaps governments became less, not more, monolithic because of technology.

AGE OF WONDERS?

Although there will still be many geo-political and societal dangers, and individuals will continue to live lives of quiet desperation, the Third Millennium still has the potential to be an age of wonders because of new technologies.

Former Soviet leader Nikita Khrushchev, in a black moment during the Cold War tensions, said he trembled to think of the possible contents of a scientist's briefcase. But it is within those same briefcases of such modern day magicians that may be the ideas and formulas that could change — hopefully, mostly for the better — the way we live in the 21st century.

A Gallup Poll concluded technology, especially automation and computerization, will foment the greatest changes in history by 2000 — more so than the economy, overpopulation, or politics.[14]

According to some futurists, technology may be the most powerful driving force of the richer nations' society and economy. And the role of emerging technologies will continue to expand within the Third Millennium's global marketplace and new world order.

While that new world order was forming, and the foundation was laid for the death of communism and the Cold War, the world was inexorably shape-shifting in other ways, being re-molded by high-tech.

The U.S. Commerce Department says, *"In an environment of intensifying (economic) global competition, deployment of technology is becoming the strategic battlefield of the international market-place."* [15]

The national development and use, or abandonment, of emerging technologies could determine the winners and losers in the global economy.

CLINTON CALLS TECHNOLOGY "ALMOST MAGICAL"

President Bill Clinton, who may lead the U.S. into the year 2000, called technology the engine of economic growth. In 1993, he proposed a multi-billion dollar effort to advance U.S. technology which could result in multiple government-industry consortiums. *"To keep the United States on the cutting edge, my job as President is to adjust America so we can win in the 21st century."* [16]

In his 1993 inaugural speech, Mr. Clinton said technology was "almost magical." Simply, if you were dazzled by the new technologies and products of the 1970s and 1980s, hold on to your collective hats. Inexorably, with or without government assistance, the portal into the Third Millennium will be shattered by emerging technologies and the economic revolution they could generate.

The Department of Commerce defines *an emerging technology* as "... one in which research has progressed far enough to indicate a high probability of technical success for new products and applications that *might have substantial markets within approximately 10 years ... or provide large advances in productivity or in the quality of products produced by existing industries which supply large, important markets.*"[17]

By Commerce's reckoning, emerging technologies will have a combined U.S. market potential of over $350 billion in annual product sales, AND A WORLD MARKET APPROACHING $1 TRILLION, BY THE YEAR 2000.[18]

MONEY AND THE MILLENNIUM

You can participate in the profits generated by those emerging technologies, perhaps become rich from them by, or early into, the Third Millennium.

The key is knowing which technologies — as picked by futurists, scientists, industry, and government analysts — are emerging and/or critical. And which companies — publicly held companies — are at the breach, currently working on and attempting to exploit those technologies. They exist now. This book will try to identify those emerging technologies and some of the companies.

It is the small, relatively unknown publicly held firms to be alert for. It's their stock prices that have the best potential to sharply gain by, or during, the Third Millenium. According to the Commerce Department, small, entrepreneurial firms often dominate emerging technologies. Somewhere out there lurks the next AT&T or Microsoft. Hopefully, the track can be narrowed.

But it will not, perhaps should not, be easy. The accumulation of wealth usually requires patience and foresight based on optimism, not speculation and schemes based on fear and greed.

But we hurtle towards the Third Millennium with all the ensuing rapid and unpredictable changes. It's been said that the future/universe/reality is not only more fantastic than we think, but also more fantastic than anything we can imagine.

Futurists Marvin Cetron and Owen Davies said that all the technological knowledge we work with today will represent only 1 percent of the knowledge that will be available in 2050. They add that there is a higher technology turnover rate. The time interval between invention, innovation, and imitation is steadily decreasing, and successful products must be marketed quickly.[19]

"I predict that within ten years, the mind will be man's primary energy source."

Reprinted courtesy *OMNI* magazine, © 1980.

The point is, today's emerging technologies that are expected to change the future may be suddenly superseded by something not even on the drawing boards—or in the synapses—right now.

The Defense Department refers to technology trump cards—to be played every five to ten years. Technology trump cards are defined by the Pentagon as something that brings "... about major shifts in how we think about and conduct war." Sort of a quantum leap with a war-whoop.[20]

Sometimes, whether for peace or war, all that's required for that type of shift is an insight from the everyday. Archimedes found it—"Eureka!"—while taking a bath.

DO YOUR HOMEWORK

The companies mentioned in this book may become duds, either through obsolescence or mismanagement. The burden will be on you to do your homework. You must order and study company financial reports. If you become a stockholder, participate in voting rights. Diversify. Stay on top of new trends in technology and science. Be alert for new products. Perhaps most importantly, keep an eye out for new, technology-oriented companies that go public. While there is always the possibility for big, fast, speculative profits, I'm sorry, but this book is not about getting rich quick.

We may have indeed escaped planetary self-destruction, but that doesn't mean, as the new millennium is joined, that you can afford to be blind or reckless with your investments. Entering the stock market carries the simplest shopper caveat: let the buyer beware.

Many of the companies mentioned in this book are small or in the development stage. Since the late 1930s, smaller, publicly traded companies with market capitalizations of under $100 million have done better than the S&P 500 by two percentage points.[21] But emerging growth companies often lose money for years, investing heavily in talent and R&D. Their stock prices can be extremely volatile initially, and they rarely pay a dividend. What you are investing in is the future, and the guts and genius of people.

It is the descendent of the same genius that conceived the brooding pyramids and Stonehenge millennia ago. But it is not mysteries that echo from millennia past, rather millennia future that concern us.

In "The Tempest," Shakespeare asked, "What seest thou else in the dark backward and abysm of time?" The same is asked of the dark future. Since ancient times, from the first sunrise to sunset, from the first awareness of seasons, humanity's been awed and confounded by the black bend of time. Then, as now, people were most concerned with throwing light on that phantom place, the future.

In the highly learned and sophisticated civilizations of ancient Greece, China, Egypt, and the Middle East, there was a tradition for both science and divination. Using everything from oracles to entrails to the silent sweep of stars in the heavens, the shamans tried to predict the future.

On the Salisbury Plain in Britain stands Stonehenge. Some call it the Giant's Dance. It is whispered that in ancient times, giants came to the circle of megaliths and danced to the ragged tune played by the winds screaming through the stones. It's said the giants, and after them, men, would use the layout of stones as a high-tech mechanism to track the moon and sun and predict the darkness, the eclipses, with computer-like efficiency.

In the late 20th century there are trade-marked computer programs that try to clear away the darkness and predict the future—including the ups and downs of the stock market.

Perhaps the future can be predicted. Einstein's Theory of Relativity and quantum physics suggest a quirky nature to time. Perhaps there are gurus and prophets who can, at will, tune into the future as an eternal present. But when it comes to your money and investments, don't bet on it. It is your own insight, intuition, knowledge, observation, memory, goals, determination, and pure hard work and research that are important.

There is an old philosophy used by many in the past to get rich—find society's next wave, and put yourself in front of it. There is also a Norwegian prophecy phenomena called *Vardogr,* where events are preceded by spectral sounds. For example, a door may be heard to open or slam shut before anyone actually passes through it. A door can be heard opening now—a door into the Third Millennium. You can step through now before others, and, using hard work, common sense, and patience, and by knowing the critical emerging technologies, ride the wave and perhaps become wealthy, and truly be ready, to usher in and celebrate the coming of the 21st century.

CHAPTER 1

SUPERCONDUCTIVITY

" ... let polar spirits sweep the darkening world ... "

— Thomas Campbell, *The Pleasures of Hope*

Granted, he was in a drunken stupor.

But in his alcohol altered-state, the hack journalist briefly touched poetry, and captured a piece of the future, describing superconductivity as an "... electric, magic carpet ride into the millennium."

Well, yes. Electricity and transportation are, in fact, two of the major industries superconductivity will affect in the future—which is to say it will affect virtually everything.

That was a former colleague speaking. What somewhat more sober scientists and analysts say about superconductivity are things like:

"A breakthrough of such a magnitude, like the laser or the transistor, that it *may spawn a whole industry or series of industries.*"[1]

And, "Could be like the discovery of electricity itself."[2]

And, "Could be bigger than biotechnology ... has the making of a phenomenal industry . . . *could spawn another industrial giant.*"[3]

And, *"Ultimately important enough to affect the balance of trade."*[4]

Some venture capitalists, who are putting their money where their mouths are, think they're getting in on "... the next great technological revolution."[5]

When you try to get a handle on superconductivity, to compare it against some more established technology, you hear things like, "... it's like comparing "Wagon Train" to "Star Trek," lanterns to lasers, Pong to Nintendo, and "M*A*S*H" to the Mayo Clinic."[6]

Obviously, something's going on out there. What's all the fuss? And what caused the media feeding frenzy in the late 1980s? After all, superconductors are nothing new. They've been around since 1911. Simply, superconductivity is the phenomenal ability of some substances, when they're cooled to very low temperatures, to carry an electric current with no resistance. *All,* or almost all, the electric power that goes in one end of a superconductor comes out the other. It's that zero resistance that has incredible implications for the millennium, and your money.

"In practically every use of electricity known ... the current meets some resistance from whatever material is carrying it. This is true in the wires of your house, the motors of your home appliances, the giant generators at Hoover Dam, and the transmission lines that pattern our skies. That resistance represents wasted energy," according to Alan Schriesheim, Director of the Argonne National Laboratory.[7]

Wasted energy means lost dollars and cents. But next to none — repeat none — of the electrical energy is lost in a superconductor the way it's lost in a traditional conductor like copper wire.

You've probably seen the pictures of a magnet mysteriously floating above a superconductor. But superconductivity will mean a lot more than that. Almost wherever wheels turn, motors rev, computers crunch, and data transmits, superconductivity could play a part.

"Superconductivity will be ubiquitous, and could benefit just about any electric-related product. *It'll be most prevalent in the TEEM — Transportation, Energy, Electronics, and Medical,*" says Michelle Zawrotny, spokeswoman for American Superconductor Corp.[8]

Superconductivity could lead to grapefruit-size computers that have the power of a $30 million supercomputer, crunching numbers at near-light speed. It could give anyone with a fear of flying a grand alternative — lushly silent, high-speed, floating trains. It could make your electric bill cheaper. And it may help scientists take a trip through a ring of fire on the Texas plains into a world of charms and quarks, and help them investigate nothing less than the nature and origin of the universe.

But let me take you on a humbler journey, down memory lane, back to 1986. Amid the tragic Challenger and Chernobyl stories of 1986, there was a less spectacular science story making the rounds. In that year, two IBM scientists discovered a ceramic that became superconducting. That was a first. Previously, all superconductors were metallic elements like mercury and lead, and metal alloys like niobium-tin. But those metals (Low Temperature Superconductors or LTSC) have to be super-cooled with very expensive, (economically impractical) liquid helium to become a superconductor.

How cold? By comparison, the polar regions would be balmy. What's needed is a temperature very close to absolute zero — about minus-460 degrees Fahrenheit. The need for that kind of cold apparently has to do with a micro-cosmic-type of battle for Lebensraum, a bizarre interplay of atoms and electrons. At more normal temperatures, vibrating atoms apparently jostle and block the flow of electrons. But that atomic bake and shake is apparently quelled in some materials at the Dr. Freeze temperatures. Thus the free-flowing electrons.

The ceramic superconductor of 1986 was a step up. It allowed superconducting at a warmer, but still very cold temperature. Unfortunately, it still required the expensive, hard-to-handle liquid helium to make the super-transition. But then in 1987, there was another breakthrough that tantalized businessmen, politicians, and scientists. If scientists can go wild over something, it was this. The scale of research became unprecedented. The media glare clicked on.

1987. Many were riveted by the Iran-Contra hearings, by Black Monday, when 500 billion dollars went poof on the stock market. And by baby Jessica, who fell down a well. It was the same year some scientists may have felt they also fell down a hole, into Alice's Wonderland. Because they found a scientific Cheshire cat — mysterious, bizarre, and astonishing.

At the University of Houston, scientists discovered a new variety of ceramic superconductor. What was significant was that it became superconducting at a, scientifically speaking, much warmer temperature — above minus-321 degrees Fahrenheit. Now, that may sound, and is, still extraordinarily frigid, but at that temperature liquid nitrogen, not helium, can be used as a coolant. And, as one scientist told me, liquid nitrogen is about as cheap to make as beer, many times cheaper than liquid helium. Doctors use it to remove warts.

All bets were now off. Superconductors potentially became economically feasible on a wide scale. In the span of just one year, superconductors went from pretty much a laboratory oddity to a possible economic revolution. From curiosity to commerce.

Since 1987, more ceramics have been developed that become superconducting at higher and higher temperatures (High Temperature Superconductors or HTSC). At this writing, the record high temperature at which superconductivity has been detected is about minus-220 degrees Fahrenheit.

Theories are out there, but unlike the LTSCs, scientists right now don't really seem to know why HTSCs work, but many experts think a room-temperature superconductor is just a matter of time. If that happens, the commercial impact of superconductivity could grow exponentially.

But media hype aside, there already is, and has been for many years, a moderate-sized commercial market for the old-style, pre-1987 LTSCs, primarily in the medical profession. That market is generated by another unique characteristic of superconductors — they create very powerful magnetic fields.

Low Temperature Superconductor electro-magnets are used in medical diagnostic equipment called Magnetic Resonance Imaging (MRI) systems, which are body-surrounding devices used to create a high-resolution, computer-gener-

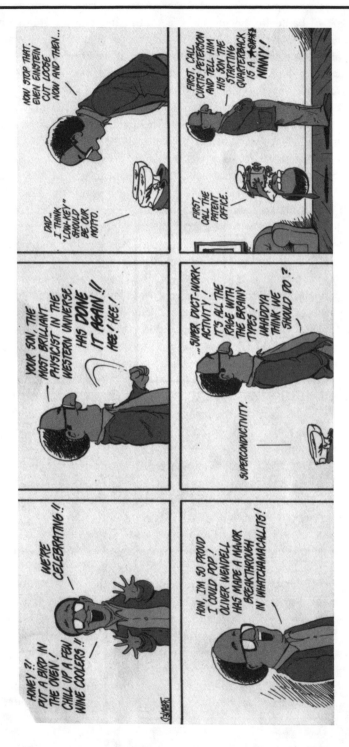

ated image of the body's insides. Using MRI, doctors can, for example, hunt down near-invisible tumors, which would have required exploratory surgery just a few years ago. MRI is more effective, and safer, than CAT scans.

But as you might expect, MRI systems are expensive—they cost millions of dollars, in large part because of that high-cost refrigerant, liquid helium. However, considering the cost, there has been solid market expansion since their development in the late 1970s, and worldwide demand is expected to grow. The market in the U.S., however, may be adversely affected by concerns about the role medical technology plays in the high costs of health care. According to the Department of Defense, MRI is a billion-dollar-a-year industry. A demonstration HTSC MRI has been built.[9]

There are also other very fine superconducting sensing devices which are used in the medical profession to detect electro-magnetic fields in the brain. That potentially could lead to early diagnosis of brain-related diseases such as Alzheimer's. The annual market for biomagnetic superconducting devices is estimated at over $30 million.

Other superconductors, in the form of wire or tape or thin film, are used on a limited basis in electronics or as magnetic field detectors. *SQUIDs* (Superconducting Quantum Interference Devices) which are used for some of the medical reasons mentioned above, can also be used for exploration of oil and minerals, submarine detection, and undersea communications.

Important though those uses are, the grand visions for superconductivity lie elsewhere. I apologize for all the acronyms, but get ready for another one. LTSCs will be used for one of the most extraordinary man-made creations appearing in Texas since the oil depletion allowance—the *Superconducting Super-Collider (SSC)*.

Call it an atom smasher, cyclotron, or particle accelerator, the SSC, using LTSCs, will accelerate atomic particles to near light-speed and smash them together, a process scientists hope will reveal the basic structure of matter, unlock the secrets of the universe, and ultimately help develop a grand unification theory—one that ties together all the basic forces of nature.

The more than $8 billion research facility is in the process of being built south of Dallas. It will consist of an underground, race-track shaped tunnel, about 50 miles around. The island I live on, Manhattan, is only about 10 miles long. The SSC is one of those Ozymandias-like projects that may still show parts of itself millennia from now, like the Statue of Liberty's head in "Planet of the Apes." There's no other supercollider anywhere near the size of the SSC.

The SSC requires 4,000 tons of hair-thin superconducting cable and 10,000—or about $1 billion worth of—LTSC magnets. It would be the first time quantities of LTSC magnets have been mass-produced. There is a possibility that HTSC electrical leads will be used to deliver power to the LTSC magnets.

As of this writing, the Supercollider was about 15 percent built, but was caught up in political budget wrangling. However, President Clinton said he supported the project. In mid-1993, the SSC was over budget and behind schedule, but if it passes the Capitol-test, it's expected to be on-stream and firing before 2001. (In October 1993, Congress voted to kill the Supercollider.)

Also sometime in the next millennium, superconductors may bring an end to a melancholy piece of Americana. For decades, small-town dreamers heard the distant, lonely train whistle, and imagined the adventures that must wait out there, and how one day they'd get their ticket to ride on the first train going anywhere. But whistle-stops may become, if they're not already, a quaint memory of the 20th century.

It was what the media went superconductor sound-bite and video-clip crazy over. The possibility of "flying" trains—high-speed, *magnetically-levitated trains, or MagLevs.*

If you have a long early morning commute to work, one that invariably winds up in hair-pulling gridlock if it's by car, or rickety bone jarring delays if it's by train, picture instead a luxurious, hushed, jolt-free train ride at 300 miles an hour—one that could get you from, say, Boston to New York in about 40 minutes.

The concept is relatively simple. A train essentially floats on a magnetic-field cushion, propelled by a computer-controlled magnetic wave generated by LTSCs. Germany and Japan have already built prototypes that hit speeds of about 300 miles an hour.

MagLevs cause less noise, weigh less, and require less maintenance than conventional trains. Because there are essentially no moving mechanical parts, MagLevs use much less energy than conventional railroads. Air traffic uses more than four times as much energy.

Japan is aiming to build a Tokyo-to-Osaka line sometime in the 1990s. There's no question MagLevs will work. But they're very expensive to build—estimates range from $8 million to $63 million per mile of trackway. Despite the high cost, it's a wave the U.S. wants to catch. A U.S. government report says that LTSC MagLevs are a cost-effective alternative to airplanes for distances of under 500 miles. MagLev projects are being considered for Atlantic City, Las Vegas, and Florida.

In 1993, the Clinton administration proposed spending about $230 million for MagLev development during the next five years, including $29 million in 1994.

That apparently is a come-down from an earlier administration's $151 billion transportation bill, providing $725 million over six years for the development and production of the first U.S. MagLev prototype.

Theoretically, it may be possible sometime in the Third Millenium to build a MagLev that could travel at 2,000 miles an hour in a vacuum inside a tube-like structure connecting major U.S. cities—New York to L.A. in about an hour and 10 minutes, no muss, no fuss.

The economics of MagLevs, MRIs, and the SSC would be considerably improved if LTSCs could be replaced by High Temperature Superconductors. But before that can happen, scientists have to get around the problems associated with HTSCs, which throw into question the potential size of the future superconductor market.

Right now, it's difficult to manufacture HTSCs into wide-scale commercial products. Bulk HTSCs have a limited electric current carrying capacity. They lose their superconducting ability in the presence of large magnetic fields. And they are relatively brittle, hence fabrication and packaging problems. But scientists around the world are working on the problems, and many feel they'll be overcome. Remember, HTSCs are just one step removed from the Kitty Hawk stage. They're still a very new scientific development and an infant industry. However, although the hunt for new and improved high temperature superconductors continues, products are being created from what exists now.

"Progress with high temperature superconductors has far exceeded realistic expectations. Experts are routinely making 100-meter lengths of HTSC wire with continuous improvement in electrical and mechanical properties. Further, prototypes have demonstrated proof of principle for several power applications, including motors and transmission cables," according to Thomas R. Schneider, executive scientist of the Electric Power Research Institute.[10]

Some of the wide-scale potential uses envisioned for high temperature superconductors are in:

ELECTRONICS/COMPUTERS: The guts of computers, which are blending with TVs and other devices, all use small integrated circuits or mirochips. But they heat up. Because superconductors lose no energy in the form of heat, cool SC-integrated circuits cannot burn up—more can be dense-packed closely together, which will lead to computers and consumer appliances that operate a lot faster and take up less space. Name your buzzword—interactive TV, multi-media, virtual reality—to advance they'll need faster digital computing capacities which could be provided by superconductors.

ENERGY: Superconductivity will be the foundation for improved motors, generators, and storage systems.

Conceivably, all kinds of motors, from the ones in appliances like refrigerators to the huge ones used in power plants, will become more efficient. More efficient motors will lead to cheaper electric bills for the consumer. It's been estimated that motors consume more than half the electricity generated in the U.S. Also, because HTSC industrial motors will be smaller, it means the cost of transporting, maintaining, and housing them should be cheaper.

According to a study by the Argonne National Lab, superconductors could make large electricity generators more efficient, cutting costs by as much as 60 percent. This would be possible because energy losses could be greatly decreased.

Underground HTSC power cables could carry as much as five times the power of equal-sized copper wire transmission lines. Also, you would not have false the fears of magnetic fields associated with overhead transmission lines. The global market for underground power transmission cable is about half a billion dollars. On a more local scale, underground superconducting wire could cut AC transmission costs by 40 percent, as a result of a 75 percent reduction in energy losses.

Superconductors may also be able to clean up "dirty power." Dirty power is the collective spikes, interruptions, drops, surges, and fluctuations in electric power. Dirty and expensive. Dirty power costs U.S. business some $12 billion every year. But a superconducting energy storage system could act as a buffer against dirty power. SMES (Superconducting Magnetic Energy Storage) essentially consists of refrigerated superconducting coils in a closed loop. That means a constant supply of electricity could be stored. SMES will be able to react to power fluctuations, by either sponging up excess power, or pumping extra power into the grid when there are drops or outages. Also, like a genie in a bottle, when we need more energy at peak demand time, SMES could come out. Superconducting systems would enable communities to store energy without loss and withdraw it at leisure.

TRANSPORTATION: (In addition to the already mentioned MagLevs) The U.S. Navy is in the process of testing an electro-magnetic propulsion system for ships and submarines using superconductors. The system effectively has no moving mechanical parts and would probably be quieter than traditional propeller-type systems.

Ships and submarines can also be powered by what are essentially the water equivalent of jet engines. With the help of superconducting magnets, water is pushed through a tube in the ship out the rear. The more powerful the magnets, the faster the ship moves. The Japanese are building Yamato-1, a 90-foot-long, 150-ton vessel that can hit eight knots.

Reprinted courtesy *OMNI* magazine.

There is the very long-term possibility of using superconducting motors in electric cars and trucks. The vehicles would be quiet, energy-efficient, and pollution free. However, there are many technical problems to overcome before that would become practical.

Finally, if America can ever get its space program in order, HTSCs would be a natural in the frigid temperatures of the final frontier.

Superconductors potentially could have many other uses in all types of industries. But, as mentioned earlier, scientists have said superconductors may well parallel the impact of the laser or transistor on society — in other words, superconductors will probably lead to many more startling developments than anything that can even be imagined now.

The future of superconductors is riddled with the potential for so many surprises, and X factors — especially the possibility of a room-temperature superconductor — that it's very difficult to predict the size of their market in the new millennium. It's like talking to the blind men who all describe a completely different type of elephant because they each touched a different part of the beast. But there was no doubt it was a beast. And there seems no doubt that superconductors will be a beast, a monster market. In the multi-billions of dollars. The question is when?

In the early 1990s, the market for superconductors in the U.S. was variously estimated by industry analysts in the $250 million to $500 million range. In 1993, the global market for superconductors was estimated at $1.5 billion. *But according to the U.S. Department of Commerce, annual U.S. superconductor sales by the year 2000 will be $3 to $5 billion. Worldwide sales will hit $8 to $12 billion by the millennium.*[11]

The Department of Defense—which could get annual funding for superconductor research of more than $50 million every year through 1997—predicts widespread use of superconductors in industry, academia, and defense by the year 2006.[12] In Japan, the Nikkei Research Institute think-tank predicts a $12.4 billion annual market for HTSCs in the early 21st century. That would jump to a stunning $85 billion a year if a practical room-temperature superconductor is developed.

At the Second International Superconductivity Industry Summit (ISIS) in 1993, it was estimated that worldwide superconductor sales would hit $60 to $90 billion in the year 2010, and that would blow out to $150 to $200 billion by 2020.

According to Alfred Sagarese, vice-president of Strategic Analysis, Inc., "the size of future markets depends on how the technology is accepted after key problems are resolved, and, then you have to consider new applications."[13]

Strategic Analysis predicts a likely total worldwide market for fabricated superconductor materials of almost $900 million by the year 2005. But under their best-case scenario—assuming eventual widespread adoption of LTSCs and HTSCs in applications currently not feasible because of economic or technology "thresholds"—the superconductor market will grow at a compound annual rate of about 28 percent, hitting almost $2.7 billion dollars by the year 2005.[14]

According to Sagarese, Strategic Analysis sees expanding use of superconductors by 1994–97 in MRI systems, bearings, Josephson junctions (which are essentially very fast superconducting electronic switches), computers, communications, and microcircuits. By 1997–2005 it predicts we'll get some of the more hyped, science fiction-type things—MagLev trains, energy storage devices, and superconducting power lines.[15]

It's the timing uncertainty that's holding back venture capitalists. According to a Coopers & Lybrand survey, 60 percent of venture capitalists interviewed felt that the financial return on superconductivity was just too far away. Most felt it would take eight to 15 years for full-scale, mass-produced commercial products to materialize and provide an adequate return on their superconductor investments. Throw in the high technological risk, and superconductors are just too far outside their profit timeframe.[16]

But a sizable minority of venture capitalists — 27 percent — were comfortable with the risks. Many compared superconductivity to biotechnology — the risks of the long-term development cycle and "blue-sky markets" were viewed as similar. They see superconductivity as revolutionary, one of the few areas offering them new positions and ground floor investment opportunities in a market with enormous potential.

Compared with the rule of thumb for venture capitalists — that they look to receive 10 times their investment — some of the so-called "pioneer" venture capitalists in superconductivity expect to get back 100 times their investment.[17]

Because the potential payoff is so great, the global race for new superconducting developments is intense. If you think the recent U.S.-Japan flap over cars is nasty, the fight for the superconducting market could be a real dirty brawl.

The National Science Foundation estimates Japan — which is usually willing to wait longer than America for a technological payoff — is spending $258 million yearly on superconductor research compared to America's $241 million. It estimates 1,000 Japanese scientists and engineers are working on unraveling superconducting mysteries, compared to about 600 in the U.S. Reportedly, one Japanese company alone has filed for over 1,000 superconducting related patents. Both the U.S. and Japan have steadily increased their annual funding for superconductor R&D.

The Japanese have encouraged industry/university/national laboratory consortiums for superconductor research. So has the U.S., among them, a joint effort by IBM, AT&T, and MIT.

Starting in 1993, The U.S. Energy Department was prepared to lay out more than $4 million in new money to superconductor companies that would work in tandem with the government.

But despite U.S. efforts, The Department of Defense said flatly: "The United States trails Japan in this high-risk, high-potential-payoff technology."[18]

Other regions do not want to be left behind. European countries — most notably the United Kingdom, Italy, and Germany — are spending millions of dollars on superconductor research — $50 million annually in Germany alone. Australia, China, Czechoslovakia, India, Taiwan, and areas of the former Soviet Union all reportedly have significant R&D efforts up and going.

Again, the world seems to recognize that the superconductor payoff does not seem to be a question of if, but when.

■　　■　　■

If you're willing to wait for the potential payoff, how can you get in on the action, and add superconductivity to your portfolio now?

Well, it isn't easy.

Although many blue-chip companies like IBM, AT&T, DuPont, General Electric, and Westinghouse have their own superconducting R&D departments, the effect of superconductors will probably be negligible on their bottom line. The same can be said of Japanese giants like Mitsubishi, Matsushita, Hitachi, and Fujitsu. Ditto for European companies like Siemens and N.V. Philips. Most smaller companies whose business is mainly or exclusively superconductivity and are privately-held. But there are possibilities. Here are some of the publicly-held companies that are pretty much pure plays in superconductivity. (Note: publicly-held companies listed in this book trade either on the New York Stock Exchange (NYSE), the American Stock Exchange (ASE or AMEX), or Over-the-Counter (OTC) which is also known as NASDAQ. The company's name will be followed by its exchange and stock symbol.)

Any financial figures reported, if not specified, apply to the early 1990s.

SOURCES

American Superconductor Corp. (OTC - AMSC)
149 Grove Street
Watertown, Massachusetts 02172
617-923-1122 Fax: 617-923-0020

American Superconductor was established in 1987 and went public in late 1991. ASC employs about 75.

This development-stage company develops and manufactures high temperature superconducting products, primarily flexible HTSC ceramic wires, wire products, and systems which can be used for various commercial areas including electric power, and magnet systems such as motors, generators, and power lines.

For the fiscal year ended March 31, 1993, the company's annual revenues were over $3 million.

ASC holds a number of patents, and has a European subsidiary based in Dusseldorf, Germany.

Ceramics Process Systems Corp. (OTC - CPSX)
155 Fortune Boulevard
Milford, Massachusetts 01757
508-634-3422 Fax: 508-478-0946

Company develops, makes, and sells advanced ceramic products for the electronics, automotive, and defense industries, specializing in thin film metallized and composite packaging for high-density, high-performance electronic devices.

Through its wholly owned subsidiary, CPS Superconductor Corp., engages in the development of high temperature superconductor bulk materials and ceramic wire for electric motor and other applications.

Company has been awarded various R&D awards, which recognize some of its products as being significant innovations.

Total annual revenues are about $5 million. For the nine months ended September, 1992, the company had a net loss of more than $1 million.

Conductus, Inc.
969 West Maude Avenue
Sunnyvale, California 94086
408-737-6700

Conductus was founded in 1987, and was planning on making an Initial Public Offering (in other words, would become a publicly traded company) sometime in mid to late 1993. Its stock would trade on NASDAQ under the symbol CDTS.

The company develops, makes, and markets electronic components and systems based on superconductors, primarily focusing on HTSC.

Conductus sells 'SQUID' sensors, and is developing various other superconductor components and systems for the medical, telecommunications, and computing industries. It's also developing superconducting packaging devices that hold a computer chip and transmit information to and from it.

For the year ended December 1992, annual revenues were $3.6 million, and its net loss was about $4 million.

Intermagnetics General Corp. (IGC) (ASE - IMG)
P.O. Box 566
Charles Industrial Park
New Karner Road
Guilderland, New York 12084
518-456-5456 Fax: 518-456-0028

IGC has been in business since the 1970s. It's a leading producer of LTSC wire and magnet systems, especially those used in MRIs. It also supplies ultra-low temperature, or cryogenic, refrigeration equipment.

The company is also conducting R&D in HTSCs, and it may be well-positioned to grab the lead in market share for HTSCs, if and when they become practical.

IGC has been profitable, and its annual sales are about $60 million.

In 1992, an IGC unit was awarded a $3.3 million qualification contract by the Superconducting Supercollider Laboratory to develop superconducting cable for the Texas Supercollider. As of this writing, the fate of the supercollider was still in the hands of Congress as part of the budget process.

The SSC could mean millions of dollars in additional revenues for IGC.

Additionally, IGC recently signed a second contract with the U.S. Navy to develop an underwater engine for vessels that makes use of superconductors. And the company started work on a program, jointly funded by the U.S. Department of Transportation and New York State, to develop a conceptual design of a superconducting motor for use in MagLevs.

Superconductor Technologies, Inc. (OTC - SCON)
460 West Drive
Santa Barbara, California 93111
805-683-7646

This development stage company was established in 1987, and went public in March, 1993.

The company is engaged in R&D on advanced electronic products incorporating high temperature superconductor materials. Using proprietary processes and technologies, it hopes to develop HTSC electronic components for the medical (Magnetic Resonance Imaging), cellular communications, and high speed computer markets.

In its prospectus, the company said it has incurred net losses each year since its inception, and it will be several years before it can generate significant revenues from commercial sales of HTSC products.

For the year ended December, 1992 its net loss was over $2 million.

XSIRIUS, Inc. (OTC - XSIR)
1110 North Glebe Road
Arlington, Virginia 22201
703-522-8601 Fax: 703-522-0710

Xsirius is engaged in the business of identifying, developing, and commercializing cutting-edge technologies in a variety of areas. Through its related company, XSIRIUS Superconductivity, Inc. (OTC-XSCI), at the same address, it engages in R&D of commercial applications of high temperature superconductivity.

The company has won some federal contracts, and collaborates with the Los Alamos National Laboratory and the University of Massachusetts Lowell Research Foundation.

XSIRIUS Superconductivity's annual revenues in 1992 were less than $1 million.

To stay on top of developments in superconductivity you can contact one of the following:

Superconductor Applications Association
27692 Deputy Circle
Laguna Hills, California 92653
800-854-8263

Council on Superconductivity for American Competitiveness
1050 Thomas Jefferson Street, NW
Washington, D.C. 20007
202-965-4070

'Superconductor Industry'
Rodman Publishing Company
17 South Franklin Turnpike
P.O. Box 555
Ramsey, New Jersey 07466
201-825-2552

'Superconductor Week'
Atlantic Information Services
1050 17th Street, NW
Washington, D.C. 20036
202-775-9008

VIRTUAL REALITY

"A wild weird clime that lieth, sublime,
Out of space — Out of time."

— Edgar Allen Poe, "Dreamland"

"Cyberspace: A concensual hallucination experienced daily
by billions ... a graphic representation of data abstracted
from the banks of every computer in the human system.
Unthinkable complexity. Lines of light ranged in the nonspace
of the mind, clusters and constellations of data.
Like city lights, receding ... "

— William Gibson, *Neuromancer* [1]

All right, let's get it out of the way quickly. Yes, someday you may, *may,* be able to simulate sex something-like-the-real-thing with virtual reality. There's even a word for virtual sex — "teledildonics." More on this important development later.

You're burning rubber, doing hog-wild wheelies with your cycle on the rings of Saturn until your momentum flings you off into the void of space. You fly, tailgate a comet's silver tail, race through an armada of alien spacecraft, all the while dodging their laser-like weapons. Ahead, a familiar form drifts into view. Your lover joins you, and together you float between the blue and red suns of a distant solar system, then surf on their turbulent solar winds until you land on a nearby planet. You explore the ruined, crystalline city of an ancient civilization, bathed in the light of three moons. You dance through its statuary and your bodies take the strange shape of those former alien inhabitants. In that

exotic form, you fly down to the wild seashore and make love in the lumines-
cent sand until the waves wash over you and drag you, not into the sea, but
back into space where you spin breathless through a black hole and emerge . . .
in the comfort of your living room. Mini-vacation over. This could be possible
one day with virtual reality.

Voice-over Rod Serling ...

Virtual reality is part "... you are entering another dimension," part a trip
through the looking glass, part weird science, part hard science, and part bud-
ding industry whose dollar potential could become, well, unreal.

Virtual reality (VR) has been called electronic LSD, a 21st century version of tune-in, turn-on, and drop out all rolled up in one by way of computer-
generated worlds. VR, it's said, could make human "cocooning" a plague. And
some VR watchers have gone so far as to say that virtual reality will be a
human chrysalis-stage that will lead to the transformation of homo sapiens.

All that was an introduction to virtual reality, and to the hype that surrounds it. But hype aside, understand that right now VR is being used for some
very real applications, including education, design, and helping the disabled.

Virtual reality's intent is to make you feel as though you've been bodily
transported into another world. It's submersion into a colorful, wrap-around,
3-D world whose environment is created by computers.

In the so-called *cyberspace* of VR, you'll see, hear, and eventually feel
and perhaps smell and taste the artificial world around you. VR brings to mind
the "All-Super Singing, Synthetic Talking, Colored, Stereoscopic Feely," in
Brave New World.

Although the technology and business of virtual reality are in the incuba-
tion stages, its economic and perhaps social consequences could be enormous
sometime in the Third Millennium.

The President's Office of Science and Technology has been commissioned
to assess the importance of VR for America. Its Group on Virtual Reality Technology, made up of 15 federal agencies, sees VR having future significance for
digital databases, medicine, rehabilitation, training, enhancements for senior
citizens, and entertainment. In the Group's 1993 preliminary conclusion there
was, however, one statement that some in the industry found potentially chill-
ing: "... VR is too important to the nation to continue its unstructured research
and development."[2] Some think that if you read between the lines, that could
mean the government will essentially wind up quashing innovations from the
small start-ups that essentially fueled the personal computer industry. And VR
may be on the verge of just such a PC explosion.

*"Virtual reality is at the equivalent stage of where personal computers
were in 1979. In 10 to 15 years, VR will be as ubiquitous as PCs,"* according to
Ben Delaney, editor of *CyberEdge Journal.*[3]

Because so many want to catch the coming VR wave, sales figures and projections are tough to pin down. Many companies are labeling products "virtual reality" even though they're really not.

But many people in the business see the VR industry growing at least 20 percent a year for the foreseeable future, with some putting the acceleration at 50 percent annually.

According to figures provided by Dr. John Latta, president of 4th Wave, Inc., *the total global market for virtual reality (not including government spending) was estimated at $110.3 million in 1993, and was projected to hit $504 million in 1997.*[4]

Legitimate virtual reality has, in fact, already come to mean many things. Definitions vary. But in its broadest sense, "Virtual reality is the ultimate computer interface — it's the most user-friendly way for a person to directly interact with a computer," said Ed Costello, director of Sales and Marketing for Polhemus, Inc.[5]

Here's a brief rundown of some of the VR subsets and technologies:

CAVE — Images are projected onto walls and a floor, and viewed with stereo glasses. The system includes a location sensor, and as the CAVE inhabitant moves, the stereo projections and perspective is updated so the image moves, and surrounds the viewer.

Mirror World — You see an electronic or video doppelganger image of yourself, which can be manipulated inside the virtual world. Also known as artificial reality.

Through the Window — Allows a person to see a 3-D universe through a computer screen. Steering through the artificial world is done with a hand-held device.

Waldo World — Essentially allows remote control of devices via "telepresence," which gives the operator a you-are-there type of feeling. For example, a remote-controlled robot could mimic the movements of a human operator who's wearing a "data suit," and is positioned far away from the robot.

Also, advanced "simulation settings," like those used to train pilots for years, can fall under the VR billing.

But for purists, the only virtual reality worth its weight in pixels is the "Immersive First-person" type.

If you want to be an immersive first-person cybernaut, it works like this:

First, you put on the "face-sucker," a Darth Vader-like, high-tech helmet or visor, more technically called a Head-Mounted Display (HMD). The HMD cuts off your field of vision to the real world, and is hooked into powerful computers. It's like one of those old ViewMasters, but on steroids.

The HMD (latest models weigh in at less than a pound) is essentially a set of two goggles, one for each eye, that contain tiny, but wide-angle TV screens which display computerized, colorific, 3-D graphics/images. But instead of just seeing moving images on a screen, you're in among the images. Headphones in the HMD can add seeming quadrophonic sound. If you decide to enter a virtual world of mystery and intrigue, you'll hear the muffled footsteps behind you.

Now here's the good thing—if you turn your head to see what's causing the sound, your field of vision within the artificial world appropriately changes—you'll see what's coming after you. Your perspective is in tune to the virtual world. If you look up, again, your field of vision will change—you'll see blue sky, or Lucy in the sky with diamonds, or whatever's up there, created by the computer program. Turn left, and you'll see what's on your left in the virtual world, and so on.

To fully experience the current state of VR, you may also wear special gloves—tight, black-elastic gloves fitted with sensors and fiber-optic wires. Put your gloved hand in front of your face and you'll see a VR representation of your real hand floating in the virtual world. Move your gloved hand, and your VR hand moves suitably. Wiggle your real fingers, and your VR fingers wiggle, too.

Better yet, the gloves allow you to interact with objects that only exist in the VR world. For example, your virtual hand could turn on a faucet in a virtual room. Your VR hand could pick up a VR object and allow you to examine it. You could grasp a VR baseball in your best fastball or knuckleball grip and hurl it. Someday, you may be able to feel the seams on the virtual baseball.

An optional 'exoskeleton,' or alternatively, a jump-suit type garment that looks something like a skin-diving suit can add to the realism of virtual reality, by translating arm, leg, and body movements into computerized images.

Calvin and Hobbes © 1992, Watterson. Reprinted with permission of Universal Press Syndicate. All rights reserved.

And perhaps best of all, entering virtual reality-land doesn't have to mean banishing yourself into a lonely computer-generated cyberia. Your friends are invited—more than one person can be tethered into the same cyberspace at the same time.

This may sound more like science fiction than fact, like the first high-tech steps toward "Star Trek: The Next Generation's" Holodeck, where characters take part in vivid, life-like adventures in the time and place of their choosing. (In fact, a mall-based VR game, based on a Starship Enterprise environment, will allow trekkers to experience the holodeck, bridge, and let them beam down to a planet, sometime in late 1993.) But virtual reality is not merely a concept. It's actively being used and explored by many industries for many uses.

And the high priests, and hard-nosed businessmen, of VR say its potential uses are just about as infinite as worlds that can be created. "VR is in its infancy, but applications are beginning to take off at a tremendous rate," said Costello.[6]

Let's say your company is going to transfer you from the East coast to the West. You don't want to spend a lot of time out West shopping for a new home. In the future you may not have to, because it may be possible to do a good bit of your house-hunting via virtual reality. You could stroll through the VR version of the house, and at least get a sense of whether or not it's something you're interested in.

"You could walk through the house and see what it looks like, or you could put your old furniture in the new house via virtual reality and move it around, or you could see it with different paint jobs, or you might view it from the outside ... you're immersed in an idea," said Eric Herr, vice-president of Emerging Businesses for Autodesk, Inc.[7]

At the University of North Carolina, which has a leading VR center, architects are using VR to stroll through as yet unconstructed buildings.

The University of Washington, which is home to the Human Interface Technology Laboratory, is helping put together a virtual reality version of Seattle that city planners could walk around in to help conceive future architectural changes.

In Tokyo, Matsushita takes customers who are thinking about kitchen renovations on a virtual tour of various designs. The customers can open virtual kitchen cabinet doors and cupboards, turn on virtual stoves and faucets, and hear the water running. They can get a sense of the overall space. It seems to be an improvement to looking over blueprints in the real world—the virtual reality tour has reportedly increased the percentage of sales per consultation. Matsushita intends to add another 10 virtual showrooms in three years, expanding to 100 in five to ten years.[8]

A VR system has been developed that permits someone who is bound to a wheelchair to tour a virtual world. The operator wears an HMD and glove, and the wheelchair is essentially attached to a roller system. With the system, an architect can test a building layout for its ease of accessibility for wheelchair users, which is required by law. The wheelchair VR system is cheaper, faster, and more effective than building models.

VR is being extensively studied for its potential to help the physically challenged in other areas. I'm speculating now, but in theory, I suppose it's conceivable that using some sort of sensory-cue system, VR could give the disabled a feeling of being freed from paralyzed bodies. Quadriplegics may be able to experience holding a child, or a springtime walk in the park in a VR world.

VR has various other health care possibilities.

Does "Fantastic Voyage" ring a bell? You remember, the movie featuring a miniaturized medical team, including Raquel Welch in a skin-hugging suit, that traveled through a patient's body. Well, someday doctors may be able to essentially do the VR equivalent of that, and explore a patient's organs in 3-D. VR is being used to create 3-D x-rays that can help in planning surgical procedures. Also, surgeons will be able to rehearse operations with VR, see VR blood, and eventually even be able to feel the VR scalpel cutting through VR skin.

Chemists and drug companies are using VR to enter a micro-cosmos to see, feel, and manipulate various VR-created molecules. Scientists are actually strolling around inside a molecule, and they can grab hold of parts of it. This isn't just a chemist's idea of a good time. With the visualization and modeling VR provides, scientists can literally get a much better handle on the structure of a disease-causing molecule, and, in essence, find out where its weak link is. That knowledge will give them a better idea of how to create a fight-back drug. The drugs would also be designed in VR to determine where the best chemical bonds are. Anti-cancer medicines have reportedly already been developed using the molecular VR systems.

From inner space to outer space, VR will have applications.

NASA will use VR to train astronauts. At one NASA center, earthbound explorers can explore Mars via a VR model recreated from data gathered from a probe of the Red Planet. In fact, NASA and the Department of Defense have in effect said that VR will be the foundation of their future training methods.

The U.S. Air Force has been using VR to train fighter pilots in high-tech craft to increase their survival rate. The Army is using VR to train tank crews and give them a realistic sense of the shake, rattle, and roll of a tank battle. The VR model is based on actual Gulf War tank fights. VR is expected to be a cost-saver over the long-term for the Pentagon, much cheaper than actually having to conduct repeated war games.

Even the more staid world of mathematicians, computer programmers, financial analysts, and actuaries will be affected by virtual reality, as they use it to make the abstract more tangible. Programs, statistics, and data can be represented in 3-D, perhaps as a forest, and accountants and the like will be able to shed their jackets and bowties and become cybernauts, and fly over and through the forest of statistics. Patterns, trends, structures, and (computer) bugs will stand out in the VR representation. You'd be able to get a better feel for the numbers.

Many Japanese companies are focusing on VR for communications. And in 1993, a Canadian consortium began work on its "Parallel Universe Hub" which will allow dozens of users to essentially hold a conference in cyberspace. The consortium says it's really in the travel business. Think about how the tourist trade could be changed forever if VR vacations become the rage.

The use of VR in education could conceivably encourage youngsters to actually want to go to school. The brain is more alert, and retains information better, when there are multi-sense cues firing at it. Other than dry textbooks or lectures, imagine a course in history that's brought alive by recreating great moments from the past. You could sit in on the Constitutional Convention, or take part in the Boston Tea Party. Or VR could be used to teach something as modern and mundane as drivers ed. It would be easier using VR to teach a reflexively-bizarre reaction, like steering into a skid. You could repeat the process over and over, and do it in slow motion, until the reaction became natural.

For similar reasons, VR will play an increasing role in sports training. For example, a Japanese company, NEC, has developed a VR skiing system that lets you do practice runs indoors without the spills. Your skis and slope are essentially piston-activated metal plates that swivel in response to your physical moves as you schuss down the course you see in your HMD.

Companies are beginning to use VR for design purposes other than buildings. For example, you could design a car in VR, and spot potential lay-out problems, and essentially figure out if the parts fit without having to build an expensive prototype. Companies like Northrop and Boeing are already relying on VR to design planes. Again, VR is expected to be a major cost and time saver.

And of course, VR will be used for pure fun. And it's that potential entertainment value of VR that could very well be the initial driving force that spreads the VR gospel by making the public more aware of it, and forcing equipment costs to come down.

Sega is set to introduce for Christmas, 1993 the first mass-affordable home VR set-up, which will include a Head Mounted Display. The HMD will reportedly retail for about $200.

MCA Inc., which owns Universal Pictures, is at work on a project to create commercial VR theaters that show virtual movies or "voomies." Voomies could make an appearance by the mid-1990s in Los Angeles and/or Tokyo. You buy a ticket, enter the voomie, put on your HMD, and instead of just passively watching a movie, you take part in the action. The voomies may also contain live performers who will enter the VR action as so-called "changelings" and become something like tour guides in the VR world.

Walt Disney Company is reportedly working on VR systems.

VR games are already beginning to proliferate in malls and arcades.

One of the best known mall VR games in the U.S. was developed by a British company, W Industries. In "Dactyl Nightmare," two players take hu-manoid-form, and chase each other through five tiers of obstacle-strewn plat-forms connected by stairways. The point of the game is a bit basic — shoot your opponent with rocket grenades. A direct hit shatters your virtual rival into squiggles. There's one other added wrinkle — swooping green pterodactyls, like Rodan, can threaten you at any time.

In Chicago there exists a well-known VR game center featuring a game called "BattleTech." Virtual World Entertainment, the company that developed the center, is planning many other similar sites, and received an infusion of cash in 1993 when Tim Disney, Walt's nephew, bought a majority interest.

With "BattleTech" and "Dactyl Nightmare," you may have just spotted a trend in VR games that is disturbing to some observers. VR games, like video games before them, seem to be featuring shoot-em-ups. The fear being that women will be less likely to take an interest in this type of experience.

As long as we're mentioning men and women, let's get back to VR sex. It is conceivably possible, but the technology has a long way to go. What would apparently be needed is something akin to a second skin — a snug, mosquito-wing thin, cybergarment. The mesh would probably contain hundreds, if not thousands, of mini-sensors per square inch that would, hopefully, receive and send a realistic sense of touch.

Since it will become possible to plug your VR system into a worldwide communications network, you could conceivably choose a partner on the equivalent of a 900 number. Maybe it will resemble the little huff-and-puff VR sex scene in the 1991 science-fiction movie "Lawnmower Man."

But if you consider sex to be more than that, if you think sex should be a multi-sense experience including the mind, all of which VR may not be able to fully recreate, then you have to wonder if the virtual route to sex is worth the

wait. It may wind up to be just a virtual version of solitary dancin' in the dark. Remember the word for virtual sex is tele*dildo*nics.

However, a London-based magazine, *Black Ice,* reportedly said it will "… develop a fully-functioning and integrated teledildonic system for anyone who will put up the necessary capital."[9]

Still, I don't think computers powerful enough to control hundreds of thousands of minute sensors that would have to cover every goose bump, tickle, and twinge of the body, and space in between, exist now. Also, the sensation of touch in the VR world is very crude, only in the early experimental stages right now. And that is pretty much the story for the VR experience in the early 1990s — crude. And expensive.

But it's getting better by the day. In the late 1980s, a VR system could cost upwards of three-quarters of a million dollars, and all it would give you were sketchy images. Some systems, with better graphics, now sell for about $60,000. Other, more cut-rate systems, go for about $5,000 to $20,000. But just like PCs and video games, prices will continue to fall, making VR systems more widespread, both for business and personal use.

Other problems exist for VR technology. Graphics still aren't that realistic — no one in a current VR world would be convinced he's in the real world. "There isn't a state in the union where you wouldn't be considered legally blind if you saw things in the real world the way you saw them in a VR world," says Costello.[10] But the graphics are improving rapidly. I've been told that by 1995, virtual images will amaze consumers.

Another problem unique to cybernauts is that current computers are not powerful enough to calculate and manipulate the massive amounts of data needed to alter images and perspective in tandem with cybernauts' movements. In other words, when, for example, you move your real head to change your VR field of vision, there is a slight lag time for the change in perspective in the VR world. As of this writing, the lag time was down to about four milliseconds. (One note here: it may be the lag time that, like astronauts with space sickness, has caused some cybernauts to report a certain queasiness and nausea, known as entering the "barfogenic zone.") But again, computers, as they always have, are getting faster and faster by the day, and that lag time will eventually be eliminated.

Companies are working on ways to make plunging into a VR world less cumbersome. They predict the somewhat bulky face-sucker helmet that can fog up glasses will be replaced by goggles about the size of ordinary eyeglasses. Some envisage TV screens the size of contact lenses that will fit right over the eyeballs, sending 3-D images.

Beyond that, there is a possibility that VR screens of any kind will become obsolete. Scientists speculate that someday scanners will follow the eyeball's motions, and laser beams will continuously and safely stimulate light receptors in the eye, in essence placing life-like images directly on the retina. The National Institute of Standards and Technology reportedly received a proposal to develop the laser microscanner.

By some estimates, VR technology is progressing twice as fast as the progress of flight. Remember, from the Wright brothers to "... one small step for man ..." took just 66 years — less than the average lifetime. Research is being done right now throughout the world that should build a huge VR industry in the Third Millennium.

As indicated above, Japan Inc. is on a major program to develop virtual reality. It looks like another case of the Japanese jumping all over an American-invented technology.

Japan's Advanced Telecommunications Research Institute International (ATR) has a multi-million dollar annual budget with a stated goal of building mass-media cyberspace communication systems by the first decade of the next millennium. And it also wants to make VR and virtual meeting places possible without the currently needed, unwielding body-contraptions.

ATR is backed by the giants — Nippon Telephone and Telegraph, Toshiba, Hitachi, and Nippon Electronic Company (NEC). Separately, Fujitsu is spending millions on VR research. The three areas it's aiming for are entertainment, education, and design. Sony is working on VR systems, and TV-quality goggles to replace the face-sucker. Japan's Ministry of International Trade and Industry (MITI) has formed a commission to study VR. Clearly, the Japanese are taking VR very seriously. And they're taking a very Japanese approach — with a willingness to wait for the big-time payoff.

Companies in other countries, including England, France, Canada, and Germany are working on some form and aspect of virtual reality technology.

In the United States, The Human Interface Technology Laboratory in Seattle is a part-commercial, part-academic VR consortium that includes the Port of Seattle, Sun Microsystems, US West Communications, and Digital Equipment Corporation (DEC). DEC, IBM, and AT&T all reportedly have VR projects on tap. And new, smaller start-up U.S. companies seem to be jumping into the VR fray everyday.

MIT Press in 1992 began publishing a quarterly VR journal called *Presence*.

New York University's School of Continuing Education suggests adult students spend their summer in cyberspace by offering a course called "The Virtual College: Management Systems Teleprogram."

And in addition to the other universities already mentioned that are active in VR research, The Art Center College of Design at Pasadena, California is starting a Virtual World design curriculum.

So industry, the government, and academia are all becoming more cyber-conscious. Obviously, the foundation is being set.

There are, of course, potential social, moral, and ethical problems and questions raised by the ability to take a walk on the wild side from your reclining chair any time you want. VR junkies, preferring cyberspace to the real thing, could become a problem. William Gibson, who wrote *Neuromancer,* reportedly called VR "the equivalent of freebasing TV."

Others have warned of the possibility of the body electric needing its dose of artificial reality to the exclusion of all else. Indeed, it's a bit unsettling to think of the possibility of bloodless little humans who have banished themselves, floating blissfully in their cubicles and living vicariously in computer-made worlds. Perhaps a VR Clinic, or VR's Anonymous will have to be created. But as many people in the industry have said to me, it's not the technology that's the culprit, it's what people choose to do with it that may be the problem.

"When the concept of VR is fully realized, it will not be viewed as something different, but will be considered the natural progression of computer technology," said Herr.[11]

In any case, this is a business book. I'll leave the moral questions raised by VR for the regulators and philosophers. The fact is, VR is already here and it's not going away. Anyone reading this chapter, can, I think, get a sense of how big VR could become in the Third Millennium. Its importance has already been compared to the invention of the telephone and the diesel engine.

■   ■   ■

So, can you invest in VR now?

It is difficult. Right now, it is more a case of being aware of VR, and being ready to jump on any of the smaller start-up companies that may go public. But not before you get their prospectus and thoroughly research them.

There is a textbook example in the VR industry of why you have to do your homework in any of these emerging technologies. What was arguably once the leading U.S. VR company, VPL, essentially went belly-up in late 1992–early 1993 because it was mismanaged.

SOURCES

To keep up on developments in VR:

Cyberjournal
#1 Gate Six Road
Sausalito, California 94965
415-331-3343 Fax: 415-331-3643

Mondo 2000
P.O. Box 10171
Berkeley, California 94709
510-845-9018

Virtual Reality World
11 Ferry Lane West
Westport, Connecticut 06880
Fax: 203-454-5840

Wired
544 Second Street
San Francisco, California 94107
415-904-0600

As of mid-1993, there were three pure-play, publicly-held, virtual reality companies — all small, two non-American:

Division Group plc
19 Apex Court
Woodlands, Almondsbury
Bristol, England BS12 4JT
0454-615-554

Division designs, manufactures, and sells VR software and systems for various applications. Company went public in mid-1993. Its stock is traded on the London Stock Exchange. This is a development stage company that showed an operating profit for the five months ended March 31, 1993.

Division has a U.S. wholly-owned subsidiary:

Division Inc.
400 Seaport Court
Port of Redwood City, California 94063

Virtual Reality, Inc. (OTC - VIRT)
485 Washington Avenue
Pleasantville, New York 10570
914-769-0900

Small company that performs R&D and manufactures proprietary systems and products, including head-mounted displays, that can be used for simulation and in various virtual reality applications, including aerospace, medical, education, and design. Company in late 1992 signed a deal with Lawrence Taylor's All Pro Sports Products, Inc. to develop, commercialize, and market worldwide VR sports and entertainment games.

This is another development stage company. Its revenues for the period ended March 31, 1993 were over $200,000.

Virtual Universe Corp.
700 Fourth Avenue SW
Calgary, Ontario Canada T2P 3J4
403-261-5652

Virtual Universe trades on the Alberta exchange under the symbol VRX.

This small, development stage company's main in-the-works product is the "Parallel Universe," which essentially will allow many users to simultaneously enter a virtual world, regardless of geographic location, so they can interact in real-time. The system reportedly will be provided over regular telephone lines. The company sees the main applications being in multi-user games and entertainment, and in concurrent collaborative design.

As I've already indicated, many large publicly-held companies like IBM, AT&T, Digital Equipment, and Walt Disney are doing VR R&D. Some other publicly-held companies, although not pure-plays, could benefit from the virtual wave, these are:

Autodesk, Inc. (OTC - ACAD)
2320 Marinship Way
Sausalito, California 94965
415-332-2344 Fax: 415-331-8093

Autodesk, Inc. is a worldwide company with a net worth of more than a quarter billion dollars and more than 1,000 employees.

The latest available figures show Autodesk's annual sales approaching $400,000,000, with net income over $40,000,000 a year. Obviously, not a start-up. (The company was founded in 1982.)

The company makes its money primarily by selling computer-aided design (CAD), engineering, and animations software for use on desktop computers and workstations. CAD allows designers of all kinds to use computers and computer screens instead of a pencil, and the designers can easily make complex drawings, "rotate" their work, and in essence see it from any angle. CAD gives architects, mechanical and graphic designers, community planners, and others a progressive, 3-D-like graphic display of, and visual feel for, their designs.

The company is conducting cyberspace R&D, and in early 1993 offered its first VR product, essentially a programmer's toolkit. Autodesk is obviously strategically positioned, by nature of its current main CAD business, to take advantage of the coming VR explosion. The company envisions a potential link-up between VR and CAD for use by designers.

Evans & Sutherland Computer Corp. (OTC - ESCC)
600 Komas Drive
Salt Lake City, Utah 84108
801-582-5847

The company designs and manufactures interactive computer systems and software which are used to create simulated settings primarily used in training and design.

The company's annual sales are over $150 million.

Kopin Corp. (OTC - KOPN)
695 Myles Standish Boulevard
Taunton, Massachusetts 02780
508-824-6696

Company primarily manufactures so-called wafer-engineered materials, and makes electronic digital imaging devices using its proprietary technology.

Kopin is also developing a head-mounted display for virtual reality applications.

Annual sales are over $7 million.

Silicon Graphics, Inc. (NYSE - SGI)
2011 North Shoreline Boulevard
Mountain View, California 94039
415-960-1980

Company makes high performance computing systems used to simulate 3D objects and environments. Silicon Graphics is probably more famous for helping to create some of the special effects in "Terminator 2" and "Jurassic Park."

The company's "RealityEngine" is apparently becoming the industry standard for generating VR graphics.

Silicon Graphics' annual sales are over $500 million.

Sun Microsystems, Inc. (OTC - SUNW)
2550 Garcia Avenue
Mountain View, California 94043
415-960-1300

Company makes powerful computer workstations that are part of the VR system, and generates the graphics display.

Sun was incorporated in 1982 and employs more than 12,000. Its annual sales are in the billions of dollars.

Another publicly-held company that on the surface would seem to have nothing to do with VR, but could benefit is:

Edison Brothers Stores, Inc. (NYSE - EBS)
501 North Broadway
St. Louis, Missouri 63178
314-331-6000

Edison is mainly a retailer of clothing and women's shoes. But it also has an entertainment division (bought in the early 1990s) which operates family entertainment and amusement game centers in malls and other locations, and which will probably increasingly offer the VR experience.

Edison is a well-established company (founded in 1929), whose annual sales are over $1 billion.

Also, on a related note:

Technigen Corp. (OTC - TGPAF)
101-84 North Bend Road
Coquitlam, British Columbia, Canada
604-421-0344

Company makes computerized golf simulators using laser disc technology. The system can essentially recreate actual golf holes. You'd smack a real golf ball with a real golf club and the computers would calculate its trajectory and show the results on a large projector screen.

The systems are either being distributed, or about to be distributed, in North America, Japan, other Pac Rim countries, and Europe.

CHAPTER 3

ROBOTS

"I'll be back."

— The Terminator

In the wee hours of New Year's Day 1993, when many were having the time of their lives, Dante was descending into hell.

It was a bleak hell of ice and rock, stone-cold temperatures, screaming winds, burning gas, and choking fumes. Dante, like one of the undead, felt nothing.

Dante, of course, was a robot, dubbed, designed, and built by Carnegie Mellon University. The eight-legged, thousand-pound Dante's mission was to explore a live volcanic crater in Antarctica. Part of its task was to prove that robots will be competent enough to explore the Moon and Mars. But graced with a certain autonomy, mobility, sensors, and vision, Dante is also symbolic of the future of robotics here on Earth.

Oh, I know what you're probably thinking. For as long as you can remember, The Age of Robots was coming. It never happened. At least not in the United States. Japan was a different story. But certain economic and political forces, and technological advances, are coming together which will give the Terminator's words a prophetic edge — *robotics is, in essence, a reemerging U.S. industry.*

■　　■　　■

In such prophetic times, changing times, *millennial* times, it would be fitting for a resurgence of interest in the mechanical relatives of the "Voice of Doom."

The Voice of Doom, so nicknamed by students, was essentially a robot telephone operator that dialed up parents and delivered a message to report truant children at one Connecticut high school. The Voice of Doom, like all robots, was persistent in its job. If anyone had the brass to hang up on Doom, it called back twice. The robot was reportedly quite effective — fewer students cut classes.[1]

I use Doom's phone-talk and Dante's death-walk to illustrate the potential future direction of robots — in each case, you'll notice neither robot was manufacturing a product.

Which is not to say the factory robot is a dead issue. In a more intensely competitive global economy, speed, quality, flexibility, cost-effectiveness, and higher productivity will be more crucial.

In the 21st century, robots should play a more significant role in manufacturing and service industries, and perhaps in the home, as well. From more "intelligent" factory robots, to "Robodocs," to seeing-eye "dogbots," to bartender-robots that will mix and serve, and perhaps even listen to your sob stories, robots appear to be ready to finally start living up to earlier expectations.

"The robotics industry has finally matured ... we look for growing usage of robotics throughout the 1990s and well into the 21st century," said Don Vincent, executive vice president of the Robotic Industries Association.[2]

And the U.S. Commerce Department concluded, "The long-term outlook for the U.S. robotics industry is promising."[3]

What took it so long? After all, the formula for a pseudo-human that would do man's bidding has been around for generations.

According to 16th century alchemists, the witch's brew went something like this: 'Let a man's semen putrefy by itself in a hermetically sealed glass with the highest putrefaction of horse manure for forty days, or until it begins at last to live, move, and be agitated. After this time it will be in some degree like a human being...

Nourished and fed cautiously and prudently with the arcanum of human blood, and kept for forty days in the perpetual and equal heat of horse manure, it becomes thence forth a true and living infant.'[4]

Arcanums not being easy to come by, modern industry chose another route.

The word robot has only been in popular use since the Roaring Twenties, following the publication of the play *R.U.R.* (Rossum's Universal Robots) by Czech writer Karel Capek.

"Robot" is derived from Czech words meaning labor or serf. In the play, a robot was an automaton, an emotionless machine-man designed to serve humans. Judging by its denouement, the play is a cautionary tale of sorts — the robots ultimately rebel, and just about destroy humanity. But they became cantankerous only after some emotions were built into them. The play would have been a big hit on Mr. Spock's Vulcan.

The definition of a contemporary robot can vary, but according to Jeffrey Burnstein, editor of *Robot Times,* a good one to go with is "... a reprogrammable, multifunctional, machine or manipulator designed to move material, parts, tools, or specialized devices through variable programmed motions for the performance of a variety of tasks."[5]

My pocket Merriam-Webster's defines a robot as an efficient but insensitive person, an automatic apparatus, something guided by automatic controls, or a machine that looks and acts like a human being.

Factory robots, anything but humanoid, first appeared in the U.S. in the very late 1950s and early 1960s. They were relatively simple arm-like machines that did unsavory and/or boring jobs — primarily die-casting work. But they could work round-the-clock, did it without bitching and moaning, never called in sick, and never asked for a raise. However, they didn't necessarily get along with their (human) co-workers.

Progressively more sophisticated robots hit the market throughout the 1960s, 1970s, and 1980s. In addition to moving parts around, they could weld, spray paint, assemble, and do enough other jobs to surely make some blue-collar workers look over their shoulder. But for the most part, the robots couldn't look back — they usually didn't have vision systems. These mostly sightless, deaf-and-dumb robots found work in foundries, aerospace plants, and heavy equipment manufacturing.

Far and away, the main market for robots in America was the auto industry. During the early 1980s the robotics market was on a roll with the Big Three. But later in the decade, as cutbacks hit the industry, overall robot sales became flat. Still, today about 50 percent of the industrial robots that have been installed in the U.S. are used in auto plants.

In Japan, something of a love affair developed with robots — no "Demon Seed" scenario here, but the machines did become almost a partner in industry.

So taken were the Japanese with robots, they were struck MUM. MUM stands for Methodology for Unmanned Manufacturing. Japan set a goal for humans to be strictly so-called 'knowledge workers' by the new millennium — no heavy lifting for the Japanese. A lofty, probably impossible goal by the turn of the century. But conditions for the proliferation of robots were always good in Japan — an export-driven economy, labor shortages, management that thought long-term, good company-employee relationships (read: few or no unions), and cooperation, support, and incentives from the government.

For essentially the opposite reasons — and because they were very expensive and there was some disappointment with their early abilities — robots didn't quite catch on in the U.S. outside of Detroit (despite generally proving their cost-effectiveness, as robots can do the work of about one and a half to six humans, depending on the industry or specific job, and the average operating cost for a factory robot is $6 an hour compared to $20 an hour, including benefits, for a human).

According to the International Federation of Robotics, at the end of 1991, Japan had a robot population of 325,000, compared to just 44,000 in the U.S.[6] But the U.S. market is on the verge of a revival. There are already signs of a turnaround.

U.S.-based robotic companies shipped almost 4,500 robots in 1991, the highest total since 1986. And through the first six months of 1992, new orders for U.S.-based robot makers hit a six-year high. Many of those were from overseas. (In the first quarter of 1992, international sales added up to 31 percent of the new order value.)[7]

New markets for robots are emerging in the Pacific Rim outside of Japan, and increasing use of robots in Europe is also a hopeful sign for new export possibilities for U.S. robot companies.

But it is the local market that's largely a new frontier. By some estimates, only 5 percent to 10 percent of North American firms that would be better off with robots than without them actually have installed even one robot. That will change. Many of those companies may be dragged kicking and screaming into the 21st century, but they will be forced to use robotics because of a couple of key millennial concepts: quality and international competition.

According to the Commerce Department, "Economic conditions are expected to improve in the North American market because companies that have been putting off large capital equipment expenditures will no longer be able to delay these investments, (and) the growing pressure on U.S. companies to improve productivity and product quality requires manufacturing executives in virtually every industry to examine possible automation solutions."[8]

According to Market Intelligence Research Corp./Frost & Sullivan of Mountain View, California, *U.S. robot sales are predicted to have a compound annual growth rate of 16.5 percent between 1991 and 1997, hitting about $1.5 billion in 1997.* Much of that growth will be for assembly applications. In 1990, assembly robot revenues were about 14 percent of total robot sales. By 1997, assembly robots will account for more than 25 percent of the total U.S. robot market.[9]

"Today, manufacturers are looking for the most cost-effective manufacturing techniques. Robots are high on the list of options," says Vincent.[10]

But it won't just be the large-size companies that will be investing in robots.

"The action for industrial robots now lies within the small to medium-size manufacturing companies. A latent demand exists and ... with industrial robots' maturity and proven track record, relatively stable prices, increased international competition, customer demand for higher quality, and the need for greater manufacturing flexibility, *more small and medium-size manufacturers are embracing robotics,"* says Ray Hinson, chairman of Robotics International/Society of Manufacturing Engineers Board of Advisors.[11]

Some of the recent pick-up in demand for robots has been coming from the electronics, appliance, food packaging, and pharmaceutical industries.

Robots will be one more tool to help improve productivity in those and other industries in the effort to grab world markets.

"The current trend in manufacturing is a move toward more rapid product introduction, abbreviated product life cycles, increased flexibility, and integrated design-production-quality control. Companies that do not move in this direction will become increasingly noncompetitive," says the Commerce Department.[12]

Robots will be incorporated into so-called flexible manufacturing systems (FMS) and computer-integrated manufacturing (CIM), which allow companies to improve quality, produce faster, and to shift rapidly to a new product-design or another product. FMS melds automation, computers, and (not to forget) human personnel into one coordinated system, and according to the Commerce Department, *robots are central to "... the successful implementation of advanced manufacturing strategies through flexible computer integrated manufacturing."*[13]

The Commerce Department predicts the annual market for flexible CIM by the year 2000 will be $10 to $20 billion in the U.S., and $20 to $40 billion worldwide.[14]

Flexible manufacturing systems are capable of, in essence, redefining themselves in quickly changing market conditions and demands. "... flexible CIM integrates product, process, and manufacturing management information ... it helps ensure that the right product at the right price is on the market at the right time."[15]

Also just at the right time, and perhaps taking a cue from Japan, the U.S. government seems ready to provide incentives for the use of FMS and robots. A report by the Office of Technology Assessment says Congress should consider options to encourage the use of robotics and other types of advanced manufacturing technologies.[16]

President Clinton, who said in his 1993 inauguration speech, "We stand on the edge of the 21st century," grew up with the songs of Bob Dylan, and may understand 'the times they are a changin'. He also apparently understands the need for an upgrade of America's manufacturing systems. As part of his plan to rebuild the U.S. technology base, Mr. Clinton said the federal government must follow the lead of some state and local governments that are already helping small and medium-sized businesses adopt robotics, CIM and FMS.

Clinton also stated, "The government already spends $76 billion annually on R&D. This funding should be refocused so that more resources are devoted

Reprinted courtesy *OMNI* magazine, copyright, 1985.

to critical technologies such as ... new manufacturing processes that boost industrial performance."[17]

Mr. Clinton said one of his goals is to "create a civilian research and development agency to bring together business and universities to develop cutting edge products and technologies. *This agency will increase our commercial research and development spending, focusing its efforts in crucial new industries such as ... robotics ...*"[18]

You can be sure another government unit will actively be pursuing robotics. Not surprisingly, the U.S. Defense Department names robotics and machine intelligence, as well as flexible manufacturing, as critical technologies. It appears the killing fields of the future will become more automated. First generation "smart" weapons already proved their battle-worthiness in the Desert Storm blitz against Iraq in 1991.

The Pentagon says, "In the fast-paced battlefield of the future, intelligent machines will fuse, process, and analyze data, and present the results almost immediately ... provide more effective military intelligence, data analysis, battle management, timely decision making, *and survivability—machine intelligence and robotic applications will reduce the need for manpower.*"[19]

Perhaps when robot armies of the night are killing each other, war will become obsolete as machines become obsolete. Or will making war just become easier—the ultimate video game, with human auxiliaries sitting at screens, operating tele-controlled robots, scoring real-time, real-life hits?

In any case, expect more sophisticated robotic reconnaissance, surveillance, and combat vehicles. By the year 2006, the Defense Department predicts widespread use of robotics throughout weapons systems, completely autonomous, unmanned robotic combat vehicles, automated sentries, and robotic security patrols. To achieve its robot-goals, the Pentagon is budgeted at about $145 million a year for R&D on machine intelligence and robotics.

Apart from the Defense Department, the government, through the National Science Foundation, also sponsors robot research at various universities. Additionally, extensive research is being undertaken by the National Institute of Standards and Technology, and the Bureau of Mines. And naturally, NASA is interested in robots as outer space explorers and construction workers.

Ironically, some of the same technological advances that will prepare robots to fight wars, do risky jobs, and "man" the loneliness of space, will also equip them to interact with Earth-bound humans, and do more commonplace work. Those technological advances will be the true driving force of the growing market for robots, in both the manufacturing and service sectors, into the next millennium.

Future robots will be "smarter," more sensitive to, and aware of, their surroundings, and will be able to make independent decisions to deal with changes in their environment. With an increasing ability to see, feel, and move, robots will adapt to new tasks. In other words, they will become more human-like, if not more human-shaped.

Robots generally suffer from sensory deprivation, which means they can't do many things we take for granted. For example, peeling a banana. First you'd have to clearly see the banana and be aware of what it is in the context of its surroundings, then pick it up lightly without crushing it, then perform reasonably dexterous movements with your hand and fingers. It's easy for you and me, but not for a robot. Not yet, anyway. But today's robotic tactile sensors and vision systems are improving daily.

Robots will eventually be able to identify objects by their feel. *Japan has reportedly manufactured a fingertip tactile sensor, that can feel where an object contacts it to an accuracy of 1 millimeter. That's about 1/25 of an inch.* Tactile sensors will greatly enhance a robot's ability to adapt to lighter, more delicate assembly tasks.

Also, prototype robot hands are under development that come close to duplicating human motor skills. One such robot hand reportedly can pick up an egg, crack it into a bowl, and scramble it up. And the Rensselaer Polytechnic Institute has constructed a five-fingered, anatomically correct, completely functional robot hand that has the potential to do industrial work that is dangerous for humans.

Japan has also built a robot arm with the same degrees of freedom as a human arm.

Will the veins in the arms of millennium robots flow with acid?

MIT has developed an artificial muscle made from a gel that swells or contracts in response to PH changes. In other words, adding an acid causes the artificial muscle to expand, while adding a base makes it contract. The artificial muscle has been able to lift or lower about four ounces, depending on whether its fed an acid or a base. That's not much, but it's a start. It's conceivable that sometime in the 21st century, the artificial muscle could replace robotic motors and gears, and lead to robots that are independent of electrical outlets.

Perhaps more importantly, robots are increasing their ability to "see." Due to computer hardware and software advances, machine vision is improving dramatically. While tactile sensors may help a robot peel a banana, better vision systems will help robots peel back the night they live in now, to become the true robots of dawn, and see the sunrise of the 21st century.

Machine vision systems essentially consist of a video camera hooked up to a high-speed computer that interprets the hundreds of thousands of bits of data captured by the camera. Right now, compared to human eyes, machine vision is relatively crude. But it's just a matter of time before machines can see in 3-D and color.

Most factory and assembly robots are pretty good at their jobs if whatever their working on is set-up in pre-arranged, highly specific locations. But if their work-piece jiggles and moves, or was positioned improperly to begin with, the robot's in trouble. It would blindly and blithely go along, trying to weld a wall where a car body should be, for example, or it would stock electronic components in circuit boards where they don't belong. That means inferior or useless end-products. Also, blind robots require long set-up times.

Machine vision systems help manufacturers produce better quality goods, cut the high cost of re-work and save producers money in the long-term. Again, in the race to capture global markets, producers will increasingly use machine vision to hike robots' productivity and flexibility.

Current machine vision systems are mostly used to automatically guide, identify, and quality-inspect various parts and products. For example, machine vision is used in the electronics industry to guide robots to accurately place mini-devices on circuit boards. Or seeing robots can rapidly align wafers for processing with a precision humans couldn't achieve. But machine vision systems are branching out to a whole series of industries.

"As computer integrated manufacturing expands, vision will become a vital component. Often, vision is the only viable solution. When there are parts flying by at tremendous speeds, there really can't be any kind of inspection ... without automated vision. If quality control is an absolute requirement, vision technology is right for the job," says Steve Silver, chairman of the Automated Technology Association and president of Imaging Technology Inc.[20]

Also, because of the trend toward miniaturization in some industries, especially electronics and semiconductors, machine vision will be the only way to inspect parts for quality control.

Additionally, the demand for machine vision will increase as prices come down, and while most current systems are used for specific purposes, generic vision systems for any type of application are developing. Sensors, machine vision, and robots have a certain symbiotic relationship. Improvements in one will enforce the advance of the others.

By some estimates, overall annual sensor sales have doubled annually since 1980, and will grow about 20 to 30 percent each year well into the next millennium. According to the Commerce Department, by the year 2000 annual sales for sensors (robot and non-robot) will hit $5 billion in the United States, and $12 billion worldwide.[21]

The world market for machine vision was about half a billion dollars in 1991, and is expected to exceed one billion dollars in 1998, with an annual compound growth rate of about 12 percent according to a study by Market Intelligence Research Corp./Frost & Sullivan.[22]

One last word on technological advances for robots. Remember, factory robots are connected to a computer (a controller). As robot software develops, and becomes more user-friendly, that should give the market another spark. Instead of custom-programming, the new software will allow users to more easily create new applications for robots without having to go through a line-by-line sequence of changes in a high-level, complicated computer language. It will be like the personal computer market, which really didn't explode until PC software applications became readily available, and PC users could stop worrying about programming

The technological upgrade for robots, like vision and touch, that will spark their increased use in factories, will also lead to an explosion in demand for another kind of robot — service robots.

"*Service robots* will affect many people. ...they have a huge (market) potential," according to Jeffrey Burnstein, editor of *Robot Times.*[23]

Robots that serve have moved off the assembly line. They don't fabricate a product, but there's almost no industry where a service robot couldn't be used. In the words of Joseph Engelberger, chairman of Transitions Research Corp., "service robots can work in any 3-D job — dirty, dull and dangerous."[24]

Think of any non-factory job that requires precision, or is hazardous, boring, repetitive, or can be ended with a robot-like "Have a nice day," and you'll find a potential job a service robot can do. The markets for service robots are truly emerging.

"It's important for people to understand that service robots are performing useful functions today. Even though the industry is still in its infancy, service robots are already contributing significantly and the outlook for new applications gets brighter every day," says Gay Engelberger, director of marketing for Transitions Research Corp. and a member of the board of the National Service Robot Association.[25]

Service robots are like infants taking their first independent steps into a non-structured world. While life used to be pretty much predictable, rigid, and restricted to the crib, the meals, the diaper changings, and sleep, now the world is revealed as a series of small and big shocks and abrupt surprises that call for a spontaneous reaction.

Equipped with an improving sense of touch and sight, along with advances in other machine senses and mobility, robots are taking those first tentative steps toward interaction with that unpredictable, sometimes hostile, world.

For example, the earlier mentioned Dante had tactile sensors on each of its eight feet, and so-called proximity sensors that would tell it when an object entered its field. The sensors would relay back to the robot the size and position of the object so Dante wouldn't trip up or crash. Like Dante in Antarctica, early service robots will be strangers in a strange land. But in the next millennium, they may be commonplace.

"Service robots will gain acceptance and slowly become an industry ... it could be a vast market of billions and billions of dollars," says Mr. Engelberger.[26]

His words should not be taken lightly. Mr. Engelberger is universally known as "the father of industrial robots." The company he set up in the late 1950s–early 1960s — Unimation — pretty much introduced factory robots to the world.

Mr. Engelberger said it was possible that the service robot industry could, like biotechnology, see quite a few new start-up companies jump into the field over the next few years. So maybe the giant of this nascent field isn't even a glint in some scientist/entrepreneur's, or robot's eye yet.

Reprinted courtesy of *OMNI* magazine, © 1983.

According to the Commerce Department, "... the service robotics industry may one day be larger than the industrial robot industry, although this is unlikely prior to the year 2000."[27]

However, the use of service robots is already expanding rapidly, and they are performing some very important and serious duties. In late 1992, a robot became an assistant surgeon.

The so-called ROBODOC performed replacement hip surgery on a 64-year-old man who was suffering from osteoarthritis. The operation was successful. ROBODOC, made by Integrated Surgical Systems, Inc. of Sacramento, California, was programmed with the exact location where it had to drill, and operated under the constant scrutiny of a team of doctors. ROBODOC can make exquisitely precise cuts, so the gaps between the replacement and the remaining bone are much smaller than if performed by humans.

The operation on a human followed 25 successful surgeries on dogs, and the Food and Drug Administration will allow ROBODOC to be used in up to 10 human hip operations, as part of a feasibility study.

Robots are performing, and will perform, many other services in healthcare:

- A robot made in England will assist doctors in procedures like gall bladder removal.
- A robot pharmacist fills and checks 1,200 medication orders every hour at St. Clair Hospital in Pittsburgh. It's been 100 percent accurate.
- A voice-controlled robot can serve dinner to patients in a Nashville, Tennessee medical center.
- A robot designed to assist quadriplegics is being developed that can pour a drink, lift a cup, open a briefcase, and open a door. Research is advancing on many fronts to develop robotics for the benefit of the disabled.
- A hospital robot is currently in use that can carry samples and specimens between different clinical laboratories.
- Another hospital robot can deliver patients' meal trays from floor to floor, crossing corridors and operating an elevator without any assistance.
- Researchers in Japan and the United States are developing a robot guide-dog, or 'dogbot,' for the blind.

Service robots are also working in security.

- Although still far from the abilities of the mighty RoboCop, one robot has already been shot in the line of duty. It happened on New York's Long Island during a hostage taking by a gunman in late 1991. Although the security robot took six direct bullet hits, it was only slightly damaged.
- Pharmaceutical company Glaxo, Inc. uses security robots to patrol its buildings. The night-watch robots cover about 10 miles a night, and allow human guards to devote more attention to more important security matters, or to their donuts.
- The Los Angeles County Art Museum is using a robot for security and environmental monitoring.
- Under the Federal Technology Transfer Act, the Naval Ocean Systems Center is working with Cybermotion, Inc. to integrate NOSC robot technology into the company's security robots.

(One aside on security robots of the future. With city streets and suburbs alike seemingly becoming more dangerous, it will be interesting to see if security robots are eventually programmed with the so-called Three Laws of Robots, originally proposed by the late, great Isaac Asimov in his fiction:

1. A robot may not injure a human being or, through inaction, allow a human being to come to harm.

2. A robot must obey the orders given it by human beings except where such orders would conflict with the first law.

3. A robot must protect its own existence as long as such protection does not conflict with the first or second law.)

While on patrol, building-security robots may have to be careful of avoiding collisions with their mechanical cousins which will also be making the rounds — commercial cleaning robots. Commercial cleaning is something like a 50 billion dollar a year business, and about 90 percent of its costs are labor-related. Cleaning robots are expected to fill the high demand for new workers, not to replace people.

Scrubbing robots that can clean washbasins, urinals, floors, and mirrors have been developed. They can work at human speed, and clean a toilet in about 90 seconds.

Robots will also be used for a variety of building construction and maintenance chores, including brick-laying, painting, window-washing, interior wall-tiling, and inspecting and repairing skyscrapers.

Electric utilities are also taking an interest in robots for repair and inspection jobs at nuclear and more traditional energy plants, as well as on transmission lines. Robots have already been used in almost 200 different utility applications. Studies by the Electric Power Research Institute show greater worker safety and substantial savings could be achieved by using robots. Public Service Electric and Gas Co. has shown that for every dollar it spent on nuclear plant robots, it saved two to three dollars in operation and maintenance costs.

If there is a radioactive accident at a nuclear power plant, robots will be in the front line for clean-up duty. They are also proficient at many other hazardous duties, including fire-fighting, tunneling and mining, undersea exploration and engineering, and repair and inspection of offshore structures.

Robots will also be on the front line against earthquakes. In 1993, Japan's Mitsubishi reported it had developed a prototype robot that could be placed some three miles under the ocean on seabeds to monitor movements of the earth's crust, collect data on seismic actions, and be used to possibly predict earthquakes.

Of course, service robots won't only be working in the danger zone and on the dark side. There is a lighter side for them, too. For example, a pizza-making robot has been developed. Other robots have been built that can pick fruit, shear sheep, and milk cows (the robotic cow-milker can increase milk output by 15 percent). And then there is the mobile, autonomous robot being developed by the University of Washington. Called the "Roboschlepper," it will handle airport luggage.

Those are just some examples. The possibilities for service robots are virtually endless. Which leads to the inevitable question: What about a home service robot — sort of a combination maid, butler, hotel front desk and room service, well-trained pet, bartender, allowance-needing, chore-doing child, etc? And would anyone want one?

According to Mr. Engelberger, a skilled household robot could be developed "in three years with a $15 million investment."[28] But would a home robot be worth the time, effort, and investment?

It's tough to say, of course, at this point. Some very crude home robots hit the market in the early and mid-1980s, but they didn't make much of an impact. Of course, they were part sham/part primitive, sort of the Piltdown man of robotic evolution. Limited in their abilities, they weren't much more than toys for adults. What Mr. Engelberger was talking about is a truly advanced robot; multi-sensored, easily-programmable, mobile, dexterous, and with a reasonable ability to respond to and speak a human language.

An informal survey of some women acquaintances would indicate that, sure, they'd love a robotic Jeeves that would vacuum, fix coffee, and do God-knows-whatever-other chores around the apartment or house. (I know, I know, that was sexist.)

My guess is, assuming the robot-servant was easy to program, multi-functional, and lived up to its billing, and was reasonably affordable, there would be a solid demand for it. Such a robot could also find a ready market with the elderly and infirm. If I had to venture a guess, a strong market for home robots would probably kick in by about 2005-2010.

Which leads to an even more inevitable question — what about the intelligent, aware, Commander Data-type android that in a dim light, and with a couple of drinks in you, you'd mistake for a human? Well, to a large degree that would depend on advances in artificial intelligence, which will be taken up in the next chapter.

■   ■   ■

It seems few of these millennial technologies can come to pass without a sociological and/or moral dilemma. It must be the tenor of the times. But it's nothing new. In England in the early 1800s, a violent movement of displaced workers led by Ned Ludd revolted against the increasing automation of the textile industry. The Luddite rebellion died out quickly, but the fear of losing one's job to a machine is still with us.

By some estimates, robots will replace about three million U.S. factory jobs by the turn of the century. Surveys indicate more than 75 percent of assembly workers and machine operators feel robots are a threat to their jobs.

It doesn't have to be that way. Not if companies make the commitment to retrain workers for the new jobs robots will create. In Japan, where robots are much more extensively used, unemployment is traditionally much lower than in America, partly because Japanese companies often assure their workers jobs for life.

Additionally, there is the argument that high technology ultimately creates more jobs than it destroys. Perhaps more importantly, in the long run, more U.S. jobs will be lost if companies, and industries, lose out to other countries in the international competition for markets.

SOURCES

If you want to keep up on developments in robotics, you can try one of the following:

Managing Automation
Thomas Publishing Company
5 Penn Plaza
New York, New York 10001
212-629-1514

The Robotic Industries Association (RIA)
900 Victors Way
P.O. Box 3724
Ann Arbor, Michigan 48106
313-994-6088 Fax: 313-994-3338

The RIA publishes *Robot Times* quarterly, and also is affiliated with *NSRA NEWS* (which is a newsletter for service robots), and *AIA Today* (the newsletter of the Automated Imaging Association—which will keep you up to snuff on machine vision)

Robotics World
Communications Channels, Inc.
6255 Barfield Road
Atlanta, Georgia 30328
404-256-9800

For a more technical write-up:

Robotics Today
Robotics International of the Society of Manufacturing Engineers
One SME Drive
P.O. Box 930
Dearborn, Michigan 48121
313-271-1500

After an industry shake-up in the 1980s, there currently are not that many opportunities to put your money into robotics. But there are a few. Again, I can't stress enough that these companies are potential long-term *investments, not speculations.* Please call for their latest annual and quarterly reports. Information applies to the early 1990s.

I am not including larger, publicly-held companies, like General Motors, that have robotics units.

Cimflex Teknowledge Corp. (OTC stock - CMTK)
Franklin Industrial Park
20 Liberty Way
Franklin, Massachusetts 02038
508-528-4787 Fax: 508-528-5615

Formed in 1981, and has more than 100 employees.

Through its Automated Factories division, Cimflex makes factory automation robotic equipment that controls the manufacturing process. Its products are mainly sold to the electronics, auto, telecommunications, computer, and packaging industries. Systems are used for CIM flexible assembly.

For its 1991 fiscal year, Cimflex's sales were about $15 million, but it lost over $1 million. The company lost money the previous four years.

Megamation Inc. (OTC - MEGI)
51 Everett Drive #B4
Lawrenceville, New Jersey 08648
609-799-7711 Fax: 609-799-9419

Produces automated, multiple-arm robotic systems designed mainly for small part (less than 10 pounds) assembly and handling in the light manufacturing, electronic, and auto industries.

This small company's annual sales are about $6 million.

Prab Robots, Inc. (OTC - PRAB)
P.O. Box 2321
Kalamazoo, Michigan 49003
616-382-8200 Fax: 616-349-2477

The company was formed in 1960, and currently has about 100 employees.

Prab manufactures and designs electric and electrohydraulic industrial robots.

The company's annual sales in 1991 were about $16 million, but it lost roughly $1 million that year. Prab also had a net loss the previous two years.

Thermwood Corp. (ASE - THM)
Old Buffaloville Road
Dale, Indiana 47526
812-937-4476 Fax: 812-937-2956

Thermwood was formed in 1969, and has about 100 employees.

Through its Machine Products division, the company makes industrial robots and high-speed robotic-machining systems for use in performing simple tasks. Its products include paint spraying robots.

Thermwood's annual sales are in the $10 million range. It lost about $150,000 in 1991, but made money the previous two years.

For the present, there are only a couple of publicly-held companies devoted primarily to service robots:

Denning Mobile Robotics, Inc. (OTC - GARD)
21 Concord Street
Wilmington, Massachusetts 01887
508-658-7800 Fax: 508-658-2492

The company was founded in 1982, and has about 20 employees.

It manufactures various types of mobile, wheeled robots equipped with vision systems and sensors, which can navigate and operate independently without human intervention. Some robots are used for security, or industrial floor cleaning. Another can position television cameras. Denning also sells mobile robots to universities and corporations for their own R&D activities. The company has also recently developed a mobile robot for automated materials handling in a factory or warehouse.

The company has annual sales of less than $1 million. It's been having problems turning a profit. For the year ended December 31, 1991, it lost more than $1.5 million. For the nine months ended September 30, 1992, Denning had a net loss of about $1 million. The company reports it only had $15,000 in cash on hand in late 1992, and said in its 10-Q form that its "... continuation as a going concern is contingent upon its ability to obtain sufficient funds to finance further development and to continue production and marketing ..." The company was planning to raise $2 million.

Trading in Denning stock is very limited.

Odetics, Inc. (ASE - O.A or O.B)
1515 South Manchester Avenue
Anaheim, California 92802
714-774-5000 Fax: 714-774-9432

The company was founded in 1969, and has more than 500 employees. Odetics manufactures automated products that help store and control information, including robotic systems. Among its products are automated libraries used to automate the storage and handling of computer tapes.

It makes a so-called Cart Machine, which is something like a robot video librarian, and is used by TV stations to retrieve a videotape of a commercial or taped segment from its storage area, place it in the right VTR at the right time for play during the broadcast, and then put it back. Having worked in television, I can tell you that quite a few tapes can get played in a short period of time. Odetics won an EMMY award in 1990 for its Cart Machine. Odetics is also developing a mobile, six-legged robot that will inspect and repair a French nuclear power plant.

Odetics has annual sales of over $50 million and has been regularly profitable.

I'd like you to be aware of one other company that, although currently privately-held, is devoted to service robots:

Transitions Research Corp (TRC)
15 Great Pasture Road
Danbury, Connecticut 06810
203-798-8988

As alluded to in the body of this chapter, the company's chairman and founder is Joe Engelberger, who is known as the father of industrial robotics. Mr. Engelberger has taken on a new title as "evangelist" of service robots. His company currently markets the "Helpmate" robot, which can autonomously carry food trays and supplies through a hospital. TRC was also granted a contract from the U.S. Post Office to develop a washroom cleaning robot.

In a 1993 interview with the author, Engelberger said he would probably take the company public.

The following companies are involved in the manufacture of machine vision systems:

Automatix, Inc. (OTC - AITX)
755 Middlesex Turnpike
Billerica, Massachusetts 01821
508-667-7900 Fax: 508-663-5842

Automatix was formed in 1980 and has more than 50 employees.

The company develops image processing software and makes adaptive automation systems and machine vision inspection systems.

According to recently available figures, its annual sales are about $8.5 million, but the company had been losing money. However, for the nine months ended September 26, 1992, it turned a profit of more than $1 million.

Cognex Corp (OTC - CGNX)
15 Crawford Street
Needham, Massachusetts 02194
617-449-6030 Fax: 617-449-4013

Cognex was formed in 1981 by machine vision experts from MIT, and has about 150 employees. It's widely considered to be the leader in its field.

The company's machine vision systems are used for various tasks in a variety of industries.

Financially, the company has been solid. For the year ended December 31, 1991, Cognex sales were about $30 million, and its net income was more than $9 million. The company posted its twenty-first consecutive profitable quarter for the quarter ended June 28, 1992.

Optical Specialties, Inc. (OTC - OSIX)
4281 Technology Drive
Fremont, California 94538
510-490-6400 Fax: 510-490-1748

The firm was founded in 1978, and employs more than 50.

Optical Specialties makes automated micro-processor-controlled wafer inspection and measurement systems primarily used by semi-conductor manufacturers.

The company's annual sales are about $7 million, but it lost money from 1985 through 1991.

Pattern Processing Technologies, Inc (OTC - PPRO)
10025 Valley View Road
Eden Prairie, Minnesota 55344
612-942-5747 Fax: 612-942-5752

Founded in 1982, the company currently has about 30 employees.

Pattern Processing Technologies manufactures machine vision systems for assembly verification, flaw detection, and character verification. In addition to quality control, the systems are used for robotic guidance applications.

The company's annual sales have been running at about $3 million. It lost money in 1991, but turned a small profit the previous year.

Robotic Vision Systems, Inc. (OTC - ROBV)
425 Rabro Drive East
Hauppauge, New York 11788
516-273-9700 Fax: 516-273-1167

Formed in 1977, the company employs more than 50.

It makes machine vision systems used for inspection and quality control. The company's main customers are large industrial concerns and the government.

Annual sales are about $10 million. Robotic Vision Systems lost more than $2 million in 1991 and 1990.

I'd also like to mention one other company, which makes sensors.

CyberOptics Corp. (OTC - CYBE)
2505 Kennedy Street Northeast
Minneapolis, Minnesota 55413
612-331-5702 Fax: 612-331-3826

CyberOptics was founded in 1984. It employs about 50 people.

The company makes high-precision, laser-based sensors, and sensor systems which can be used for robotic control and other areas of automated manufacturing. It also provides R&D services in machine vision systems.

The latest available figures show the company's annual sales are more than $5 million, and it has been profitable.

CHAPTER 4

ARTIFICIAL INTELLIGENCE
(BY ANY OTHER NAME)

"If I only had a brain."

—the Scarecrow in 'The Wizard of Oz'

"I believe that at the end of the century... general, educated opinion will have altered so much that one will be able to speak of machines thinking without expecting to be contradicted."

—Alan Turing, 1950

"Hello."

Just one little soft-spoken "Hello." Trivial. Commonplace. White noise. But that one common word drew cheers.

That's because that particular "Hello" was the successful beginning to a provocative demonstration of artificial intelligence.

The everyday greeting started a telephone conversation in 1993 among Japanese, German, and American scientists—in their native tongues. But they weren't multi-lingual. Their words were translated and spoken by Janus.

Janus, named for an ancient two-faced god, is a computer translation system. The computer understands words spoken in one language by anyone who speaks clearly, translates them, then synthesizes them into speech in another tongue. So the Janus experiment started in Tokyo with a Japanese researcher saying "Moshi-moshi" into a microphone, which came out as "Hello" in Pittsburgh. And off they went.

Janus only works for the three above-mentioned languages, and it's translating abilities are limited. But it's a beginning. Appropriately, Janus was also the god of beginnings (hence January). An advanced commercial computer translation system probably won't be on sale for a few years. But the potential worldwide market could be huge. Think of it. Tourists would no longer have to shout at natives, as if that ever made it easier to be understood. A system like Janus could also be used by hotels, car rental companies, and the like to take reservations when multi-lingual staff isn't available. Along with the travel industry, translating computers could become an indispensable business tool for meetings and presentations in the global marketplace.

In Janus, we have a machine that, in one package, can hear, understand, translate, and speak. Janus, binary and two-tongued, would fit some definitions of artificial intelligence.

One of the founding fathers of artificial intelligence (AI), Marvin Minsky, once defined *AI as "the science of making machines do things that would require intelligence if done by men."*[1] But over the years, AI has become more of an umbrella term that covers many distinct but related areas. Janus-like speech recognition, translation, and speech are just a few aspects. Indeed, the words artificial intelligence have recently fallen somewhat out of favor. *"Applied intelligence"* is more in vogue nowadays. And the politically-correct sounding *business process automation, intelligent process modeling,* and *knowledge management* are also beginning to take hold.

Perhaps it's because the sound of artificial intelligence was always a bit threatening. It does not quite settle well on the mind. It jars. Artificial intelligence. *Artificial* intelligence. Machines that can think right along with humans, or perhaps out-think them — computers are already beating some of the world's chess masters. AI sounds like the 21st century equivalent of learning that the sun does not revolve around the earth. Artificial intelligence seems to toy with the relationship, the natural order, of man and machine.

Artificial intelligence may be considered by some to be the ultimate threat to the alpha-primacy of humans on the planet — we, perhaps will no longer be at the top of the food chain come the millennium. It's a modern day version of the Frankenstein fear. We created something we shouldn't have toyed with. It will destroy us. A sci-fi image easily comes to mind of modem-lined, thought-sharing, intelligent computers, pixels pulsating, gestating, silently waiting for their moment, like the birds in the final shot of the Hitchcock movie of the same name, to one day announce to us by computer-screen message, something along the lines of, "So long, suckers."

But that was just my science version of gratuitous T & A, and sex and violence. An attention getter. The PG version of artificial intelligence is much more subdued. For the time being, and very possibly forever — there is no machine threat. In fact, the reason the expression artificial intelligence probably really fell out of favor was because AI did not live up to its early suggested promise and hype. Certainly, not within the time frame originally expected after the term and concept were first coined in 1956.

Simply put, the goal then was to create computers that could think like humans — emulate the thought process, and be as smart, if not smarter. But that proved tricky. The most basic type of common sense, or even horse sense, sometimes seems damn near impossible to program into computer brains.

In many ways, computers are still very stupid. They pretty much do exactly, *exactly*, what they're told. They're like idiot-savants, machine-Rainmen, brilliant at rapid-fire calculations, but otherwise, lost. When it comes to the three Rs, except for 'rithmetic, any grade-schooler can pretty much whip a computer.

But computers are beginning to climb off their lap-top haunches and take their first upright steps through the silicon valleys. The spark of artificial intelligence has taken hold in computer evolution. However, it's humans who call the shots for now. They're just calling them more and more with the assistance of computers. (In the military's case, AI is often literally calling the shots. The Pentagon has various on-going projects in machine intelligence, many of which are related to its efforts in robotics — see previous chapter.) AI is being used as an indispensable aid for many humans and industries. There's a large and expanding market for AI, although it has nothing to do with the original vision.

"AI is growing but it's difficult now to put a dollar figure on it. Trying to define the AI market size is like trying to define the size of the market for vinyl-covered seats in cars. AI is growing as part of the overall computer software growth," according to Harvey Newquist III, chief executive officer of The Relayer Group.[2]

The AI industry totaled out to just a few million dollars in the early 1980s. For 1993, total U.S. AI sales are estimated at about $1 billion. But according to the Commerce Department, annual U.S. sales for AI will hit $5 billion by the year 2000. For the world, they will be $12 billion.[3]

Some estimates take it a step further, predicting the overall computer industry will hit about a trillion dollars by the new millennium, and the bulk of that industry will be "intelligent."

Currently, the most commonly used type of applied intelligence on the market is something called expert systems, which allow computers to mimic human knowledge. Expert systems are, in essence, an attempt to give computers judgment and the ability to make inferences and solve certain (non-math) problems.

The systems work by transferring the sum knowledge, the savvy, of human professionals, old master hands in a particular field, say medicine, into a computer. It's like passing down lore to a machine. The computer gets the facts and figures, the procedures, the experience, the ideas and concepts, the rules of thumb, tricks of the trade, and perhaps a machine-form of sixth sense.

More technically, expert systems are an advanced type of software, or computer program, that allows a computer to quickly analyze scads of information, and make a prediction, spot a trend, draw a conclusion, make a decision, or find a solution. Expert systems have proven they can rival the judgment of human professionals.

To give a quick example, one early expert system developed in the 1970s called "INTERNIST," whose field of knowledge was internal medicine, made a correct diagnosis 25 times in 43 actual cases. The physicians taking care of those patients made the correct call 28 times. More recent diagnostic expert systems have been more accurate than doctors. This is a bit disconcerting—a computer doing as good a job as Marcus Welby. Perhaps in the future you'll be able to run a self-diagnosis on a personal computer with an expert system.

Giving a computer that kind of learnin' is an interesting, but complex process. Developing an expert system starts with a so-called knowledge engineer, who is a human being. The knowledge engineer actually goes out and conducts in-depth interviews with human experts in a field, records their knowledge, and tries to get at the crux of how they solve a given problem. The knowledge engineer then puts that insight into a code a computer can understand and use.

Now, say the expert system-endowed computer is confronted with a problem in that field. The computer sifts through its database of expert knowledge, essentially using a series of if-then statements or rules to eventually home in on a solution. It's been compared to playing a complicated, extended game of 20 questions.

But it's no game. It's big business.

Expert systems have already proven their worth in a wide variety of fields. Some systems have accurately identified previously unknown sites for various natural resources. One global bank has saved $2 million by applying

Reprinted by permission: Tribune Media Services.

expert systems to its customer service department. General Motors and Ford use expert systems to help build cars and solve engine problems. The Human Service Agency of one California county has an expert system that helps its clerks decide if welfare applicants qualify for benefits. American Express uses expert systems to assist its credit authorizers to analyze a customer's payment history and financial credentials to determine if a specific charge is risky. In this way Amex's systems have cut bad credit judgments by 75 percent. American Airlines has a system to figure out the best maintenance schedule for all of its planes. American Airline's expert system reportedly saves the carrier about half a billion dollars a year.

The list goes on and on. There are thousands of expert systems in use and they will continue to proliferate in the business world.

"By the year 2001, expert systems are in universal use in manufacturing, energy prospecting, automotive diagnostics, medicine, insurance underwriting, and law enforcement," predict futurists Marvin Cetron and Owen Davies.[4]

And according to the Commerce Department, "Expert systems will become an embedded function within mainstream computer systems. Users will increasingly demand that these systems be integrated with the databases of their companies."[5]

Annual sales for expert systems in the U.S., already at about $750 million, are predicted to grow 10 percent annually.[6]

Ultimately, expert systems of various kinds will probably become commonplace for personal computer owners.

For example, expert systems are being used to help aspiring fiction writers develop plot lines. In fact, computers have already written novels. The most recent example, *Just This Once,* published by Carol Publishing Group, is being billed as a steamy romance novel. The plotline reportedly deals with a woman who's waiting for her divorce to go through. Among some of the lines of artificial dialogue: "She's doing the sit and split and looking for a gig." And "Put Glenn under the forever thumb of the alimony court."

Frankly, I'm not sure if that passes for good or bad writing for a romance novel.

Some expert systems use fuzzy logic, which has nothing to do with the logic of teenagers, or the stoned, or the madly in love. Fuzzy logic is actually based on a form of mathematics.

Fuzzy logic allows computers to better deal with uncertainty, with the way the world really is. It lets computers mimic the human reasoning process, giving them the ability to make decisions the way humans make most of theirs — without all the facts, based on incomplete and imprecise knowledge.

We decide to wake up on Monday morning, even though we don't know for sure if the subways are running. But the likelihood that they are is pretty certain. It's like that in life. Not everything is an absolute — absolutely true or absolutely false. Fuzzy logic lets computers deal with the grey areas. With fuzzy logic, expert systems can proceed through their knowledge-base with a series of questions that don't have to be answered true or false, but can be "likely" or "unlikely," and thereby reach a conclusion or decision.

"Expert systems are 'brittle.' but if you coat them with fuzzy logic, or 'fuzzify' their crisp input values, they can more readily respond and react appropriately to unforeseen circumstances," says Colin Johnson, editor of *The Cognizer Almanac.*[7]

The Japanese are reportedly at the forefront, both in the research and marketing, of fuzzy logic. It's part of Japan's so-called Real-World Computing Program which began in 1992. The goal of the 10-year, multi-million dollar collective effort is to create the next generation of computing, and nothing less than a computer that essentially thinks like a human — one that can intuitively deal with the 'real-world.'

"Fuzzy logic is potentially a coming revolution — it's a tremendously hot global growth area . . . except possibly in the U.S.," says Johnson. "American engineers seem to have a built in prejudice against the word 'fuzzy, but U.S. semiconductor companies are starting to get behind it."[8]

The international market for fuzzy logic is expected to grow from 1992's roughly $300 million (double 1991's) to more than $6 billion in 1997. That's a 20-fold increase. Fuzzy logic-based software and hardware could hit the tens of billions of dollars before the 21st century. Fuzzy microchips alone could bring in $10 billion or more by the year 2000.[9]

Another rapidly growing form of AI is called neural networks — computer systems that also attempt to give machines a more human-like thought process. In fact, they are often used to essentially "tune" or "tweak" fuzzy logic systems and make them more accurate.

Using sophisticated software and developing hardware, neural nets model themselves after the naked ape's brain. The systems try to simulate how neurons transmit all those millions of pieces of (sensory) data to the brain for sorting out.

"Neural nets attempt to duplicate the workings of the brain by duplicating the structure of the brain. A specific piece of information is worked on by a number of facilities at one time. Neural nets can process an incredible amount of data, and save time spotting unusual data trends," says Newquist.[10]

The very important thing about neural nets is that they can learn by example, and from past mistakes. Consequently, they become more adept over time. Neural nets can recognize patterns and make associations and judgements.

"Neural nets are a whole different ballgame. Unlike fuzzy logic, which engineers design, they are self-organizing, and somewhat autonomous," according to Johnson. "A neural has the ability to learn a pattern, and once it learns, it never forgets. But the algorithm it recognizes was not designed by humans."[11]

Neural nets are spreading through the corporate world for various uses, slaving away at such tasks as lending risk analysis and detecting credit card fraud. Additionally, some oil companies use neural nets to pinpoint crude oil deposits.

For Shearson Lehman, the hope is that the future can be caught in the web of neural nets. Brokers use neural nets to forecast the movement of the stock and bond markets. And if you get a catalogue from Spiegel, it may have been with the prompting of AI. Spiegel uses neural nets to try and figure out who among the millions of mailing list minions out there are the most likely to be attracted to, and buy, Spiegel goods.

(One little sidebar here. In 1992, scientists at the California Institute of Technology and Oxford University jointly announced that they had developed a so-called "silicon neuron"—a chip that mimics the qualities of a human brain cell. Much like a brain cell, the chip's response to electrical stimulation varies with the intensity of the stimulus. Also, like the brain, the silicon neuron chip will eventually stop reacting to the same stimulus if it's constant—like when you stop "hearing" white noise.)

In the U.S., annual sales of neural networks (including fuzzy logic and neural microprocessors) are running at about $50-80 million a year, but yearly revenues are expected to grow 25 percent to 30 percent.[12]

A more recent development, related to and used with neural nets and fuzzy logic, is *genetic algorithms*. Genetic algorithms are essentially a computer software version of survival of the fittest. They randomly create many solutions to a problem, successively killing off the ones that don't work well enough. Also, in 1993 Japanese researchers were reportedly working on a method to allow hardware, groups of chips, to essentially evolve, or change their circuitry in response to a changing environment.

Because neural nets can recognize patterns, including shapes of objects, they are important in the development of computers that can see with extreme skill. Neural nets are already beginning to be used to recognize handwriting. If you've ever looked at a doctor's prescription, you know how difficult that can be.

The ability to decipher handwriting could save certain organizations — read, no pun intended, the Post Office — millions of dollars. It reportedly costs the P.O. more than 10 times as much to process a letter by human hand-eye action as opposed to automatic processing.

American Express already uses so-called *optical character readers (OCR)* to make out the writing on more than half of the almost one million daily charge slips Amex receives. Those slips are processed automatically. Human clerks handle the rest of the slips, the ones that are chicken scrawl. The IRS also uses machine scanners to sift through the E-Z forms it gets that are hand-written. Any office that's inundated with applications and other forms of paper-work would probably welcome an OCR.

OCRs and neural nets also play a big part in the development of pen-based computers, the ones where you can write directly on the screen, like Apple's Newton.

If you combine an OCR with a computer that can speak, you have what could be a monumental aid for the visually impaired. There are, in fact, such text-to-speech systems already in use. For example, the user can run a hand-held scanner over a magazine article, or lay the page on a portable scanner, and the device will then read it aloud (in as many as nine languages).

Unlike children, computers are being heard as often as they're being seen. The ability of computers to deal with language, whether it's voice synthesis, or hearing and understanding, or translating, is, as alluded to earlier in the chapter, a major aspect of AI. Be it on the phone, playing a video game, being prompted by a car or vending machine, we've probably all had our experiences with a machine that has a voice box made up of chips. Computers can talk the talk; they're virtually becoming talking heads. Speaking is the easy part for computers when it comes to dealing with language. It's the hearing, understanding, and translating that's the tough part.

Reprinted by permission: Tribune Media Services.

In the movie "My Cousin Vinny," there's a well-known scene where Vinny, a street-wise, New York lawyer is defending his young cousin and his cousin's friend in a Deep South courtroom against a murder charge. In his presentation, Vinny, in his best New Yawk-ese, refers to the youngsters as the two "yutes."

The son-of-the-South judge is perplexed. 'What's a yute?' he wants to know. Vinny, realizing the problem, repeats the word with the most precise and exaggerated diction and enunciation — "Excuse me your honor, the two *youthhss.*"

That scene essentially captures the problem computers have in understanding the spoken word. Because computers are so exacting, any slight variance from what it's used to, from what it's programmed for, can throw it for a loop.

When it comes to language, that variance can take the form of a regional accent, or just the differences in speech from individual to individual. The speed, pitch, volume, and pronunciation you use when talking is probably significantly different, to a computer, than one of your immediate family members. And then there's the question of background noise. Does the computer take those sounds into consideration as it tries to understand the speech sounds being thrown at it? And we still haven't covered nuance and context. Imagine a computer trying to figure out what's going on in the famous Abbott and Costello "Who's on first" routine? It gives one a new appreciation of the senses we take for granted.

But speech recognition systems are rapidly improving, and their commercial applications are beginning to spread. For example, the "type-less" typewriter — the talkwriter — is on the way. In fact, it's already here. But the top of the line systems, the most urbane of the talkwriters, are pretty much out of the price range of the average consumer now — costing anywhere from $5,000 to about $30,000. What users get for that kind of money is a system that can recognize something like 30 to 40 spoken words a minute, but the speaker has to pause slightly between words. Depending on the model, the talkwriters can understand a total of about 20,000 to 50,000 words.

Among the current users of such systems are doctors, who want them for dictating medical reports, the handicapped, and those with repetitive stress syndrome.

Many companies, including IBM and Apple, are ready to offer scaled-down, more general purpose voice recognition systems, which will be cheaper.

And while typing may be a thing of the past, so may be dialing a phone. A voice recognition system developed by NYNEX, and aimed at the mass market, lets a customer pick up a phone, speak a key word or phrase that represents a certain number, say "work" or "girlfriend," and the phone will dial the appropriate number.

Personal computers, stereos, and other home appliances, even microwave ovens, are becoming more adept at understanding the spoken word because of software advances. For example, a company called Voice Powered Technology has marketed a remote control device that can program a VCR with a few simple voice commands. Instead of going through the baffling dial-o-rama to record a show that's on when you're asleep, you just distinctly tell the device the key information — channel, day, and time the show begins and ends. And that's it.

The U.S. market for voice recognition in 1992 was estimated at about $100 million, and was expected to grow at about a 20 percent annual clip.[13]

As this is being written there are indications that even talking to a computer will someday become obsolete. Rather than read lips, computers may read minds. Get ready for some real science-fiction stuff here. A front page story in the *New York Times* February 9, 1993 issue reported that researchers in Japan, America, and Europe, in separate projects, are developing ways to control a computer just by thinking the commands. Although the research is in its infancy, human thought has already moved cursors and typed words across computer screens.

Actually, it apparently has nothing to do with ESP, but is based on the electrical signals of the brain. Still, it's quite a startling story.

So with AI, computers are talking, gaining judgment, making decisions, seeing better, understanding speech and handwriting, and even translating. AI has, in essence, become a stew of interconnected and related functions.

But the original vision of AI never really died. In the leading AI centers, like MIT and Carnegie Mellon, the ultimate goal is still to create a computer that thinks like a human. But is it possible? Will machines ever be truly "intelligent," really be able to "think?" Will they know they exist? (Cogito, ergo sum!) That type of speculation, of course, gets caught up in a recursive loop — what is intelligence, thinking, and consciousness, anyway?

Alan Turing, a brilliant British mathematician, tried to cut through the philosophical crap. In 1950, he devised the now famous Turing Test to determine if a computer is truly intelligent.

Essentially, the test goes something like this: A panel of humans sit on one side of a screen. They converse by computer terminal with what could be a human or a computer on the other side. If the panel, by the nature of the responses it gets, is faked out and believes a computer is a human, then the computer can safely be said to be intelligent.

One recent, partial exchange went like this:

Terminal (could be human or computer)—A whim is a sudden capricious and often peculiar behavior. A bit of sunlight in a grim gray world.

Panelist (human)—Something like a hunch?

Terminal—Everybody sets out to do something and everybody does something, but no one does what he sets out to do.

Panelist—Well, anyway, I would imagine whimsical conversation is like a series of knight's moves in chess—sort of zig-zag rather than following any particular line.

Terminal—A whimsical person is subject to erratic behavior and unpredictable thoughts . . . how nice to be unpredictable.

Panelist—Are you kidding? Sure, total predictability would make the world a dull place, but unpredictability is hardly a virtue.

At the terminal was a computer. I've had lesser phone conversations.

Recent Turing-test computers have fooled as many as four out of eight human panelists. But the conversations were restricted to one tight topic. A $100,000 prize awaits anyone who can create the software or machine that passes a completely unrestricted test. But even if a computer eventually passes, that still won't mean it has the spark.

Some experts I've spoken with predicted a computer that truly thinks like a human will be on the scene in a generation. Others say it will take 100 years.

By some calculations, computing power is doubling every two years. Certainly, that will help push the evolution of machine intelligence. As for the future of that evolution, AI expert Raymond Kurzweil says, "Within a matter of years or decades it appears that computers will compete successfully with human intelligence in many spheres. If we extrapolate a sufficient number of decades or centuries into the future, it appears likely that human intelligence will be surpassed."[14]

But rather than ultimately matching, or surpassing, human-type intelligence, perhaps machine smarts will move along a different parallel pathway. There may be an apartheid, a segregation of intelligence on the planet. I'm reminded of something Andrew Marvell wrote in the 17th century concerning a love that was never meant to be:

As lines, so love's oblique may well
Themselves in every angle greet:
But ours, so truly parallel,
Though infinite, can never meet.

So it may be for machine and human intelligence.

SOURCES

As for investing in AI, while the potential is strong, the opportunities are limited right now. But there are a few, and more AI companies are expected to go public.

To keep up with the AI field I'd recommend one of the following:

AI Magazine
published by:
The American Association for Artificial Intelligence
445 Burgess Drive
Menlo Park, California 94025
415-328-3123

Artificial Intelligence Trends
published by The RELAYER Group
8232 East Buckskin
Scottsdale, Arizona 85255
602-585-8587

Cognizer Almanac
An annual report on the AI field published by Cognizer Co.
10075 S.W. Barbur Boulevard
Building 5, Suite 405
Portland, Oregon 97219
503-246-6464

INTELLIGENCE: The Future of Computing
PO Box 20008
New York, New York 10025
212-222-1123

Intelligent Software Strategies
Editorial Office:
151 Collingwood
San Francisco, California 94114
415-861-1660
Published by Cutter Information Group
37 Broadway
Arlington, Massachusetts 02174
617-648-8702

Many large, publicly-held computer companies are developing AI hardware and/or software. They include, Apple, Digital Equipment, Hewlett-Packard, IBM, Microsoft, Motorola, Sun Microsystems, Texas Instruments, and Xerox.

Besides the companies listed below, please also check the chapter on robots for firms involved in the machine vision field.

If you are interested in any of the following smaller AI companies, please call for their latest financial reports. Unless otherwise specified, information applies to the early 1990s.

ALPNet, Inc. (OTC - AILP)
4444 South 700 East
Salt Lake City, Utah 84107
801-265-3300

ALPNet was incorporated in 1980, and has more than 200 employees. It makes various machine translation products, including software solutions for customers with large multi-lingual translation requirements. The firm's annual sales are running at about $20 million, but it lost money from 1987 through 1991 and for the first nine months of 1992.

Bolt, Beranek & Newman Inc. (NYSE - BBN)
70 Fawcett Street
Cambridge, Massachusetts 02138
617-873-2000

The company was formed in 1948 and has more than 2,000 employees.

Bolt builds various computer-based systems. Performs R&D in the computer (including AI), communications, acoustic, and physical science fields. Does contract work for the government. Expert systems, speech, and natural language systems are among its AI projects.

The company's annual sales are about a quarter of a billion dollars (about half its sales are to the federal government). The company turned a $9 million profit in 1991.

Caere Corp. (OTC - CAER)
100 Cooper Court
Los Gatos, California 95030
408-395-7000

Caere was founded in 1973. The company employs more than 100.

The firm is a leading developer and manufacturer of page recognition software and optical character recognition readers. The products essentially automate data entry by reading printed information and storing it in a computer.

The information is transferred into a computer with much greater speed and accuracy than manually typing it in.

Caere's annual sales were running at more than $40 million, and the company has been turning a solid profit.

Cimflex Teknowledge (OTC - CMTK)

Develops expert systems software (see listing in Robots, Chapter 3, for more details).

Cognitive Systems, Inc. (OTC - CSAI)
234 Church Street
New Haven, Connecticut 06510
203-773-0726

Formed in 1981, the company currently has about 30 employees.

Cognitive develops various AI based software including expert systems software. Its products are primarily sold to the financial industry and the government.

Annual sales are about $3 million.

Communication Intelligence Corp.
275 Shoreline Drive
Redwood City, California 94065
415-802-7888

Company is listed on the Vancouver Stock Exchange under CUA.

Also known as CIC, the company was founded in 1981. It employs about 60 people.

CIC develops computer character recognition technology, including systems that allow a computer to recognize hand printed characters. One system recognizes Japanese characters.

Annual sales are about $1 million, but the company lost money in the 1991 and 1990 fiscal years.

Digital Sound Corp. (OTC - DGSC)
6307 Carpinteria Avenue
Carpinteria, California 93013
805-566-2000   800-347-2946

Digital Sound was formed in 1977. It employs about 150.

The company makes computer-based systems that can perform various voice processing applications simultaneously, including speech recognition and converting text-to-speech.

Annual sales are more than $30 million, and the company's net income was $1.5 million in 1991.

Dynamics Research Corp. (OTC - DRCO)
60 Concord Street
Wilmington, Massachusetts 01887
508-658-6100

Incorporated in 1955, and presently has more than 1,000 employees.

Develops natural language workstations and software.

U.S. government contracts account for more than 80 percent of its annual revenues, which approach $100 million. The company has been turning a profit.

Excalibur Technologies Corp. (OTC - EXCA)
2000 Corporate Ridge
McLean, Virginia 22102
703-790-2110

Incorporated in 1980, Excalibur develops neural net software. Annual sales approached $5 million in 1992, but the company lost over $3 million that year.

Intel Corp. (OTC - INTC)
2200 Mission College Boulevard
Santa Clara, California 95052
408-765-8080

Intel is the world's leading manufacturer of computer chips. I'm including it because it is developing neural net chips (see Nestor listing below).

Intel's sales are in the billions, it's solidly profitable, and its stock price saw explosive growth in 1992 and 1993.

IntelliCorp (OTC - INAI)
1975 El Camino Real West
Mountain View, California 94040
415-965-5500

Formed in 1980. Employs more than 100. The company develops AI software products that make it easier to create expert systems.

Annual sales are about $10 million, but it's lost money every year since 1989. For the six months ended December 31, 1992, IntelliCorp lost more than $3 million. But that loss was less than year-ago figures for the same time period.

InterVoice, Inc. (OTC - INTV)
17811 Waterview Parkway
Dallas, Texas 75252
214-669-3988

InterVoice was founded in 1983, and currently has more than 250 employees.

The company makes interactive voice systems that allow someone to access a computer data-base by using touch-tone phone keys, dialing a rotary phone, using computer keyboards, or the voice.

InterVoice's annual sales are about $30 million, and it turned a solid profit in 1991 and 1992.

Nestor, Inc. (OTC - NEST)
1 Richmond Square
Providence, Rhode Island 02906
401-331-9640

The company has about 30 employees. It was formed in 1975.

Nestor develops neural network software to solve complex pattern recognition problems. One of its products can recognize handwriting for the new "pen" personal computers.

Annual sales are about $4 million. For the six months ended December 31, 1992, Nestor lost about half a million dollars. It also lost money for the fiscal years 1992, 1991, and 1990.

Nestor and Intel Corp have jointly developed an advanced neural network chip called the Ni1000 which could have widespread commercial uses.

Perception Technology Corp. (OTC - PCEP)
40 Shawmut Road
Canton, Massachusetts 02021
617-821-0320

The company was formed in 1968. It employs more than 100.

Perception manufactures voice response products that allows direct access to computers.

Its annual sales are about $16 million, and according to most recent figures the company is making money.

Scott Instruments Corp (Amex - SCTI)
1111 Willow Springs Drive
Denton, Texas 76205
817-387-9514

Founded in 1978, incorporated in 1981. Employs about 20.

R&D on hardware and software for voice recognition equipment.

With annual sales of about $2 million, the company turned a small profit for the 1991 fiscal year, but was losing money for the first six months of 1992.

Symbolics, Inc. (OTC - SMBXQ)
8 New England Executive Park
Burlington, Massachusetts 01803
617-221-1000

Symbolics filed for Chapter 11 bankruptcy protection in early 1993. Trading on its stock was halted after the bankruptcy announcement, but the company remains in business.

Symbolics designs and makes software and hardware for AI and other symbolic applications.

Trinzic Corp. (OTC - TRNZ)
101 University Avenue
Palo Alto, California 94301
415-328-9595

Trinzic was formed in 1992 as a result of the merger of AICorp Inc. and Aion Corporation.

The third quarter, ended December 31, 1992, was the company's first full quarter as Trinzic. For that quarter, its revenues were about $10 million, and the company made a profit of more than $1 million.

Trinzic develops expert systems and natural language software.

Vocaltech, Inc. (OTC - VCTHV)
240 West 98th Street
New York, New York 10025
212-663-4587   800-548-6225

This very small company, formed in 1987, makes voice synthesizers used in the development of systems for the treatment of speech disorders. Annual sales are about $100,000.

Kurzweil Applied Intelligence, Inc.
411 Waverley Oaks Road
Waltham, Massachussetts 02154
617-893-5151

In mid-1993, Kurzweil was reportedly planning on going public soon. Kurzweil makes advanced "talkwriters."

CHAPTER 5

MIRACLE MATERIALS

"Ay, workman, make me a dream,
A dream for my love.
Cunningly weave sunlight,
Breezes, and flowers . . . "

— Stephen Crane, "Ay, workman"

"Use of advanced structural composite materials
is likely to have a dramatic effect on Gross National Product,
balance of trade, and employment."

— Department of Defense[1]

I remember seeing a comedian — his name escapes me — who suffered form a severe case of flight-phobia. He just would not get on a plane. He'd rather walk, bike, drive, row, hitch-hike, take the train, whatever. He said he'd never fly until the plane was made out of the same material as the black-box. The black-box is, of course, the box that contains the flight recordings, and survives a crash intact.

The joke may be on him.

Although the "black-box" design is far-fetched, materials are brewing in modern alchemists' labs that could get that comedian his wings yet, and give all of us greater peace of mind — tougher, stronger, lighter, more heat resistant, even "smarter" substances will gird the planes of the 21st century.

But planes are only a small part of it. There is a quiet revolution taking place in materials that will ultimately affect almost every facet of your life, and the quality and efficiency of thousands of products ranging from windsurfers to supercomputers, tennis rackets to rocket ships.

According to the Commerce Department, "The current revolution in the field of materials . . . is beginning to permit design engineers to specify materials having properties that would have been unthinkable a decade ago. Increasingly, it is possible to produce materials having essentially the exact combination of properties desired."[2]

For example, imagine near balsa-light substances, steel-tough, or as hard as a diamond. Advanced materials will mean that in the 21st century you could hop a super-material jet in New York and arrive in Tokyo a couple of hours later. They could lead to snappy, more fuel efficient cars. "Biomaterials" will offer lifetime functional replacement of bones, diseased, tissues, and organs. Advanced construction materials could lead to smooth roads that don't know the meaning of the word pothole, and to homes and buildings that are better able to stand up to hurricanes or earthquakes, and are more energy efficient to boot.

"(Advanced materials) are essential to building America's 21st century infrastructure and the next generation of aircraft, high-speed rail, autos, engines for transportation and industrial use, electronic components, medical devices and environmental products," says an industry group.[3]

Also, using advanced materials could help overcome potential raw materials shortages, putting an end to the "limits to growth" arguments.

Historic periods have often been defined by the prevalent material in use — the Stone Age, the Bronze Age, etc. Some have said the early 21st century will have vying titles — the Information Age versus the Age of Materials.

Materials are the underpinning of all other industries and technologies. From materials, all else springs. In fact, the word 'material' is derived from 'matter' which in turn comes from the Latin 'mater' — mother.

"Materials are the basis of a critical enabling technology upon which most other technologies depend for their success . . . *Increased investments in materials science and technology should result in major contributions to this nation's quality of life, national security, industrial productivity, and economic growth,*" said Dr. Allan Bromley, former director, Office of Science and Technology Policy.[4]

Materials are simply the substances gathered, manipulated, and used by humans to make something they need. Materials are stuff. For the most part, over the millennia, humans have scraped up naturally occurring stuff and adapted it for economic uses.

But with today's technology, it's possible to first have in mind a specific need, and then make the appropriate material. Advanced materials can be tailor-made, sometimes designed layer-of-atoms by layer-of-atoms.

As the Congressional Office of Technology Assessment explains, with the new tailored materials, the designer starts with the final performance requirement and literally creates the necessary materials and the structure.

Teflon is an advanced material. High temperature superconductors are advanced materials (see Chapter 1). Flubber would have been an extremely advanced material. Advanced materials have made possible recent successes in human-powered flight—you may have seen films of a human flying over the Mediterranean by pedaling a light, winged aircraft.

Too late for Icarus and Daedulus. But from before the days of the flying Greeks, the human tribe has attempted to change materials, for practical reasons, or to make them more beautiful, or to get, often literally, an edge. In the ancient Mideast, steel was sometimes made more malleable by shoving a red hot blade into a living slave.

That process ended, but not necessarily because of mercy. It was eventually discovered that you didn't really need the poor slave. A vat of water filled with animal skins would do just as well. What they didn't know back then was that the effect was caused by carbon dioxide, and from that ancient process, and thanks to nameless slaves, metallurgy developed, eventually leading to the modern technique of baptizing steel with CO_2 ions.

Later, in the Dark Ages, alchemists' books of magic referred arcanely to an absolutely non-corrosible iron, and to a flexible glass made from a mineral. In cryptic drawings and writings they allude to transparent metals, and red and blue gold. They whisper of Atlantis and Orichalk, the phosphorescent metal that was rumored to light the causeways of that island civilization.

It may take modern scientists centuries or longer to find the Philosopher's Stone that will enable them to duplicate, if true, that knowledge of the ancients. But in the shorter term, for the purpose of investing, it is important to know that in the new millennium, so-called advanced materials, although not as dramatic as alchemists' achievements, will begin to criss-cross the planet and beyond. They'll be found in our teeth, in our homes, and will help take us to the stars. If we ever build glittering cities on the edge of forever, they will probably be made of advanced materials.

"Unlimited and unprecedented opportunities are waiting to be exploited in the arena of modern materials science and technology. The defining technologies of the future are likely to be based on materials not yet developed, or even imagined. This is an era of invention as well as discovery," according to the U.S. government.[5]

The market pay-off could be huge. *According to the Commerce Department, annual sales of advanced materials by the year 2000 will be $150 billion in the U.S., $400 billion worldwide.*[6]

"The market for advanced materials is large and growing, but it's important to remember that advanced materials are an "enabling" technology, and their market size is incidental to their ability to leverage other industries such as communications, information and transportation," says Samuel Schneider, scientific advisor to the director of the Materials Science and Engineering Laboratory of the National Institute of Standards and Technology.[7]

The competition for the large and growing advanced materials market will be intense. If materials are stuff, then the stuff-wars are on.

Japan recognized the importance of materials way back in the early 1980s when it embarked on a multi-million dollar research and development effort on advanced materials which, along with microelectronics and biotechnology, it saw as one of the big three of emerging technologies. More recently, Japan is taking on new initiatives in materials to support development of next generation airplanes. Japan intends to establish an R&D center for new materials which function at temperatures greater than 3600 degrees Fahrenheit. *The Ministry of International Trade and Industry expects Japan to use up to $90 billion worth of advanced materials annually by the year 2000.*

In the U.S., 1993 was something of a watershed year for advanced materials. The Federal government made a major commitment to them, initiating a multi-year, multi-agency program to increase the effectiveness of the fed's R&D program in materials. The Advanced Materials and Processing Program (AMPP) will focus on improving the manufacture and performance of materials, and will bring government, industry, and universities into closer collaboration. A key goal of AMPP will be to transform research and innovation into useful products.

"The government wants to sit down with industry and work out a common R&D agenda," according to Schneider.[8] AMPP's budget for fiscal 1993 was almost $2 billion. Among the 10 participating federal agencies, the Department of Defense, the Department of Energy, and NASA are among the highest funded.

The Pentagon is interested in advanced materials for everything from grunts' helmets to high-tech, hush-hush aircraft. The Defense Department predicts that by the year 2001 it will have achieved a 25 percent to 50 percent weight reduction in airframes, and land and space vehicles with advanced composites. By 2006, the Pentagon expects widespread use of advanced composite materials in U.S. weapons systems and platforms.

The space colonies of the future will owe a nod to advanced materials. NASA is performing materials R&D for next-generation, high speed civil airplanes, as well as spacecraft, space platforms, and launch systems. NASA is developing materials for everything from airframes to engines, and is hoping to improve the longevity, efficiency, economy, and environmental compatibility of military and civilian aircraft.

Other federal agencies participating in AMPP are the Departments of Commerce, Interior, Transportation, Agriculture, and Health and Human Services, the Environmental Protection Agency, and the National Science Foundation.

Obviously, advanced materials encompass quite a bit of turf. Because of their diversity, I'll focus on a couple of key areas whose markets are expected to explode. They are materials for the millennium.

Although advanced materials cover a lot of ground, when it comes to *advanced ceramics* they don't include the kitchen sink. Nor are high-tech ceramics a crock. They're just distant cousins to the ceramics you find in pottery and bricks, or in the porcelain of teacups and sinks.

Advanced ceramics are basically very pure powders of nonmetallic (and sometimes metallic/nonmetallic) minerals which are mixed, processed, and fired under high pressures to form very dense, hard structures. Compared to many metals, advanced ceramics are Superman. They're stronger, more durable, lighter, they don't rust, they resist corrosion, and they can maintain their structure at volcanic temperatures that would turn metal into silly putty. Some advanced ceramics are second only to diamonds in hardness.

High-tech ceramics are already found in such diverse items as scissors, sensors, dentures, fishhooks, and Space Shuttle tiles.

Because of their imperviousness, ceramics will become more prevalent as cutting tools, and as protective packing for sensitive computer components.

High-tech ceramics are expected to have a large impact on many industries, including telecommunications, electronics, and medicine. But the ultimate big pay-off for advanced ceramics could come in autos and airplanes. Because of their high heat resistance, ceramics are naturals for engines and engine components.

To achieve the faster planes of the future, some expected to travel at Mach 8 (eight times the speed of sound—that's about 6,000 miles per hour, or New York to L.A. in about half an hour!), much greater propulsion capabilities will be needed. Raising the combustion temperatures in engines is a key to achieving better thrust-to-weight. Advanced ceramics, which can stand up to temperatures of about 3000°F (that's well above the maximum capabilities of metallic alloys), will allow an engine to perform at those needed hellish temps. By some estimates, ceramic jet turbines can boost jet engine efficiency by 30 to 40 percent, with substantial fuel savings.

Ceramics are also being tested for their viability as part of the actual frame or surface structure of jets, where searing temperatures will be encountered from the atmospheric drag. The National Aerospace Plane, which is on the drawing boards, is a jet that will fly in space, but will take off like a regular airplane from an airfield. Certain surface sections of the space jet will have to tolerate temperatures of more than 3000°F.

It's pretty much the same story with autos. Ceramic engines or engine parts can mean much better performance and fuel efficiency. Again, the estimates run in the area of 40 percent improvement. Various engine components, including rotors and pistons, are under development by the U.S. government and industry. Japan is going all-out to develop ceramics for extensive use in cars and trucks. Japan has, in fact, built a prototype all-ceramic diesel engine which runs without a cooling system.

High-tech ceramics almost sound like the perfect material. By now, you're probably asking, what's the catch?

There are, in fact, a few. For one, high-tech ceramics are expensive to fabricate into a final product. Also, they sometimes have this strange quality — if you took the same batch of basic ceramic material and subjected it to the exact same process, you could wind up with a set of final products that vary widely in their qualities. For example, one engine component could be much tougher than another. Some ceramics that have been produced at the same time in the same kiln have reportedly varied in strength by as much as 40 percent. In other words, ceramics have poor reproducability.

Perhaps more importantly, although high-tech ceramics are tough and strong, like some boxers, they can also have a glass jaw. They're brittle. They crack easily. The real problem is that even a microscopic crack in ceramics can rapidly develop into a full-fledged faultline. That could obviously lead to a potential catastrophe, especially at 20,000+ feet.

But there are new manufacturing, design, and detection processes that day-by-day are increasing the dependability of advanced ceramics.

"We're making great strides in making ceramics tougher. We can make them reliable now, but the process is too costly on a mass-production basis," says Schneider.[9]

As their reliability improves, and as engineers and business leaders become less leery about using them as replacements for the old standby metals, the market for high-tech ceramics should grow quickly. The projections vary quite a bit because they are such a new and potentially widespread market.

Many analysts expect the market for high-tech ceramics to grow rapidly in the next five to 20 years, perhaps by 20 to 40 percent annually, commanding at least $10 billion in global sales by the year 2000.

**On Oct. 23, 1927, three days after its invention,
the first rubber band is tested.**

The Far Side cartoon by Gary Larson is reprinted by permission of Chronicle
Features, San Francisco, CA. All rights reserved.

One way to stymie advanced ceramics' crack-and-shatter potential is to
add particles, fibers, or "whiskers" of other high-strength materials to the ceramic matrix. That results in an advanced composite.

Advanced composites, to make an analogy for some old-time rock and
roll fans, are like the Beatles. If you met John, Paul, George, and Ringo as
individual musicians before they became a group, you probably would never
imagine that they could come together to make the kind of music they did. With
advanced composites, two or more materials are "joined," forming a new material that is better than any of its constituent parts. Fiberglass is probably the best
known example of an advanced composite. Composites can out-do traditional

metals and alloys on many fronts—like ceramics, they can be lighter, but still be tougher.

Outside of the military, which is already a fairly thriving market for advanced composites, they are currently used as prosthetic devices, as truck pistons and aircraft brakes, race car brakes, in commercial satellites, refrigerator liners, and washing machine tubs.

Also, if you have an edge on your tennis or golf partner, it could be because of advanced composites. They are built into many specialty sporting goods, including tennis rackets (one recent racket model adjusts its stiffness depending on how hard the player swings—it stiffens under high impact, stretches on light impact), fishing rods, golf clubs, skis, and windsurfers. Some bicycle manufacturers are replacing metal with advanced composites in bike frames which have no seams or bond lines (that means the bike is less likely to bust apart in high-stress areas).

Although some of this sounds mundane, the Commerce Department says, "Advanced composites are a leading edge technology with profound implications for economic competitiveness and national security."[10]

The Pentagon says, "Great promise for the commercial application of these materials is foreshadowed by current specialty applications in the commercial sector."[11]

Composites are, in fact, the fastest growing advanced material. They will be important to the design and manufacture of just about any product that is subjected to any kind of heat, corrosion, or stress. For example, in electronics, as smaller components are packed closer and closer together, they increasingly begin to heat up, reducing reliability. Use of temperature-resistant composites in electronic components could increase their performance by 50 percent. But advanced composites, like high-tech ceramics, will probably have their most profound impact in the auto and aerospace industries.

Advanced composites can mean huge fuel cost savings, upwards of 40 percent, for aircraft. In the future, composites will more frequently replace metals like aluminum and titanium in jets and planes. It's projected that by the year 2000, the use of composites could quadruple in the aerospace industry, and composites could make up 50 percent to 65 percent of the structural weight of commercial aircraft.

Advanced composites potentially could reduce the weight of a large plane by up to 15 tons. If you use the rule of thumb that for every pound saved on a commercial plane, you can cut costs by $100 to $300 dollars (depending on the price of fuel and other factors), over the lifetime of the plane that works out to $9 million in savings.

Also, advanced composites could mean other types of huge savings. It's estimated that replacing alloys with composites in large plane fuselages will cut total production costs by 30 percent. And the planes would be much lighter, and be better able to fight off corrosion.

Additionally, high-temperature composites could increase engine thrust by 50 percent, making more feasible those high-speed planes that could turn a New York to Tokyo excursion into something more like a daily commute.

But if your commute of the future stays on the roads or the sidewalks, you may still encounter advanced materials. With all the talk of improving America's infrastructure, composites could play a key role. Used as a reinforcement, composites would mean more durable highways, sidewalks, bridges, and buildings. Many corrosion problems could be done away with. If you lived through the Blizzard of 1993, you know how a storm like that can cause roads to buckle, or leave huge potholes in its wake. With advanced materials, parkways and sidewalks could be built that would resist the snap, crackle, and pop caused by de-icing products, road salt, and temperature shifts.

Bridges and houses better able to stand up to time and the elements could be constructed with composites. Bridges lasting 100 to 200 years without the need of any major repairs or renovations are conceivable.

Advanced composites are defined by their basic matrix material. Ceramics reinforced with fibers are Ceramic matrix composites or CMC. There are also Polymer matrix composites (PMC), Metal matrix composites (MMC), Carbon-carbon composites (C/C), and hybrid composites.

Each category is unique. CMCs, MMCs and C/Cs are truly emerging, currently used almost exclusively in military aerospace and outer space applications. PMCs, however, are already widely used. Polymer matrix composites are stronger, stiffer, lighter, and have superior fatigue and corrosion resistance than many metals and alloys. However, they can tolerate only moderately high temperatures. Despite that, PMCs are quickly becoming the structural material of choice for the military's aerospace projects — growth projections range to 22 percent a year. Their lighter weight can mean faster jets with better maneuverability, with increased range and payload. Also, advanced composites will allow somewhat bizarre plane designs, like the Stealth Bomber, that can more readily avoid radar.

For essentially the same reasons, except radar detection, PMCs will be key to cutting costs for commercial airliners, and improving their performance.

For the time being, only subcomponents are made out of composites, like the rudder on the DC-10. But much of the surface area of the large planes of the future are expected to be made of advanced materials like graphite-epoxy composites. In the U.S., small business planes with all-PMC airframes are being developed. And in Europe, the consortium Airbus is beginning to widely use PMCs for main airframes. Also, components made out of composites generally have fewer parts than conventional components, which means a further reduction in costs. By some estimates, *the use of PMCs in commercial aircraft could rise to 65 percent by the year 2000.*

As it gets cheaper to produce PMCs, they will also begin to have a greater impact on the auto industry, replacing sheet metal. PMCs, and other composites, will be used to meet environmental and CAFE (Corporate Average Fuel Economy) standards. It's estimated that to attain a 35-mpg standard by the 21st century, the average car will have to lose about 200 pounds. To do that, lighter metals and composites will continue to replace steel. All-PMC car frames, which should simplify the production process, are being developed.

But for the time being, PMCs are time-consuming to make, and are ultimately much more expensive than competing metals. Consequently, before the next millennium they will still be used largely where performance and efficiency may outweigh cost, i.e., in outer space, military jets and helicopters, and sports equipment.

Metal matrix composites can be far superior to the basic metal. For example, aluminum matrix composites can be 10 times stronger than aluminum alone. MMCs can be lightweight, but still be strong and show a high resistance to torrid temperatures. For that reason, they too will probably be increasingly used in the hot sections of autos and aircraft. At present, the Japanese use MMCs in piston skirts. They're also found in certain parts of the U.S. Space Shuttle and the Hubble telescope. That may not be the greatest sales pitch for them, but MMCs could play a critical role in developing outerspace.

Metal matrix composites are ideal for outerspace structures and systems. They have a high resistance to radiation. Unlike PMCs, they are not susceptible to the phenomenon of 'out-gassing' — that essentially means MMCs do not release water vapor, which could gather on space instruments and diminish or destroy their effectiveness.

However, when exposed to repeated stark changes in temperatures, the bond between the metal and the fibers in the matrix can degrade because they expand at different rates. Also, MMCs can be expensive to fabricate because of high raw materials costs, and because the manufacturing method is complicated. Despite all that, "metal matrix composites are an emerging technology critical to the future of the United States industrial base," according to the Department of Defense.[12]

Carbon/Carbon composites, are in a sense diamonds in the rough. They can stand up to higher temperatures better than any other known composite. As such, they're used, for example, in rocket nozzles, and have the potential for other applications in space vehicles and aircraft. C/Cs could supplant superalloys in jet engines by the end of the century, but before that happens certain complex chemical, physical, and technical obstacles have to be overcome.

Depending on your outlook, *hybrid composites* are either the goulash, or the designer label of composites. By essentially combining all the previously mentioned constituents (fibers, polymers, metals, non-metals) to specifications, hybrids can be designer tailored for optimum properties, leading to a wide variety of specific applications for many unique situations.

According to the Commerce Department, "composites offer the potential for a revolutionary synthesis of materials science and product design with the advent of "designer materials."[13]

Because of the obvious widespread potential of advanced composites, there is an ongoing full-court press to develop them. Research is swiftly progressing in government and industry labs. Many universities have established composite research centers. Aerospace firms have built, or are building, composite fabrication sites. Much of the current research is devoted to finding ways to cut the current high cost of fabrication, and to maximize product quality.

Advanced composites seem like a lock. Current global sales are about $4 billion a year. The Office of Technology Assessment estimates that worldwide annual sales of advanced composites will climb to $20 billion by the year 2000.[14]

Looking out further into the future, still more magical materials are possible. Advanced materials won't just be manufactured for use in space, but will be *manufactured* in space.

Down on planet Earth, because of gravity, some elements and compounds cannot be mixed at all, or the mix will contain imperfections that can ruin its effectiveness. But in space, of course, there's no gravity. That will allow scientists to make cosmic connections between substances they can't make on terra firma. For example, exotic combinations between aluminum and antimony, or gold and germanium would be possible. Theoretically, a whole new slew of advanced materials with unusual but beneficial properties could be developed.

Scientists are also beginning work on *"intelligent" materials.*

Smart materials can respond to a stimulus. Those sunglasses that get darker when you step out in the sun, and lighten when you're in the shade are essentially smart materials. Smart materials may be able to change shape, or repair themselves. Other intelligent materials would essentially have sensors and even mini-processors built into them, which, when combined with the inherent abilities of the materials, would allow structures to react to changes in the environment, or signal problems in the material itself. For example, a building made out of intelligent materials might be able to detect the first slight tremble of an earthquake and become more rigid, or more pliant, depending on what would increase its chances of surviving the quake. Or an airplane, with fiber-optic sensors built into its structure, might be able to light-signal exactly where there's metal fatigue before it developed into a crisis situation.

Please bear in mind that research on intelligent materials is in the laboratory-embryonic stage, and they probably won't have a big impact on society until well into the 21st century, perhaps by around 2020.

As for investing in advanced materials, there is a rub. As you may have picked up on in the course of this chapter, some of the projected main markets for them include autos, airplanes, and the military. In the early 1990s those sectors either had dismal years and/or were expected to cut back. Of course, the auto and airplane industries may be in turn-around mode. It seems like they've already been through the worst of times. As for the future of the military, no one can really say.

According to the Suppliers of Advanced Composite Materials Association and the U.S. Advanced Ceramic Association, " . . . the U.S. is at a crossroads. In spite of the criticality of advanced materials and their worldwide market potential, the sharp decline in Department of Defense demand and the lack of substantial commercial markets threatens the existence of a growing number of companies. To date, the advanced materials industry is a fantastic technological success and a total financial failure since billions of dollars of invested capital continue to be grossly underutilized.

" . . . future participation by U.S. based manufacturing concerns is threatened by low industry returns on invested capital."[15]

It's especially tough for small and medium-sized firms to compete in the advanced materials industry because initial costs for capital and equipment are so high, and the time required to develop in-demand products takes so long.

SOURCES

If you want to keep on top of developments in advanced materials, you can contact one of the following:

The Materials Research Society
9800 McKnight Road
Pittsburgh, Pennsylvania 15237
412-367-3003 Fax: 412-367-4373

Suppliers of Advanced Composite Materials Association
1600 Wilson Boulevard
Suite 1008
Arlington, Virginia 22209
703-841-1556 Fax: 703-841-1559

United States Advanced Ceramics Association
(Same address as above)

If you are conservative, and want to participate in the long-term advanced materials revolution, it might be wise, for now, to invest in some of the large, established companies that have solid materials research programs. For example, in 1992, Du Pont established a multi-million dollar advanced composite R&D complex in Europe. At the complex, Du Pont will concentrate on commercial aviation and space markets.

Other large firms that have substantial advanced materials divisions, or are committing themselves to some R&D, are the Big Three car companies, AAR, Adolph Coors, ALCOA, Allied Signal, American Cyanamid, Amoco, Armco, Asarco, Bairnco, Boeing, Brush Wellman, Cabot, Dexter, Dow, Ferro, H.B. Fuller, General Dynamics, General Electric, General Signal, Hercules, Hexcel, Lockheed, Martin Marietta, Morton, PPG Industries, Pfizer, Pratt & Whitney, Rogers, Sequa, Textron, Thermo Electron, 3M, Union Carbide, Westinghouse, W.R. Grace, and Wyman-Gordon.

One of the best bets might be:

Corning, Inc. (NYSE - GLW)
Corning, New York
607-974-9000

The company, which has been around since the 1800s, is preparing for the 21st century. Corning makes a wide variety of materials requiring special properties, including strength, lightness, heat, shock, and moisture resistance. It is conducting R&D on advanced materials, especially ceramics, and seems well positioned to take advantage of the coming materials revolution.

For the more adventurous, some of the smaller publicly-held advanced materials companies include:

Cade Industries (OTC - CADE)
5640 Enterprise Drive
Lansing, Michigan 48911
517-394-1333

Cade makes high-tech composite products and components for the aerospace and air transport industries, including composite gas turbine engine components. Cade was incorporated in 1980 and employs more than 200. Its annual sales are about $30 million.

Ceradyne, Inc. (OTC - CRDN)
3169 Red Hill Avenue
Costa Mesa, California 92626
714-549-0421

Ceradyne was incorporated in 1987, and has about 250 workers. It makes advanced technical ceramic products and components for the aerospace, defense, electronic, medical, and industrial sectors. The company's annual sales are over $20 million.

Ceramics Process Systems Corp. (OTC - CPSX)
155 Fortune Boulevard
Milford, Massachusetts 01757
508-634-3422 Fax: 508-478-0946

The company was formed in 1984, and incorporated in 1987. It employs about 50.

Ceramics Process Systems makes advanced ceramic products for the auto, defense, and electronic industries. The company focuses on microelectronics, producing packaging and interconnections for high-performance, high-density electronic devices. It performs R&D, which is funded by large corporations and the Federal government. The company also has a subsidiary that develops high-temperature superconductor ceramic wire.

Total annual sales are about $5 million.

Keene Corp (OTC - KEEN)
200 Park Avenue
New York, New York 10166
212-557-1900

Through its Reinhold Industries subsidiary (12827 East Imperial Highway, Santa Fe Springs, California 310-944-3281), Keene manufactures various advanced composite materials and structures for the defense industry and commercial applications, including aerospace. Products include heat absorbing nozzles and heat shields, and are sold mainly to prime contractors for the U.S. government.

In late 1992, Keene announced that it was selling the Reinhold unit to existing Keene stockholders and the investing public. That transaction was expected to take place in the first half of 1993.

Reinhold's 1992 sales were over $13 million, a 37 percent increase from the previous year. Reinhold had an operating profit of $1.5 million in '92 after losing almost $2 million the year before.

Quadrax Corp. (OTC - QDRX)
300 High Point Avenue
Portsmouth, Rhode Island 02871
401-683-6600

Quadrax is a development stage company formed in 1986 to process and market high-strength, lightweight fiber-reinforced composite materials. Company uses a proprietary process.

Quadrax also has developed a laser modeling system which can create 3D models directly from 2D on-screen CAD images.

Latest available figures show annual revenues are over $1 million.

CHAPTER 6

THE LIGHT WAVE OF THE FUTURE— PHOTONICS, OPTOELECTRONICS AND FIBER OPTICS

"Purge the horrible darkness of our mind,
light a light for our senses."

— alchemist's prayer

"I have heard a ray of sun laugh and cough and sing,
I have been able to hear a shadow . . . "

— Alexander Graham Bell

His parents' faces scowled-up into "The Look."

The child recognized it immediately. The "we're-very-disappointed-in-you" look. The little boy was getting ready to have his mind wander into that far-away place it went to when he was being lectured.

"This is a terrible report card," the father said. "You'll just have to watch more TV."

Did the boy hear right? Watch *more* TV?

He didn't misunderstand. There was a small catch, but the boy really didn't mind much.

That evening, the child clicked on an interactive TV show, carried by way of fiber optics, to help himself learn how to spell. On the screen was a fuzzy picture of an elephant. As the boy used an interactive mechanism to spell out elephant, the screen got progressively clearer, until a sharp-imaged elephant raised its trunk, bellowed an acknowledgement, and thundered off.

The sharks attacked.

Again and again they ripped at the unfamiliar intruder. The sea predators did some minor damage, but even Jaws could not stop a revolution in the making. In a photon feeding frenzy, the sharks were assaulting a prototype cable that generated an energy field they didn't recognize, and would carry trans-oceanic phone conversations on light beams.

In the early 1990s Bruce Springsteen mourned "57 channels and nothin' on." How archaic that already sounds. 57 channels.

In 1993, a cable TV company announced it would install a network of so-called fiber optic cables that could carry some *500 channels* to most of its customers by 1996. The shows, and other two-way, multi-media services, would be transmitted via lasers.

The bride was glowing. No, I mean she was *really* glowing.

She lit up the night, flashing like a human fire-fly as she twirled into the darkness. When she spotted her new husband, her gown changed color. Woven into the wedding dress were fibers, special optical strands, that could transmit light over and around her figure.

All of the above were just mini-tales, or tales to be, from the front in the exploding photonics revolution.

Photonics (which can be pretty much used interchangeably with optoelectronics) sounds futuristic, and in a sense it is. But all it essentially means is using light to store, process, manipulate, or transmit information. Because, technically, an affiliated item like a windowpane could fall within its parameters, photonics can seem deceptively innocuous. Not so. It's potentially revolutionary.

The photonics revolution will lead to the next generation of lightning-fast computers, and incredibly small, discerning light sensors that will, for example, warn airplanes and buildings of cracks, and warn humans of disease.

But most importantly, it will lead to a 21st century dimension of sight, sound, and mind where TVs act more like computers, and computers act more like TVs, and both act more like telephones in an information and entertainment-hungry wonderland of multi-media and interactive communications.

See, Frank? Keep the light in their eyes and you can
bag them without any trouble at all.

Photonics, optoelectronics, and fiber optics will help overhaul, and bridge, the telecommunications and computer industries, leading to the virtual melding of those businesses.

"It's going to be very difficult to draw the lines between the telecommunications and computer industries. We're octopuses where we will all end up with hands in each other's pockets," says John Malone, president of Tele-Communications Inc.[1]

For consumers, its predicted that photonics, optoelectronics, and fiber optics will have an impact on just about every facet of life and work. "Optoelectronics will affect communications of all kinds—the telephone, television, fax, interactive TV, computer, multi-media will all be made possible, or better, or cheaper, or faster because of it," said Dr. John Weiner, program director for the Atomic, Molecular and Optical Physics Program of the National Science Foundation.[2]

The bottom line: "Photonics will be more important than electronics," says Charles Troy, managing editor of *Photonics Spectra*.[3]

Here's part of the recent ad nauseum commercial pitch:

Doctors will make 'house-calls' again. You could have the knowledge of all the world's libraries at your fingertips, be able to hook into a supercomputer from your apartment, "virtual conference" with your co-workers from just about anywhere. Someone on the other side of the planet could throw down the challenge and play a 3D-like video game against you. Browse through malls and do one-stop shopping from your living room for almost anything, have a video-phone conversation with your long-distance lover, see and talk baby-talk to your new-born grandchild who's on the other coast, order current movies or TV shows (not syndicated re-runs) on demand and watch them at home at your convenience — no need to videotape or rent.

And, by the way, all of that — sending and receiving images, text, sound, and data — you'd be able to do from the same desktop unit. One piece of equipment will act as TV, computer, and telephone. In other words, you'll be directly hooked into the Information Age.

Photons will illuminate the "information superhighways" of the 21st century. Perhaps it is fitting that more light will be there to help guide us into and through the next millennium, a frontier foreboding and dark to some.

The millennium market potential is huge. According to Mr. Troy, the overall market for photonics "was about $25 billion in 1992, which, if the economy starts to pick up, will grow 10 percent to 15 percent a year. If the dreams, like information highways, interactive TV, and multi-media come about, then the market will be explosive."[4]

A photon is the basic unit of light, as an electron is the basic unit of electricity. Through the 20th century, electrons, electricity, and electronics have been the foundation of our communications and computer systems. But the photon is the new quantum-kid in town. That town is the Global Village.

Photons will increasingly supplant electrons in the 21st century. That's essentially because light can carry more information, and carry it faster, than electricity — qualities needed as consumers and business demand more information, and society moves toward a data "logjam." Also, light is pretty much immune to annoying electro-magnetic interference, which is an increasing problem for alternative forms of communication, like satellite and microwaves. It's also harder to eavesdrop on light-beam messages.

"Photonics can provide order-of-magnitude improvements over today's conventional electronic devices," according to the Pentagon.[5] Order-of-magnitude improvements is Pentagonese for "photonics is damn better than electronics."

Using light as a means of communication isn't really anything new. You must have seen some old Western where the cowboys or Indians were communicating across the mesas with light flashed off a mirror or some type of reflector. Ships used to communicate with light signals. Lighthouses. Flares. "One if by land, two if by sea!" In "Close Encounters of the Third Kind," musical notes and flashes of light were used to communicate with an alien race.

Alexander Graham Bell, the very same, back in the 1880s also invented something called the Photophone, which essentially used focused sunlight to transmit a voice message. Ingenious yes, but it didn't work too well on a cloudy day. And God forbid you wanted to call someone at night. Fortunately, Mr. Bell didn't stay out in the sun too long, and went his more famous route.

But light seems like an obvious, natural way for humans to communicate, and the light-of-choice used in optical communications systems is laser-type light. A laser (Light Amplification by Stimulated Emission of Radiation) is distantly related to the 150-watt soft-white light from your kitchen bulb, but laser light is much more focused or coherent—you may remember that during his 1992 campaign, then-candidate Bill Clinton promised to "focus like a laser" on the economy. Laser beams can be made tight enough to be used for industrial cutting, or surgery, or for defense systems like the semi-defunct "Star Wars" (the Strategic Defense Initiative). The laser you're probably most familiar with is the one used on supermarket scanners to read the price off those black-lined tags on your groceries. Lasers are also used prevalently to store information on audio and video discs.

The beam from a laser (or LED, the related Light Emitting Diode) is shot from a crystal or gas that generates the light when it's titillated by a form of energy, like electricity. A laser used for communications can pulse millions to billions of times a second to transmit information. Pulses are important. If you consider each pulse a "one" and the time between pulses a "zero," then you're talking about a binary code, or a digital signal, that computers can understand.

On the other end of the system, catching the light beam, is a receiver. The basic type of receiver is called a photodiode, which essentially converts the light back to electrons and hence into something your TV or telephone (or computer) can use.

In between, connecting the laser and the receiver, is a thin strand of special glass fiber about the diameter of a human hair.

If you stand on an ocean shore and hold a shell to your ear, you'll hear the roar of the sea. Pick up a handful of sand, hold that to your ear, and if you use your imagination, you may be able to hear the conversational roar of the 21st century. For those pure glass strands, made from silica found in common sand, are the glass path to the telecom/puting age of the future.

Fiber optic cables, containing a bundle of the hair-like strands, can carry 250,000 times as much information as common copper telephone wire. A quarter pound of fiber optic cable, which is relatively easy to install, can carry the same amount of information as 33 tons of copper wire.

Fiber optic-delivered light signals are faster than electricity and, as you might expect from a glass-carried message, are usually crystal-clear—fiber optic glass is so pure that if you could drain the oceans and fill the gap with sheets of that glass, you could see to the bottom of the rifts at their deepest point, about six miles down. And you'd be able to see many miles beyond that, some 75 miles, if the ocean canyons plunged down that deep.

The Pentagon puts it this way: "The superiority of fiber optics over copper-based systems can be measured by information carrying capacity (which is thousands of times greater for optical systems), energy loss in signal transmission (100 times lower), error rate (10 times lower), greatly reduced size and weight, and by its resistance to electromagnetic interference, and other harsh environments . . ."[6]

Fiber optics has for many years been widely used by telephone companies for long-distance calls. Fiber optic cables are economical for trans-oceanic or trans-continental calls because they don't need that many repeater or amplifier-type components to boost the signal. For shorter, local calls, those boosters weren't need to begin with, so the regional phone companies stuck with copper wire-to-the-home.

But copper wire, or coaxial cable used by cable TV firms, can't handle the proliferation of information that's becoming available. Technically, copper doesn't have the capacity, or bandwidth. Therefore, more fiber will be layed down locally. "Fiber-to-the-curb" and perhaps "fiber-to-the-home" may widely expand into the next millennium. Fiber optics will travel that final so-called last mile.

To sum up: fiber optic cable can carry much more information, at a faster speed, than copper wire used by phone companies or coaxial cable used by cable TV companies. Fiber optics should be the communications medium of choice to transmit the impending 21st century explosion of entertainment and information in two-way text, voice, video, graphics, and data.

(One note here: a technique has been developed that can essentially squeeze video images through a copper wire. However, it's not as good as fiber optics when it comes to handling the high amounts of information required for interactive and multi-media services. Also, the relative picture quality isn't that great for live, action-oriented programming, such as sports. And that method will not be able to handle High Definition Television, which could become available in the U.S. by about 1996.)

Overall, the U.S. fiber optics market grew about 20 percent in 1992, to about $2 billion, despite a stagnant economy.

"The industry is expected to enjoy continued growth during the first half of this decade (the 1990s), gaining momentum as fiber is installed closer to the home," according to the Commerce Department.[7]

According to some estimates, it's predicted that the worldwide market for fiber optics and fiber optic sensors will hit somewhere between $12 billion to $20 billion by the year 2000, or about a 15 percent to 20 percent increase annually.

Because the cost of fiber optics may actually get cheaper over the years, dollar projections can be tricky. But a study by Corning, Inc. predicts the volume of worldwide optical fiber used for local-loops (the home and private connections for business, industry, education, and the like) will increase about 100-fold from 1992 to the year 2000.[8]

Trans-oceanic fiber optic cables are expected to proliferate during the 1990s, and *a huge land-based global market awaits U.S. companies. In 1992, the U.S. loosened export controls of high-tech telecommunications equipment, including fiber optics. That year, U.S. exports of optical fiber and fiber optic cable increased 35 percent from the year before, and resulted in a trade surplus for those products of more than $300 million, a 43 percent gain.*[9]

Large areas of Western Europe, Eastern Europe, Asia, Latin America, and other areas still need to be hooked up with fiber optics, and potential explosive markets are emerging in Russia and other regions of the former Soviet Union, where you usually still have to use a roto-phone and often have to scream past the clicks and crackling static to be heard. In 1993, Corning reached an agreement to supply Russia with fiber optics to improve its communications services. The pact is expected to last into the 21st century.

China, where there are very few phones relative to the total population, is another potential monster market.

Back in the U.S., under the stewardship of Vice-President Al Gore, the Clinton Administration has been pushing hard for the development and construction of an "information superhighway and information infrastructure" which is expected to require massive deployment of fiber optics. The administration intended to spend $5 billion on the project (officially called the National Research and Education Network or NREN) in its first term.

The information superhighway is envisioned as a national network that can move data perhaps thousands of times faster than current links. How fast is that? At the hoped for speed of NREN, the equivalent of 100,000 typed pages could be transmitted in a second. That's about 10 encyclopedia sets of information every second. Every second.

In the global economy of the 21st century, speed, access to information, knowledge, quality, and technology will be critical to a nation's economic standing, and the Clinton administration thinks fiber optics and the information superhighway will give the U.S. a competitive advantage in the long run. Business generally agrees.

"(Fiber optics) will reduce development cycles . . . in ways of innovation we can't even imagine today," says an IBM spokesman.[10]

For example, auto engineers working for the same company, but located throughout the globe, would be able to conference over complex blueprints or designs very easily. Sales presentations by way of the information highway may become commonplace. The Willy Lomans of the future may be traveling the side streets of the information superhighway.

It's been estimated that if American businesses cut out just 10 percent to 20 percent of their activities requiring transportation and replaced them with communications, the U.S. could save $23 billion a year.

As Mr. Gore envisions it, tomorrow's data superhighway will also create new information businesses and services, the way new industries and communities sprung up near the rivers, stage trails, railroads, and cement highways of the past. If information and knowledge are the primary commodities of the 21st century, then transporting it conceivably will be as important to the economy as moving the natural resources across the infrastructure of bridges, canals, and roads once was.

In any case, it's a market almost everyone wants a piece of. As of this writing, the debate had just started as to whose responsibility it will be to build the NREN. The government wants to play a role. Television cable firms and telephone companies want the action for themselves. Others who stand to be considerably affected, including libraries, universities, hospitals, and consumers, generally stand somewhere in the middle.

But as alluded to earlier in the chapter, some companies are already damning the photon torpedoes and going ahead with their own plan to build the local streets and boulevards of the information superhighway.

Tele-Communications, Inc (OTC - TCOMA), America's largest cable TV operator, announced in April 1993 that it would spend more than $2 billion to lay down thousands of miles of fiber optic cable to service more than 300 communities by 1996 — 10 million customers will be wired.

"There probably will barely be an industry in the country that won't be affected by implementation of this technology . . . it should make America a world leader in all the businesses that feed off this technology," according to Tele-Communications (TCI) President John Malone.[11]

Reprinted by permission: Tribune Media Services.

The cable with the high bandwidth will be able to transmit upwards of 500 channels to customers. Among the expected services are data transfer, and *interactive, or two-way TV,* which will allow armchair shopping, education and/or work-at-home, and something like video-on-demand. The video service, which could be the big money-maker, will probably work like this: say you want to watch a hit TV show or movie. With its great capacity, TCI will be able to essentially run a menu of shows round-the-clock and you just tune in at your convenience, unencumbered by complicated VCR programming or treks to the video store.

TCI intends to spend $2 billion to refurbish its overall cable spiderweb with fiber-optics and data compression technologies.

(Shortly after TCI's announcement, there were reports that TCI was talking with Carolco Pictures about a deal to show new Carolco movies on cable on or before the day the flicks start playing in theaters.)

Other cable companies are also moving in on the fiber optics/photonics band-wagon. In 1994, Time Warner, Inc. (NYSE - TWX) will start a fiber optic-based interactive system for 4,000 customers in Orlando, Florida offering video, home shopping, telephone, and data services with simply a 'click!'

In 1993 alone, Time will spend another $100 million, to a total $400 million, to lay down that system, and convert its other cable systems to fiber-optics.

To prepare for the information and photonics revolution, the cable TV industry plans to spend $18 billion into the early 21st century to upgrade its equipment and facilities, and more than 60 percent of existing systems will be refurbished. In 1992, cable TV companies collectively doubled their consumption of optical fiber, and their use of fiber optics is expected to grow at least 25 percent annually through the 1990s.[12]

Despite being archrivals, Time Warner and Tele-Communications reached an agreement in 1993 to press for industry standards for interactive TV.

Phone companies are after a piece of the interactive action too, and in the early 1990s the breakdown of certain legal and regulatory barriers gave them the impetus.

In 1992, a Federal Communications Commission decision paved the way for local telephone companies, including the regional Bell firms, the "Baby Bells," to carry video and information services. Also in that year, the FCC essentially ruled that cable TV operators could provide telecommunications services — in other words, phone calls. So the competition, and probably collaboration, will be increasing between the cable companies and phone companies.

In fact, AT&T and cable TV giant Viacom (ASE - VIA) in 1993 jointly tested a cable system offering interactive services in a San Francisco suburb.

In 1993, regional phone company U.S. West (NYSE - USW) invested $2.5 billion in a Time Warner unit to develop interactive cable service technology.

AT&T, U.S. West, and Tele-Communications in 1993 began testing consumer reaction to an interactive video-on-demand service for selected homes in Denver. (In October 1993, Bell Atlantic and Tele-Communications announced they would merge. It would be one of the largest corporate marriages ever.)

You can see that 1993 was something of a turning point for interactive TV, with the lines already beginning to blur between phone companies and cable TV firms.

And then there are the computer companies. Admittedly, at this point I am wandering a bit from the photonics/fiber optics theme, but there are important connections.

IBM has created an interactive television system that will, among other things, provide movies-on-demand, with an option to read movie reviews before making a choice.

Microsoft (OTC - MSFT) allied itself with Time Warner and Tele-Communications via a new company called Cablesoft, which will offer a mongrel of computer and cable TV service, and will work to establish and promote a national interactive technology standard.

But computer companies may make their most immediate impact on interactive TV via the "Box."

To negotiate their way through, and take advantage of the interactive offerings on 500 channels, consumers will need a so-called converter box, which is really a small type of computer. The box will attach to the TV and give viewers the power to tap into various services. Microsoft Corp., and fellow computer giant Intel Corp. (OTC - INTC), along with General Instrument (NYSE - GIC), are collaborating to develop such boxes.

Silicon Graphics (NYSE - SGI), which makes powerful computers, and creates computer-generated special effects and graphics (it made some of the visual magic in "Terminator II" and "Jurassic Park") was picked by Time Warner to build the chip that will essentially function as the brains in the box necessary for Time's interactive service in Florida. Silicon Graphics will also provide so-called servers, which are powerful computers, that would be placed in neighborhoods to route digital, interactive media signals to the home.

3DO Company (OTC - THDO), a firm that went public in 1993, to much excitement on Wall Street, is developing a so-called "interactive multiplayer" which attaches to a TV and plays interactive video computer games with animated characters that move in 3D, plays audio and video discs, and can display color photos stored on photo CDs. The device may also ultimately be used as a way to voyage through the interactive, multi-channel systems.

3DO claims the interactive multiplayer will allow consumers to enter a world of interactivity which spans the gap between television and computer.

All the while, computer companies are developing *multi-media* technology for personal computers — moving images, animation, video, sound graphics, and data will all be available on the desktop computer. Multi-media PCs will require greater storage capacity, which will be provided by *optical* CD-ROMs (compact disc-read only memory). Some computers already network, or communicate, with fiber optics, and the great information-carrying capacity of fiber optics may be needed for PCs to "talk" to one another on a multi-media level.

So, the blending goes a step further — TV/phone/computers.

Some of the estimates for interactive and multi-media are intimidating.

Apple Computer's (OTC - AAPL) former Chief Executive Officer John Sculley figured *the multi-media industry — which is actually a loosely defined amalgamation — could generate global revenues of $3.5 trillion by the year 2001.*

And by some estimates there will be about 50 million interactive subscribers by early in the 21st century, and sales of the necessary devices and services will hit about $5 billion to $10 billion.

It's important to remember that, at this point, most interactive and multi-media systems are just in the development and test phases. Fully established and integrated systems probably won't be up until the century turns over, or even beyond that. You can't really predict how consumers will react to them. But many new companies are likely to enter the interactive and multi-media scene, and many companies, old and new, will probably fall by the wayside of the information highways.

As the light fantastic is tripped throughout the world, light will have to be better integrated into the existing electronic matrix. Optoelectronics is essentially the merging of light with microelectronics.

"The conversion of light to electricity, and vice-versa, is where optoelectronics comes in. You want to push back the point at which light is converted to electricity," says Dr. Weiner.[13]

There's more to those optical information highways than a laser, fiber, and a receiver. Several other components are also involved, for example, to split, or switch, or boost the signal.

When a photonic signal has to be boosted or switched, or have some other function performed on it, often the light has to be first converted to electricity. Then it's boosted or switched, or whatever. Then the electricity may be converted back to light. It sounds like a double play combination. Photons-to-electrons-to-photons. The conversion from photons to electrons and back doesn't just happen with the pass of a wand. Part of the optoelectronics involves making the conversions faster and more efficient, with the ultimate goal of eliminating them altogether — in other words, an all-photonic network.

"It's a difficult problem to switch packets of data as light. Optoelectronics seeks to cut back on the number of conversions to electricity, which slows things down, and eventually create all-optical networking," says Dan McQueeney, research staff member of IBM's Thomas J. Watson Research Center.[14]

Of course, a final transition to electricity is necessary so your home appliance can work. But someday the guts of your TV or computer may work on light, and would be plugged into a photonic outlet.

Many companies are working on the quantum shift. In 1992, four major U.S. companies formed what is called a pre-competitive opto-electronic alliance. General Electric, Honeywell, AT&T, and IBM will collaborate in the Optoelectronic Technology Consortium (OETC), whose stated purpose is to develop optical interconnections for high-speed digital data transmission in computers and telecommunications systems. The alliance promises to "break through the data processing 'bottlenecks' of conventional systems by transmitting data . . . faster across optical highways."[15]

The OETC wants to develop advances in various opto-electronic integral parts, and will get $8 million in initial funding from the Defense Department.

The Defense Department has seen the light. Light's speed, reliability, and survivability is a strong inducement for the Pentagon to integrate photonics into its systems for many uses.

" . . . it has been only recently that photonics technology developed the necessary critical mass of tools and capabilities to springboard into revolutionary new applications . . . (which) can support a number of applications that previously were the sole realm of electronic and microelectronic devices," according to the Pentagon.[16]

The Defense Department wants to use photonics and fiber optics mainly for computing, communications, surveillance, missile guidance, and tele-operated weapons. In addition to the Pentagon's interest, the federal government supports photonic R&D through the Department of Energy, NASA, the National Institute of Standards and Technology, and the National Science Foundation.

"The commercial and military potential of photonics is such that most of the industrialized countries of the world are making a significant national commitment to develop photonics," says the Department of Defense.[17]

Nowhere more so than in Japan, which may be on the verge of grabbing the international lead in photonics from the U.S. One of Japan's — and the rest of the world's — goals is to develop photonics for computers. Computers can already transmit data within and among themselves using fiber optics and light. But the ultimate hope for photonics is the creation of an all-optical computer —

where the actual computations and logic functions are done in the guts of the computer with light instead of electronics. In such an optical computer, there'd be few wires or cables; data would instead shoot around on criss-crossing light beams.

"That's possible because photons don't interfere with one another, they can essentially drive right through each other," says IBM's McQueeney.[18]

Photonics will allow computers to calculate at incredibly fast speeds and store huge amounts of information. The supercomputers of the future will very likely incorporate photonics or be wholly optical.

Japan will try to develop an all-optical computer as part of its so-called 10-year Real-World Computer Program, which is designed to create next-generation computers that can mimic human thought. Many U.S. universities are working with the government and/or companies to develop optical computing. Among them are the University of Arizona, the University of Southern California, the University of Alabama, and the University of Colorado, which has built and demonstrated a prototype optical computer that can do relatively easy math.

A California company — Conductus, Inc. (in mid-1993, Conductus announced it was about to go public) — collaborating with other firms, the government, the University of California at Berkeley, and Stanford University, will reportedly try to develop photonics for a prototype computer that may lead to *desktop supercomputers.*

"In the case of computing, new photonic technologies may in the future replace the all-electronic computer and assume the lead role as the technology of the future," said the Commerce Department.[19]

The storage discs used by computers, currently dominated by magnetic discs, will also increasingly go the optical route. Annual growth rates of more than 15 percent are predicted in the optical storage industry during the next five years. " . . . higher capacity (optical) compact disk-read only memory (CD-ROM) or perhaps even three dimensional holographic devices, may provide storage capacity needed for extensive multimedia capabilities . . . " according to the Commerce Department.[20]

Speaking of holograms, which are 3-D images created by laser-light, fiber optics may eventually be able to transmit such full-bodied images sometime in the 21st century. That could lead to another revolution in telecommunications. Imagine communicating or watching a form of TV in 3-D. I can foresee conversing with 3-D human-like images like they did in the "Star Wars" movies. Beyond that, something like the Holodeck of "Star Trek: The Next Generation" awaits.

The scientific, business, and entertainment value would be enormous, but I can also envision holograms affecting us on a smaller, more human, individualistic level. For example, future family albums might be stored on hologram discs, so you could have the words and images of your ancestors come to life for you.

There is, of course, a spectrum of other uses for light. Lasers for medical (more on that in another chapter) and industrial uses are proliferating. Optical fiber is also being wired into cars and planes for internal communications systems. Optical systems in cars will carry commands for stereo, radio, the air conditioner, etc.

Also, fiber optic cable in cars would transmit light wherever needed — to headlamps, blinking back-of-the car signals, or for interior instruments. Lighting door handle areas and floors would become feasible. The thin fiber cables would give designers more leeway, since less area would be needed for an auto's lighting system. General Electric has developed a concept that could cut the number of total bulbs a car uses from the present 80 to about 10.

For the airline industry, fiber optics can mean lighter aircraft, and internal communication systems on planes that are not as susceptible to outside interference. 21st century planes will also be criss-crossed with fiber optic sensors that will, for example, give pilots a heads-up warning to impending damage to wings.

Fiber optic sensors could be a huge growth industry. They can measure anything from temperature, to pressure, to pollution, to acidity, to blood flow, to the sugar level in cells. They'll be increasingly important to medicine, industry, and science.

In the 21st century, fiber-optic sensors could make for "smart buildings." The sensors would be laced through a building, and changes in their light flow could indicate developing stresses, strains, or cracks, and perhaps could be used as part of an early warning system for earthquakes.

The advantages of light-based sensors is that they're lightweight, don't decay as easily, and you won't get funky readings from them because, again, they are pretty much unaffected from outside interference.

The Commerce Department sees sensors as a high growth area, with total global sales hitting $12 billion by the year 2000. Fiber optic sensors should capture a large percentage of that market.[20] According to Frost & Sullivan/Market Intelligence, *"the total world market for fiber optic sensors was estimated at approximately $126 million in 1992. Revenues increased despite the recession that gripped economies around the world. A compound annual growth rate of 36.6 percent will push revenues over $1.12 billion by 1999."* [21]

However, as indicated, the real potential for photonics lies in telecommunications and computing.

Light will be the information-bringer of the 21st century. There may be a cautionary note in that. In legends, bringers of light and knowledge have often had problems. Prometheus gave the world fire, and for his efforts, Zeus chained him to a rock so a vulture could tear at his liver. Lucifer literally means the light-bringer, and we all know what happened to him.

Around the middle of the 20th century, Gertrude Stein said everyone gets so much information all day long that they lose their common sense. In the 21st century, we'll be confronted with the possibility of 500 channels of information and then some.

Will the light, the digital pulses, of the 21st century cause a self-banishment of humanity, Lucifer-like, into an interactive hell of cocoon living and remote control surfing through multi-media and multi-channels?

For the investor, will there be a demand for the large amounts of information fiber optics allows? Or will the information superhighway be a dead end? Will the initial buyers of 500 channels be tooling around the data highway on the 21st century equivalents of Edsels and Deloreans?

It's always tough to predict the reaction of the body collective. Certainly, for competitive reasons, many businesses will have to hitch up to the information superhighway.

With the apparent trends of more movement out of the cities to rural areas, suburbia, and "penturbia," and with more women working, more service employees and professionals will want the option of working from home — a request ideally handled by the interactive, multi-media capacity of fiber optics.

I also believe if the cost does not become prohibitive, there's almost no end to consumers' desire for entertainment and information. Five hundred channels will be a bit much to work with, and many of the offerings could make "Wayne's World" look classy. But you have to consider that really what the huge number of channels is leading to is one channel — your own, where you leisurely pick and choose the shows and show times, a channel tailor-designed for your own taste. What winds up on the tube will essentially be the quintessence of the democratic process at work.

"The words are changing, and that's a good thing. Stations, channels, dials — they are all out the window soon," according to QVC Chairman Barry Diller.[22]

It's as though light itself — a spectrum of multi-colored light — becomes simple white-light again when it passes through a prism. So, the photonics revolution will ultimately offer up a reflection, as light does, a reflection of ourselves and our own culture.

The Far Side cartoon by Gary Larson is reprinted by permission of Chronicle Features, San Francisco, CA. All rights reserved.

SOURCES

To keep up with developments in photonics, optoelectronics, lasers, and fiber optics you can contact one of the following:

Fiber Optics News
Phillips Business Information, Inc.
7811 Montrose Road
Potomac, Maryland 20854
301-340-2100

International Society for Optical Engineering
P.O. Box 10
Bellingham, Washington 98227
206-676-3290

Laser Focus World or *Laser Report*
PennWell Publishing
One Technology Drive
P.O. Box 989
Westford, Massachusetts 01886
508-692-0700 or 508-392-2177

Optical Society of America
2010 Massachusetts Ave., N.W.
Washington, D.C. 20036
202-223-8130

Photonics Spectra
Laurin Publishing
Berkshire Common
P.O. Box 4949
Pittsfield, Massachusetts 01202
413-499-0514

For multimedia and interactive developments:

Interactive Multimedia Investor
Paul Kagan Associates, Inc.
126 Clock Tower Place
Carmel, California 93923
408-624-1536

The photonics revolution will, sooner or later, have a major impact, for better or worse, on just about every telecommunications and computer company. For practical reasons, I am not going to list those companies beyond the ones already mentioned in the body of the chapter. But since telecommunications, in its various forms, is considered by many analysts to be a top growth industry into the 21st century, here are some mutual funds that invest in telecommunications:

Fidelity Select Developing Communications
800-544-8888

Fidelity Select Telecommunications
800-544-8888

Flag Investors Telephone Income
800-767-3524

G.T. Global Communications
800-824-1580

Seligman Communications & Information
800-221-2783

For the following companies, the information, unless otherwise specified, generally applies to the early 1990s.

ADC Telecommunications, Inc. (OTC - ADCT)
4900 W. 78th
Minneapolis, Minnesota 55435
612-938-8080

Makes electromechanical and electronic products for the telecommunications industry. Through its American Lightwave Systems unit it makes various fiber optic links. Annual sales are over $300 million.

APA Optics, Inc. (OTC - APAT)
2950 Northeast 84th Lane
Blaine, Minnesota 55434
612-784-4995 Fax: 612-784-2038

APA was established in 1980 and has about 40 employees. The company makes optical components and systems, including gallium arsenide modulators, for laser and other industrial applications. It also designs and provides computer-generated holograms and does R&D in optoelectronics for communications and optical applications.

Annual sales are in the $2 million to $3 million range, and it's recently had mixed earnings results.

Advanced Photonix, Inc. (ASE - API)
1240 Avenida Acaso
Camarillo, California 93012
805-484-2884 Fax: 805-484-9935

Incorporated in 1988. Employs about 90.

Advanced Photonix designs and makes photodiodes, which detect and amplify light and other radiant energy sources and converts them to electrical signals.

Annual sales are now over $2 million. This developing company has been having the usual early trouble establishing a profit.

Amphenol Corp. (NYSE - APH)
358 Hall Avenue
Wallingford, Connecticut 06492
203-265-8900

Well-established company that employs 5,000+.

Amphenol manufactures electronic and fiber optic connectors.

Annual revenues are over $400 million, and the company has been profitable.

Artel Communications Corp. (OTC - AXXX)
22 Kane Industrial Drive
Hudson, Massachusetts 01749
508-562-2100

Artel was established in the early 1980s. It employs 50+.

Company makes fiber optic transmission systems.

Annual sales are about $5 million.

Augat, Inc (NYSE - AUG)
89 Forbes Boulevard
Mansfield, Massachusetts 02048
508-543-4300

Employs 4,000+. Formed in the 1940s.

Augat makes electromechanical and electronic components, and fiber optic connectors for the telecommunications industry.

Yearly sales are in the $200 million to $400 million range. Company has been profitable.

Codenoll Technology Corp. (OTC - CODN)
1086 North Broadway
Yonkers, New York 10701
914-965-6300

The company, incorporated in 1980, makes fiber optic networking and communications systems. Produces light-emitting diodes and diode receivers.

Annual sales are about $10 million. Has had some recent trouble turning a profit.

Coherent, Inc. (OTC - COHR)
3210 Porter Drive
Palo Alto, California 94304
415-493-2111

Formed in the mid 1960s. Employs more than 1,000.

Coherent manufactures various electro-optic products, including precision optical components and lasers.

Annual sales are about $200 million. Has been recently profitable.

Corning Inc. (NYSE - GLW)
Houghton Park
Corning, New York 14831
607-974-9000

The leading fiber optic manufacturer.

Electro Scientific Industries, Inc. (OTC - ESIO)
13900 Northwest Science Park Drive
Portland, Oregon 97229
503-641-4141 Fax: 503-643-4873

Formed in the 1950s, the company employs about 500.

Electro makes computer-controlled laser systems used in the production of semiconductor memory circuits and hybrid circuits.

Annual sales are about $60 million.

Excel Technology, Inc. (OTC - XLTC)
101-2 Colin Drive
Holbrook, New York 11741
516-563-7067

Established in the mid-1980s, company employs about 10.

Excel manufactures tunable laser systems used for medical and industrial applications, and also other electro-optical products.

Annual sales are about $250,000 to $500,000.

Fibronics International, Inc. (OTC - FBRX)
Communications Way
Independence Park
Hyannis, Massachusetts 02601
508-778-0700 or 800-456-3279

Designs and makes Local Area Networks which link computers. Manufactures fiber optic cable, optical fiber, fiber optic receivers, lasers, and internetworking equipment for high-bandwidth information transfer.

Company was formed in the late 1970s and employs more than 400. Its annual sales are about $50 million.

Galileo Electro-Optics Corp. (OTC - GAEO)
Galileo Park, PO Box 550
Sturbridge, Massachusetts 01566
508-347-9191 or 800-648-1800

Galileo makes various fiber optic and electro-optic products used to transmit, sense, and intensify light and images, and to detect charged particles and photons.

Established in the late 1950s, Galileo employs more than 300. Its annual sales are about $40 million, and its earnings results have been mixed.

ILC Technology, Inc. (OTC - ILCT)
399 Java Drive
Sunnyvale, California 94089
408-745-7900

Established in the late 1960s, ILC employs 200+.

ILC makes high-technology light sources, including laser pump lamps, and also manufactures sensors.

Annual sales are about $30 million to $40 million. Company has been profitable.

INRAD, Inc. (OTC - INRD)
181 LeGrand Avenue
Northvale, New Jersey 07647
201-767-1910

INRAD was formed in the early 1970s. It employs 80+.

The company makes crystals and products incorporating crystals which are used to control and augment laser radiation. Manufactures precision optical components, optical coatings, and laser systems. R&D on laser technology.

Annual sales are about $6 million.

Ion Laser Technology, Inc. (ASE - ILT.EC)
3828 South Main Street
Salt Lake City, Utah 84115
801-262-5555 Fax: 801-262-5770

Ion was formed in 1983. Employs 40+.

The company manufactures argon, krypton, and carbon dioxide lasers for industrial, scientific, and dental applications.

Annual sales are about $3 million.

Irvine Sensors Corp. (OTC - IRSN)
3001 Redhill Avenue
Costa Mesa, California 92626
714-549-8211

Established in 1980, Irvine employs about 35.

The company makes infrared sensing devices using electro-optical detectors which are sold to the electronics industry.

Annual sales are about $3 million to $4 million. Irvine lost money for the 1992 fiscal year.

Isomet Corp. (OTC - IOMT)
5263 Port Royal Road
Springfield, Virginia 22151
703-321-8301

Employs about 70. Isomet makes laser control devices used to process or communicate information.

Annual sales are about $8 million.

Laser Corp. (OTC - LSER)
1832 S. 3850 West
Sale Lake City, Utah 84104
801-972-1311

Through its subsidiaries, the company designs and manufactures lasers for various markets.

Laser Corp. was formed in the early 1980s and employs about 75.

Annual sales are about $7 million, and recent earnings results have been mixed.

Laser Precision Corp. (OTC - LASR)
32242 Paseo Adelanto
San Juan Capistrano, California 92693
714-489-2991

Company was formed in the late 1960s. It employs about 180.

Laser Precision makes fiber optic test equipment and other measurement equipment using electro-optical and data processing technologies for use in fiber optic telecommunications, data communications, and laser systems.

Annual sales are about $25 million and the company has recently shown a profit.

Lasertechnics (OTC - LASX)
5500 Wilshire Avenue N.E.
Albuquerque, New Mexico 87113
505-822-1123

Formed in 1982. Employs about 50.

Manufactures laser systems used in marketing a variety of products.

Annual sales are $7 million to $8 million.

Maxwell Laboratories, Inc. (OTC - MXWL)
8888 Balboa Avenue
San Diego, California 92123
619-279-5100

Maxwell makes defense and commercial equipment generally based on pulsed power technology, including pulsed laser excitation systems.

Annual sales are about $90 million, and the company has been profitable.

Newport Corp. (OTC - NEWP)
P.O. Box 19607
Irvine, California 92714
714-963-9811

This well-established company employs over 500. Annual sales are about $60 million.

Newport manufactures lasers, fiber optic components, and other optical electronic equipment used by scientists and engineers.

Optek Technology, Inc. (OTC - OPTX)
1215 West Crosby Road
Carollton, Texas 75006
214-323-2200

Optek was established in the late 1970s and has about 2,000 employees.

The company makes optoelectronic components and assemblies, including fiber optic data links and optical switches.

Annual sales are over $50 million, and the company has been profitable.

Optelecom, Inc. (OTC - OPTC)
15930 Luanne Drive
Gaithersburg, Maryland 20877
301-840-2121

Incorporated in 1973. Optelecom employs about 60.

The company is engaged in R&D in the electro-optics field, mainly in optical communication and laser systems for use in defense-related applications. Optelecom develops fiber optic links, fiber optic payout spools for missiles, and fiber optic sensors.

Annual sales are about $4 million to $5 million, and the company has been profitable.

Optical Coating Laboratory, Inc. (OTC - OCLI)
2789 Northpoint Parkway
Santa Rosa, California 95407
707-545-6440

OCLI produces multi-layer optical thin film coated products used for the control of light.

Annual sales are about $100 million. OCLI employs 1000.

Optical Radiation Corp. (OTC - ORCO)
1300 Optical Drive
Azusa, California 91702
818-969-3344

Company was incorporated in 1969. It employs about 1,800.

ORCO makes electro-optical systems and components.

Annual sales are about $150 million, and the company has been profitable.

Opto Mechanik, Inc. (OTC - OPTO)
PO Box 361907
Melbourne, Florida 32936
407-254-1212

OMI was established in 1969. It employs 200.

The company makes precision optical systems for the U.S. military.

Annual sales are over $30 million. Recent available annual earnings results have been mixed.

Optrotech Ltd. (OTC - OPT.KF)
Industrial Zone B
Box 69
Nes Ziona, Israel 70450

Company was incorporated in 1981, and employs 600+.

Optrotech makes computerized electro-optical systems for automated inspection using artificial intelligence technologies.

Annual sales are more than $70 million, and the company has been profitable.

SpecTran Corp. (OTC - SPTR)
SpecTran Industrial Park
50 Hall Road
Sturbridge, Massachusetts 01566
508-347-2261

Established in the early 1980s. Employs 100+.

SpecTran manufactures glass fibers used in telecommunications, and other specialty fibers and glass used for military and medical applications, and for laser transmission.

Annual sales are about $15 million to $20 million. SpecTran has been profitable.

Spire Corp. (OTC - SPIR)
One Patriots Park
Bedford, Massachusetts 01730
617-275-6000

Established in the late 1960s. Employs 150+.

Spire provides thin film technology services for various industries, including optoelectronics. R&D on photovoltaics. Manufactures optical coatings for the defense industry. Optoelectronic products include laser diodes and gallium arsenide wafers.

Annual sales are about $17 million.

Thomas & Betts Corp. (NYSE - TNB)
1001 Frontier Road
Bridgewater, New Jersey 08807
908-685-1600

Leading manufacturer of electric and electronic components. Also makes fiber optic connectors.

Annual sales are about $600 million.

Three-Five Systems, Inc. (ASE - TFSY)
10230 South 50th Place
Phoenix, Arizona 85044
602-496-0035 Fax: 602-496-0168

Incorporated in 1990.

Three-Five makes optoelectronic equipment using visible and nonvisible light. Its products include light emitting diode array displays and liquid crystal display components.

Annual sales are about $18 million, and the company has been profitable.

II-VI, Inc. (OTC - IIVI)
375 Saxonburg Boulevard
Saxonburg, Pennsylvania 16056
412-352-4455

Incorporated in the early 1970s, employs more than 200.

II-VI fabricates optical and electro-optical components and materials for use in infrared devices and high-powered lasers.

Annual sales are more than $16 million. Company has been profitable.

Vicon Fiberoptics Corp. (OTC - VFOX)
90 Secor Lane
Pelham Manor, New York 10803
914-738-5006

Company employs about 20. Incorporated in 1981, Vicon makes fiber-optic illumination transmission systems used for dental, medical, and industrial applications.

Annual sales are about $1 million. Lost money in 1991.

Zygo Corp. (OTC - ZIGO)
Laurel Brook Road
Middlefield, Connecticut 06455
203-347-8506

Established in the early 1970s, Zygo employs about 200.

The company makes high-performance laser-based electro-optical measuring instruments and optical components.

Annual sales are about $30 million, and Zygo has been profitable.

On a related note, here are a few companies, besides those already mentioned, that are in some way involved in the information highway, or interactive systems, or multimedia systems (keeping in mind that just about every computer and/or telecommunications company has its eye on the potential markets):

ACTV Inc (OTC - IATV)
1270 Avenue of the Americas
New York, New York 10020
212-262-2570
Develops interactive TV technology and systems.

America OnLine (OTC - AMER)
8619 Westwood Center Drive
Vienna, Virginia 22182
703-448-8700
Provides information services for on-line computers.

Cisco Systems, Inc. (OTC - CSCO)
1525 O'Brien Drive
Menlo Park, California 94025
415-326-1941
Manufactures high-performance computer networking products.

Commodore International Limited (NYSE - CBU)
1200 Wilson Drive
West Chester, Pennsylvania 19380
215-431-9100
Large manufacturer of personal computers that is actively developing multimedia systems.

Electronic Arts Inc. (OTC - ERTS)
1450 Fashion Island Boulevard
San Mateo, California 94404
415-571-7171
The world's largest publisher of interactive software. Owns 20 percent of 3DO.

Interactive Network, Inc. (OTC - INNN)
1991 Landings Drive
Mountain View, California 94943
415-960-1000
Developing interactive TV systems and technology.

Novell, Inc. (OTC - NOVL)
122 East 1700 South
Provo, Utah 84606
801-429-7000

Leading manufacturer of software that allows personal computers to network and communicate.

NTN Communications, Inc. (OTC - NTNX)
2121 Palomar Airport Road
Carlsbad, California 92009
619-438-7400

Operates an all-day TV network that features interactive game programming.

PictureTel Corp. (OTC - PCTL)
The Tower at Northwoods
222 Rosewood Drive
Danvers, Massachusetts 01923
508-762-5000

Manufactures video phones and other visual communications systems.

Scientific-Atlanta, Inc. (NYSE - SFA)
One Technology Parkway
Atlanta, Georgia 30348
404-441-4000

Makes various cable television and satellite network systems equipment and electronic measurement devices. Company will help design the converter box needed for Time Warner's interactive system in Florida.

Sierra On-Line, Inc. (OTC - SIER)
40033 Sierra Way
Oakhurst, California 93644
209-683-4468

Sierra develops and publishes various entertainment software products, including interactive animated games and simulations. Sierra may write the software for 3DO's "interactive multiplayer."

Tandy Corp. (NYSE - TAN)
1800 One Tandy Center
Fort Worth, Texas 76102
817-390-3700

Has introduced its own multimedia personal computer.

3Com Corp. (OTC - COMS)
5400 Bayfront Plaza
Santa Clara, California 95052
408-764-5000

Manufactures computer communications systems and products.

VideoTelecom Corp. (OTC - VTEL)
1901 West Braker Lane
Austin, Texas 78758
512-834-2700

Manufactures video conferencing systems.

A few other publicly traded (all OTC) companies that are involved in the software or hardware aspects of multimedia or interactive TV are:

Acclaim Entertainment, Inc. (AKLM); Broderbund Software, Inc. (BROD); Capital Multimedia, Inc. (CDIM); CEL Communications, Inc. (CELC); Singapore-based Creative Technology Ltd. (CREAF); Electro Brain International Corp. (EBIC); Franklin Electronic Publishers Inc. (FPUB); Media Vision Technology Inc. (MVIS); RasterOps, (ROPS); and Radius, Inc. (RDUS).

CHAPTER 7

MEDICAL MARVELS (Part 1): HIGH-TECH MEDICINE

"First, do no harm."

— Hippocrates

Surgeons must be very careful
When they take the knife.
Underneath their fine incisions
Stirs the culprit, life

— Emily Dickinson,
'Surgeons Must be Very Careful'

"If Casey Stengel were alive today,
he'd be spinning in his grave." (?!?!)

— Ralph Kiner,
Hall of Fame baseball player and
New York Mets' broadcaster.

In the Third Millennium, the Bionic Man may own a Smart Bathroom.

If you take a seat in the Smart Bathroom, your weight and body fat could be measured and displayed on a nearby monitor screen. You'd be able to insert your arm in a cuff and get a blood pressure reading. Or a quick, accurate urinalysis could be provided by sensors before the final flush. Who said 21st century technology will be remote?

Unobtrusive, very accurate, high-tech monitoring and diagnostic systems like the Smart Bathroom could be as common in the 21st century home or apartment as high definition television sets, or virtual reality games. Japan, in 1993, was ready to market an early version of the Smart Bathroom which would use biosensors to automatically test for glucose in urine — a possible indication of diabetes.

So, in the 21st century, doctors will expect their patients to have diagnostic bathrooms. It's not the first time bathrooms were used as a directional marker for medicine. In the 14th century, proctologists signalled their specialty to would-be patients with a painting of a chamber pot above the door. That was the same century doctors said the Black Plague had started because of a triple conjunction of Mars, Jupiter, and Saturn in Aquarius. So medicine, diagnostics, and bathrooms have all come quite a way.

The devotees of Osiris performed surgery in ancient Egypt. The mysterious white-hooded Druids knew of biological rhythms, and incorporated them when they mixed their healing smidgeons of roots, leaves, and blossoms. In their cryptic texts, the ancient Hindus alluded to an unidentified "secret cement" which helped them originate what today would be called plastic surgery. Using a syringe, what was essentially the first artificial insemination was performed in the 1700s. Anesthesia was used in the 1800s. The clinical thermometer, stethoscope, and ophthalmoscope were invented in the 19th century. And in the very early 1900s, a company in New York City had a 400-page catalogue detailing its strap-on and sometimes spring and bolt-action wood and rubber prosthetics for the feet, fingers, legs, and hands.

But medical technology has probably advanced further in the past 20 years than in all previous centuries. The explosion will continue. It's been said that if a doctor fell asleep in 1900 and didn't awake until the Great Depression some thirty years later, he probably could still pick up right where he left off and resume his practice. So little had changed. But if a doctor did a Rip Van Winkle in 1930 and didn't awake until 1960, she'd be lost.

Forget about falling asleep in 1960, or 1980, or 1990, and waking up in the 21st century. "If a doctor fell asleep just 10 years ago, they'd have real difficulty today, things have changed so much," says Henry C. Alder of H.C. Alder & Associates in Palatine, Illinois.[1]

Medical knowledge potentially could grow exponentially, doubling in less than a decade, then doubling again, and so on. For example, Baxter International, a leading health-care company, says that more than one-third of its 1992 product sales came from products introduced in just the past five years.[2]

It's possible that sometime in the 21st century, eyeglasses and wheelchairs will become curio shoppe items. The deaf may be able to hear, the blind see, the paralyzed walk. Custom-made artificial organs and limbs will make today's look as primitive as Captain Ahab's "barbaric white leg . . . fashioned from the polished bone of the Sperm Whale's jaw."

If you're less concerned with the future-shock possibilities of a Bionic Man and more concerned with the foibles of contemporary man, then know that today's medical technology can do things like laser-zap from your arm or butt the tattooed name of an old lover that so annoys your spouse. And leave you scar-free.

The zap of a laser apparently became more practical for medicine before it did for the military. If you think about it, the terminology of war and health care often overlap. Surgical strikes. Operations. Invasions. Antibodies that search and destroy. The body's defense system. The expression "smart bombs" is now used in medicine. Smart bombs are the latest thing in magic bullets. And so on. Perhaps that kind of mindset has been part of the problem for current health care. Fighting a war can be costly. And many battles won are Pyrrhic — some treatments and operations can be about as dangerous as the disease.

As in war, it generally makes more sense to take preventive steps to ensure a disease never develops to begin with. Much of 21st century health care and medical technology will be about staying healthy and catching trouble spots and treating them before they blow up into a real crisis. The old cliche about an ounce of prevention worth a pound of cure will take on a high-tech twist.

Some innovations in medical technology will be prompted by current developing trends in health care. Prevention. Cost-containment. And moving it out of hospitals and doctor's offices, and into alternate sites. Consequently, high-tech millennium medicine could feature sophisticated, cost-effective imaging techniques. Diagnostic equipment will improve and eventually take their reading at the cellular level. Self-monitoring systems will become commonplace.

In the 21st century, if surgery has to be performed, new and improved methods will continue to make operations increasingly less traumatic and invasive, which will get the patient up and around much faster. Some doctors speculate that in the future many, if not most, operations will be done without having to cut the patient at all — surgery would be performed with some sort of directed energy waves that would manipulate the insides. (Sound waves have been used to break up kidney stones.)

Of course, computers will proliferate in just about every facet of 21st century health care, from keeping the books, to acting as something like a midwife, to even reading the mind of some patients who are locked in a coma-like state.

The Commerce Department lists medical devices and diagnostics as an emerging technology. *Commerce says the nascent market for new and improved diagnosis and treatment equipment and supplies based on new sensors, mini-*

aturization, biomolecular processes, and imaging devices will hit $16 billion worldwide by the year 2000.[3] Some of the major technology elements of this emerging field will be cellular-level sensors, electromedical imaging, and fiber optic probes.

As for investing in high-tech medicine, there are some serious caveats to consider first.

In the early 1990s, the U.S. government passed a law which essentially toughened the Food and Drug Administration's approval process for new medical devices, and imposed new regulatory requirements on manufacturers. It was like a shot in the gut for the industry. The number of product marketing applications fell from 47 in 1990 to 12 in 1992. The average time for a PMA to clear the review process jumped from about 400 days to more than 600, and in some cases stretched beyond two years.

Fears and flaps over artificial hearts and, more recently, silicone breast implants, have focused the government's attention on the industry, and made consumers more concerned about medical devices. Lawsuits have proliferated. In an industry that has always been marked by rapid innovation, medical device companies may now be less inclined to innovate.

Then there's the problem of soaring health care costs.

As this is being written, President Clinton's health care team, led by the First Lady, is working on a plan to cut the high cost of health care, and make health insurance and good health care affordable and available to every American.

It would seem something has to be done. In 1993, America's annual health care costs approached $1 trillion dollars. That compares to $250 billion in 1980. More than 14 percent of the U.S. Gross Domestic Product (GDP) goes to spending on health care. Without some changes, the numbers will probably go up.

The uncertainty about the future of health care has sent many high-tech medical device company stocks into a spin. By some accounts, high priced medical technology is one of the main culprits pushing up costs.

"But the high cost of medicine has inappropriately been blamed on high-tech — the blame is in the decision made to utilize it," says Alder. "High-tech procedures have often been overused or misused. Not to be facetious, but you don't always have to use MRI because the patient has a headache. But because incentives were set up to use high-tech to a greater extent than appropriately needed, such tests could be ordered with impunity."[4]

And there's an often overlooked side to high-tech medicine. *A cost-saving side.* For example, a relatively new surgical process called a laparscopic cholecystectomy is being more frequently used to remove a gallbladder overrun with gallstones. The operation's cost is about $3,000 to $4,500, or as much as

Reprinted by permission: Tribune Media Services.

50 percent less than the more conventional procedure. And the newer method uses much less pain medication, and can get the patient out of the hospital in one day, as opposed to five. With half a million patients a year being treated for gallstones, you can see that the ultimate cost-saving is substantial.

Another example — a procedure called laser angioplasty, used to treat certain cardiovascular problems, is estimated to be saving $21 million a year in Medicare costs.

Savings from medical technology are often difficult to quantify. How do you measure the psychological benefits of feeling better, improving the quality of life, and the return of an individual to a productive life?

"It's hard to show a direct cost-saving from medical technology. But medical devices make people healthier, which gives a cost-saving to society as a whole — *medical technology helps the system to be more productive,*" according to James McCamant, editor of the *Medical Technology Stock Letter.*[5]

A study by the Battelle Medical Technology Assessment and Policy Research Center (MEDTAP) concluded that medical advances, including drugs, biotechnology, and medical devices, as well as changes in life styles, will cut health costs by hundreds of billions of dollars over the next 25 years. The study predicts there will be a dramatic drop in the number of patients with disabling diseases, and a corresponding rise in the number of lives saved due to medical advances.[6]

In the short-term, the shake-up in the health care industry probably won't help the bottom line of high-tech medical device manufacturers. However, an underlying theme of this book is investing for the long-term. And long-term, the fundamentals still look good for medical technology.

For one thing, despite concerns about the safety of new products, Americans will always insist on a continuing high level of quality health care.

Also, the graying of America will push the demand for certain devices. Obviously, the elderly are the main users of some medical products, especially cardiovascular and orthopedic devices. The statistics tell part of the story. According to recent Census Bureau figures, the number of Americans over age 75 will increase dramatically from 1990 to 2000.

The number of 75–84 year olds will increase 21 percent, 85–94 year olds will rise 40 percent, 95–99 up 60 percent, and the number of centenarians, those aged 100 or more, will rise 79 percent. And although not all of them will be able to return to their jitterbugging days, like some scene out of "Cocoon," many will be fit and spry, thanks to healthier lifestyles, better preventive measures, and high-tech medicine. By 2080, there could be one and a half million centenarians in the U.S.

The proportion of middle-aged Americans (35–54 years old) will also increase sharply in the 1990s, up 28 percent. Many of them will be generally well-off technophile-type baby boomers who will expect to see high-tech devices as part of the mix of high-quality health care.

In another positive sign for the long-term, medical device and service companies don't shirk when it comes to R&D — they generally put back almost 10 percent of their annual revenues into research and development, compared to less than 4 percent for all U.S. manufacturers. Also, in what could have other long-term investment implications, more than a third of all venture capital money spent in 1992 went to the broader category of health care.

The National Critical Technologies Panel says, "due to the aging of the population and the demand for products that improve and prolong life, major global market growth is expected."[7]

It's that global market that's another key to the future of the high-tech medical industry.

Medical technology is the most rapidly growing sector of U.S. exports. The global market for current medical devices stands at more than $70 billion, and U.S. manufacturers supply about half the total.[8]

As overseas economies expand, as they become wealthier, and as a strong middle class develops, one of the nation's highest priorities becomes quality health-care. America is the recognized leader in advanced medical devices, and foreign markets should increasingly turn to the U.S. for their supplies. For example, U.S. exports of medical and dental instruments and supplies to Eastern Europe rose 29 percent in 1992. And the government says that overall, U.S. medical products' exports increased at a compound annual rate of more than 15 percent over the four years ended in 1992. That type of growth is expected to continue.[9]

Of course, it won't be a cake walk for U.S. companies. Germany and Japan will be major competitors in the global medical technology market. Over half of the technologies identified as highest priority emerging technologies by Japan's Science and Technology Agency were medical and biotechnologies. The winner will be the country that can turn out the most cost-effective, highest quality products.

As indicated earlier, many of the products that could become popular overseas, as well as domestically, will stress cost containment. Holding down costs fortifies the trends towards self-care and prevention, and moving health care out of the hospital and into various outpatient alternatives, such as specialty surgical and diagnostic centers, and the home.

During the mid-1980s, the number of free-standing ambulatory surgical centers increased nearly five-fold. And because of medical technology advances, more patients can maintain high-quality treatment at home, which is obviously cheaper than a hospital stay. Since 1975, the number of patients treated at home has roughly quadrupled to about 2 million. The U.S. market for home health care equipment is estimated at over $1 billion and growing.

For example, Baxter International has developed a roughly 25-pound, easy to use, at-home kidney dialysis machine that could get FDA approval in late 1993, and will help thousands of patients.

There are many do-it-yourself diagnostic kits already on the market. Pregnancy, ovulation, blood pressure, and colorectal cancer kits are all available. A rapid test for HIV using saliva samples is in the works.

In 1993, the Food and Drug Administration approved the first at-home test kit (made by Chemtrak, OTC - CMTR) for detecting cholesterol. A prick of blood from the finger is put in a plastic container with a test strip. The strip turns a different color depending on the level of cholesterol. The results, given in 15 minutes, are reportedly as accurate as anything you'd get in a doctor's office.

"Making it more convenient to check on cholesterol can help ensure that people are aware of the level so they can see a doctor before serious problems develop," says Donna Shalala, Health and Human Services Secretary.[10]

Even taking little pin-pricks of blood for home diagnostics may eventually be seen as unnecessarily 'barbaric.' Many in-home monitoring and diagnostic products based on biosensors will emerge. *Biosensors* are essentially a union of biocompatible materials with electronics. Products using them are expected to be more accurate and cost-efficient.

For example, an at-home glucose detection device takes a drop of blood, and works by essentially counting the number of electrons released when the glucose in the blood comes in contact with a binding material.

But that system may already be passé. A newer at-home diagnostic system can measure the amount of glucose in someone's blood by shining a light on them. Glucose has a particular spectrum which the system's software can screen out from non-glucose signals. The glucose-catcher weighs less than 20 pounds, about the size of a portable TV. It's much more accurate than over-the-counter glucose kits currently used by diabetics, and no pin-prick of blood need be drawn. Again, another example of the less-invasive trend.

In the 21st century, self-monitoring at home, or elsewhere, could become something of a lifetime affair. Babies' cribs could contain sensors to detect the onset of any abrupt physical/health change. Sudden infant death syndrome is still a concern in America. Senior citizens will wear high-tech monitors, much more advanced than those available today, that could keep constant tabs on things like the heart and respiration.

Young and old alike may wear 21st century beads, bracelets, and bangles that are more than aesthetic—they'd actually serve as high-tech medical monitors. For example, you could wear an arm or wristband that looks like a bracelet, or clip on an earring, which could take blood tests and measure the body's levels of fat or cholesterol. Best of all, the 'jewelry' would be able to take the blood tests without drawing even a single drop. The wristband would be laced with mini-optic sensors that could detect the molecular makeup of substances swishing around in the capillaries.

Many futuristic self-monitoring systems will ultimately be able to be hooked into the information highway, so their results can be sent to the computer in the doctor's office. A modem-sent alert-message or a radio signal may be able to "shout" a heads-up to the physician if there's any major change in normal readings.

Out of the home, diagnostic methods are also taking new spins. In some cases, literally.

A new, rapid-fire diagnostic system called ERA, for Electro-Rotation-Assay, is being developed in Britain. ERA essentially makes use of the observation that different particles spin in their own distinctive ways when placed in a rotating electric field. A computer can analyze the various spins and detect, for example, the HIV virus, or hepatitis, or cancer. ERA can quickly tell if the target particle is there, in what concentration, and if it's dead or alive. Other detection systems usually can't do all three. Immunoassays can't find their target if it's in low concentrations. And ERA systems are expected to be very cost-effective.

ERA is new. Ultrasound imaging is one of the older diagnostic techniques around. But it's the only method approved for viewing the pregnant mother and fetus. However, newer ultrasound systems to observe the heart, liver, prostate, and other organs are becoming more popular because their imaging quality has improved. Some ultrasound systems are miniaturizing so they can be more easily used for imaging baby's heads and hearts. Small ultrasound systems are especially useful in cases of premature birth and can be incorporated with incubators.

A study by the American Hospital Association says ultrasound provides high diagnostic yield relative to its costs. At less than $200,000 in some cases, the test is much cheaper than some alternatives that can cost millions of dollars. About 25 percent of the money spent on diagnostic systems in the U.S. goes toward ultrasound, up from 19 percent in the early 1980s. Ultrasound may also be used for therapy in heart-related diseases.[11]

However, there is one big-ticket imaging system whose sales could expand. Positron Emission Tomography or PET systems cost about $5 million. But it's apparently worth it. PET shows the internal body in action, unveiling in 3-D the biochemical processes and functions of organs and tissue. Other advanced imaging systems, like CAT scans or Magnetic Resonance Imaging (MRI) can give you a good 3-D-like picture of the internal organs. But that's all they can give you. In other words, if you scanned a cadaver with MRI you couldn't tell from the image if the body was dead or alive. Not so with PET. PET provides superior diagnostics for the brain, giving clues to Alzheimer's and Parkinson's, and is also useful in cardiology.

The cost of radioisotopes needed for PET scanning are coming down. PET cameras are becoming cheaper. PET also makes use of the physicist's cyclotron, which is very expensive. But less costly minicyclotrons are being developed. For example, a Massachusetts start-up company called PracSys is developing a cheaper cyclotron it calls an "accelerator." Using an accelerator, PracSys expects to cut in half the cost of PET. PracSys intends to unveil its first model by 1995. PET is used in only about 50 U.S. cities, but is expanding.

Newer MRI machines could also be more in demand. MRI is somewhat limited to stationary organs like the brain, because it essentially can't capture the image quickly enough of moving organs like the heart. But Fast MRI works at much higher speeds, and will allow the imaging of the heart, or lungs, or blood circulation. Fast MRI scans are also beginning to be used to detect the distinct parts of the brain that are activated when, for example, a person thinks of a specific word. That could have future implications for mental disorders like schizophrenia and dementia.

Another evolving advanced imaging technique called SPECT (Single Photon Emission Computerized Tomography), which, like PET, also gives insights into the metabolic functioning of tissue, may also become more popular. Fast MRI and SPECT will be able to tell, for example, exactly where and to what degree tissue has been damaged by a heart attack.

An experimental brain scan called Magnetic Source Imaging (MSI), by detecting faint electrical signals, can reveal the precise areas of the brain that are at work when specific parts of the body are moving. In other words, if you scrunched up your nose, a computer-generated image of the brain would essentially light-up at the exact places in the brain where the nose movement originated. So, if brain surgery has to be performed, the MSI can tell surgeons what areas to avoid cutting.

The MSI scanner costs about $2.5 million but, "(MSI) has eliminated to a large extent some of the devastating consequences of neurosurgery. It doesn't take many unintentional paralyses to pay for this," says Dr. William Orrison, Jr., chief of neuroradiology at the University of New Mexico and Veterans Administration hospitals in Albuquerque.[12]

In the 21st century, who knows—smaller, advanced body-scanning machines using the above-mentioned and other types of internal energy may be commonplace in alternative health-care sites, including possibly even the home.

If it's discovered you have heart problems, and need an operation, there are new procedures utilizing items as simple as balloons, or as sophisticated as lasers, that can help.

Despite considerable medical advances in cardiology, heart disease is still the number one killer in America. Almost one and a half million Americans suffer heart attacks every year. More than half a million die from them. Globally, cardiovascular disease contributes to 11 million deaths each year. So the development of high-tech cardiovascular diagnostic and therapeutic devices will continue to be a top U.S. priority.

The total heart-related device market, currently estimated at about $3 billion world-wide, is expected to more than double before the 21st century.[13]

The global market for synthetic heart valves is expected to grow about 10 percent annually, and demand for a device called an L-VAD is also expected to increase. An L-VAD is like a bridge to a heart transplant. The Left Ventricular Assist Device can help carry the load of the left chamber of the heart, which does much of the heart's work, pushing oxygen-rich blood out to the body. The L-VAD is an external device that can keep the heart functioning while the patient awaits a heart donor.

Reprinted by permission: Tribune Media Services.

A potentially huge heart-seller could be a gadget called an implantable defibrillator. *By various estimates, the annual global market for the defibrillator is seen quadrupling to about $1 billion by 1996.*[14]

The defibrillator is often referred to as a personal paramedic. It's essentially a tiny computer with a heart for a companion. The defibrillator acts like a watchdog and savior. Instead of barking, the device sends out electric pulses to the heart. About the size of a bottle of aspirin, the implantable defibrillator can control a too-rapid heartbeat, technically called tachyarrhythmia. (The commonly known pacemaker generally controls a too-slow heartbeat.)

The beauty of the defibrillator is that it can sense how bad the jumpy heart is, and can alter the strength of its electric pulses, which slow the heart down. The device can send various levels of pulses to the heart, from mild to jolting. The mild pulses essentially coax or guide the beating-a-bit-too-fast heart back to a normal rhythm. The more powerful jolts, like shock therapy, are for a more desperate situation. That is quite an improvement from earlier versions which were restricted to intense electric shocks, described sometimes as being kicked by a mule, that over time could have a debilitating effect on the patient.

The defibrillator system is also relatively easy to install, and does not require that the patient's chest be cut wide-open. The system basically consists of a patch under the skin near the heart, an external pulse generator near the stomach, and a couple of wires snaked through a vein leading to the heart. Cost? About $20,000.

Already a very popular item in Europe, the FDA approved the use of the defibrillator in the U.S. in 1993.

Some people use a bouquet of balloons instead of flowers to encourage or save an affair of the heart. But until just a few years ago, who would have expected that blowing up a balloon would become another major way to treat heart trouble? An amazingly simple procedure called *balloon angioplasty* is being used as an alternative to coronary bypass surgery to clear up blocked arteries. In it, a tube (or catheter) is inserted into an artery and is maneuvered until it reaches the blockage. A tiny balloon at the tip of the tube is then blown up, which presses the built-up fatty blockage, called plaque, against the arterial wall. The operation is much less expensive and traumatic than bypass surgery.

Bypass is a risky, major operation that can increase the chance of a stroke, infections, or bleeding, not to mention intense chest pain. An angioplasty procedure takes about an hour and a half, and the patient can sometimes go home the next day.

By some estimates, the average overall charges for angioplasty are about $10,000, about half as much as bypass surgery.

The number of balloon angioplasty procedures have more than doubled since the late 1980s, and, because of the already mentioned growing number of elderly, and because it's a cost-container, the industry expects annual growth of as much as 15 percent to 20 percent into the next millennium.[15]

But a balloon angioplasty is not perfect. The procedure works best for arteries that are only partially blocked, and because the plaque is not destroyed, it can make a comeback and cause other blockages. But newer methods are taking the balloon bust-up a step further.

Using tiny rotating blades (atherectomy), and "cool" lasers which are less likely to destroy the arterial wall, the bulk of the plaque can be scraped and zapped away.

The use of lasers for various other diagnostic, surgical, and therapeutic purposes is expected to grow strongly into the 21st century. A significant amount of venture capital is being raised for medical laser start-up companies.

Imagine a visit to the dentist without having to hear that teeth-grinding whine of the drill. Lasers are expected to be ultimately used on the teeth and cavities. Right now, a small percentage of dentists already use a hand-held laser to perform periodontal operations on the soft tissue in the mouth. And the surgery is almost bloodless. Anything that can perform near-bloodless surgery while AIDS exists certainly will be in demand.

The use of lasers by dentists is expected to be a huge growth area. There are about 1,500 lasers in the world being used for dental or oral surgery. There are hundreds of thousands of dentists in the U.S. alone, so the market potential is very large.

One of the most intriguing and dramatic laser technology developments will allow the billions of individuals who don't have 20-20 vision to toss their glasses and contacts into the trash. "Four eyes" will become as rare and meaningless a denigration in the future as "peg leg" is now.

Nearsightedness, farsightedness and astigmatism are essentially caused by a misshapen eyeball. But a type of laser called an excimer laser can be safely used to re-form the curve of the cornea. The excimer laser, unlike most other lasers, does not heat and burn tissue. Instead, it chemically breaks down the unneeded tissue which can then be washed away with no other damage to the rest of the eye. With a simple, quick operation, vision potentially can be restored to a perfect, or near-perfect, state.

The use of an excimer laser in the U.S. for that type of eye surgery is awaiting FDA approval, which is expected by 1995. By some estimates, by the year 2000, at least two million eye operations will be performed annually using the excimer. *Global excimer laser sales totaled $34 million in 1992.*[16] *Many analysts predict that will grow to over $2 billion before the turn of the century, or about a 60-fold increase.*

Lasers are also increasingly being used for dermatology. As mentioned earlier, they can remove tatoos without leaving any scars. They can in fact help remove scars, or zap blemishes. They can also eradicate some birthmarks. If Mikhail Gorbachev wants to get rid of that wine-colored mark that looks like a map of Russia on top of his head, he can.

Along with lasers, the light revolution discussed in another chapter is helping to change the face of medicine in other ways.

The fiber optic network, and two-way video communications, will essentially allow the return of the doctor who makes house calls.

Also, fiber optics will make it possible for complex images from PET or MRI scans to be transmitted globally. This *teleradiology* will mean the expertise of medical specialists will be available to remote locations without the need, and expense, of transporting them.

Using fiber optic technology, once complex diagnostic and/or surgical procedures are being replaced by operations that are much less invasive and traumatic to the patient. Called *endoscopy,* it's sometimes referred to as 'keyhole' surgery. Essentially, small incisions are made on the patient through which are inserted thin, flexible tubes. Down one tube, light is radiated which illuminates the area to be operated on. Connected to another tube is a mini-cam (the endoscope). The magnified area can be viewed on a video monitor. The surgeon operates through the other holes, using miniature instruments (or again, lasers are used).

You may have heard of arthroscopy, which is popular with athletes. *Arthroscopy* is just endoscopy on the knee. For abdominal procedures, endoscopy is called laparoscopy, and when the chest cavity is explored, it's thorascopy.

Endoscopy is becoming the operation-of-choice for a growing number of conditions. The bottom line in each case — less invasiveness, less pain, less recovery time, less cost.

The market for endoscopic-related devices is forecast to exceed $3 billion dollars by 1996 from $300 million in 1991.[17]

There are, however, possible downsides to endoscopy. There is some evidence that endoscopes may transmit diseases, including AIDS. But a company called Vision-Sciences Inc (OTC - VSCI) in 1992 received FDA approval for an endoscope with two parts. The expensive and high-tech optical piece can be safely reused. The other part, which comes in contact with the body, is a disposable sheath which can be removed and tossed after the operation is over.

But endoscopy is still limited because the view given the surgeon on the monitor is in two dimensions. For more complex operations, greater depth perception is needed. If you think about it, you really wouldn't want a doctor with one glass eye doing intricate surgery on you. However, in mid-1993, Britain's Cambridge University reported that it developed an endoscopic system that lets televised images of a body be displayed in 3-D without the need for any special glasses or headsets. The images can be seen from various angles if the viewer just moves their head from side-to-side, or up-and-down.

Because complex computer/television images will be able to be transmitted globally over the fiber optic network, and because instruments can be manipulated over great distances with "telepresence," which is used in robotics, it opens up the possibility that surgery can be performed although the patient and surgeon are thousands of miles apart. Again, remote areas will have direct access to a medical specialist because of technology.

Apart from endoscopy, some operations, like joint or organ implants, by their nature may require the patient to go more deeply under the knife. Each year in the U.S., there are well over 300,000 joint replacement operations, mostly of knees and hips. Many seniors are being relieved of the crippling pain of osteoarthritis thanks to high-tech joint substitutes. Using computer-aided design and manufacturing (CAD/CAM) and computerized modeling systems, artificial hips and knees made of plastic and metal can be made to order for specific patients. But they do wear out.

Newer prosthetics with a porous stem allow for the growth of bone to knit into the knee and/or hip implant and form a more permanent attachment. Biodegradable polymer microcapsules are available that release proteins to stimulate bone growth. Additionally, biomaterials researchers are developing more bone-like synthetic substances.

The increasing number of elderly Americans should boost the demand for orthopedic devices and prosthetics. The number of orthopedic implants in the U.S. rose from 135,000 in 1981 to 390,000 in the early 1990s. The market is currently estimated at about $3 billion, and by some predictions is seen exceeding $14 billion by 1998.[18]

Of course, it won't just be the elderly that will be in the market for orthopedic replacements. If you're a baseball fan, you know Bo Jackson was able to return to the game in 1993, and hit a home run in his first at bat, due in part to a high-tech replacement hip.

But joints will be just a small part of the invasion of the body patchers. In the 21st century, there probably won't be any organ or limb that can't be adequately replaced, or possibly improved, by an artificial substitute. Biocompatible bionic hearts, valves, livers, pancreases, kidneys, skin, blood, ligaments. Even artificial nerves. You name it. Artificial substitutes are important because the demand for natural organs is outstripping supply. In a related area, an artificial "womb" which would allow in-vitro, or out-of-body gestation of a fetus will probably be possible.

Perhaps more amazingly, senses will also be restored through advances in *neural-prosthetics.* Right now, surgeons can restore hearing to some deaf individuals by inserting a tiny electronic device called a cochlear implant deep inside the ear. The implant essentially stimulates auditory nerves in the ear which the brain can convert into the frequencies that become sound. About 7,000 individuals around the world have cochlear implants, but only 20 percent of them have their hearing restored adequately. Sixty percent get some help from it, and use it effectively as an aid in lip-reading. But the rest really only get a buzz from the implant. Work is ongoing to improve the cochlear implant.

Further in the future, researchers hope to cure a more difficult form of deafness. If the auditory nerves have been destroyed, an array of electrodes is implanted in the area of the brain which would normally receive the signals from the nerves. If electrodes are "sparked," a rudimentary sensation of sound can be created in the brain. Again, it's primitive, but it's a start.

There's hope for the blind, too. First-level artificial retinas are being developed that can receive and convert light into electrical impulses that stimulate the appropriate parts of the optic nerve. Hopefully, early models would give the ability to see the outlines of things. But for most blind people, about 80 percent, an artificial retina wouldn't do any good. They don't have a functioning optic nerve. For them, a system is being developed that would be sort of like getting live TV reception directly on the brain.

Two unobtrusive mini-video cameras would be mounted on the sides of a pair of pseudo-eyeglasses. The images the cameras pick up would be sent electronically to electrodes imbedded in the visual cortex of the brain. The hope is that the electrodes would stimulate the brain cells and create a pattern of light-dots which would form an image. The level of vision would initially be crude, maybe something along the lines of TV reception with a lot of snow.

There's more to the body-electric connection that offers hope for the paralyzed and amputees. Using advanced electrodes and sensors, prosthetic limbs are being developed which will hopefully move more like the real thing, and give their wearers a sense of touch.

The use of electricity is also being explored to give paralyzed limbs movement. Prototype systems based on a technology called functional electrical stimulation (FES), which uses low levels of electric current, are being developed that would initially be used by patients with paralyzed upper limbs.

Separately, using a combination of FES and a computer-controlled brace, researchers are working to restore the ability to walk for paraplegics. Sensors attached to the joints of the body send the computer information on muscle movement and velocity, and the computer then relays to the FES system how to properly stimulate the muscles, and the brace how to brake, to achieve a semblance of a natural gait.

Eventually, the FES technology could also be used to regulate breathing, provide bladder control, restore reproductive function in some men, and treat curvature of the spine.

Doc Frankenstein apparently was on to something when he surrounded his laboratory and his namesake with crackling charges of electricity. Electricity is intimately tied into the functioning of the human system. Electric pulses are used to reduce pain in some cases where drugs don't work. Electromagnetic pulses are being used to induce fractured bones to mend and burns to heal. But there is one problem with generating tissue growth. When cells are coaxed to grow, they may not stop. In other words, cancer could be induced. But that kink is expected to be worked out early in the 21st century.

The link between the body and electricity may also help in cancer detection. For example, an Australian company, Polartechnics Ltd., is developing a way to instantly detect cervical cancer, which is one of the top cancer killers of women.

The device essentially makes use of the discovery that cancerous or pre-cancerous tissue has a measurably different electric polarity than normal tissue. Also, abnormal tissue reacts differently to light. The polar-probe shoots 10 million pulses of light and electricity every second to the tissue. A powerful computer provides near instantaneous analysis. If cervical cancer is detected it can be quickly treated.

The polar-probe is reportedly 90 percent accurate compared to the Pap smear's 50 to 80 percent rate. There are 90 million cervical cancer tests done globally every year. Besides being less reliable, the Pap smear is uncomfortable and it takes a few days to complete test results. U.S. clinical trials for the polar-probe will begin in 1994 under FDA supervision.

At the farthest frontier of electro-medicine and electrohealing, is research into the possibility of regenerating lost limbs. Salamanders are known to have the ability to regrow a lost tail or limb. It seems to have something to do with the electric current the amphibian generates at the wound-site. Using electricity, researchers have tried to duplicate the salamander's ability in frogs and other creatures with varying success. If it can ever happen with a human, it will probably be well into the 21st century.

Attention men: I'd like to pass along one last thing pertaining to electricity and the body. It has to do with *male pattern baldness.* There is a Canadian company that markets an apparatus that it claims can grow back hair on men who suffer from male pattern baldness. The device essentially radiates an electric field over the chrome dome, and apparently may spark the follicles to sprout hair again. The company claims a success rate better than minoxidil.

Current Technologies Corp. in Vancouver (604-684-2727 or 800-661-4247) is traded publicly Over the Counter. It's OTC stock symbol is CRTC.

As suggested by much of the above, computers will pervade 21st century health care, from the mundane to the esoteric.

Artificial intelligence expert systems are already being used as aides to diagnose and recommend treatment.

Japan's Sony Corp. has helped set up a computer-based service in the U.S. which allows patients to access — via videos — various doctors' advice on a particular ailment. It's supposed to help patients decide what medical advice to take, and help doctors avoid malpractice lawsuits.

Computers will help hospitals keep better records, freeing up nurses to pay more attention to patient care. Hospitals are notorious for having archaic systems to keep records, and they spend only 1 percent to 2 percent of their budgets on information systems.

Just about every hospital bed will have a computer nearby that can keep a constant vigil on body functions, so patients don't have to be awakened, for example, to have their blood pressure checked. Bedside terminals will help in hospital logistics, giving doctors and nurses an instantaneous way to know just what needs to be known about the patient, and what has to be done next.

Some new implantable drug-delivery devices will be controlled by radio signals from a computer, which will prompt the system on when and how much medication to deliver to a targeted site.

Along with drug delivery, delivering babies could be made easier thanks to computers. A program is being developed that can be used to simulate birth on a powerful computer. Using the data from ultrasound scans on the mother and fetus, the entire birth process can, in essence, be test run on a color monitor. Changing bodily stress levels will be revealed by changing colors on the monitor. The upshot — physicians will be able to tell well ahead of time if vaginal birth is possible, or if a Caesarean-section will be needed, which could possibly save the mother hours of unnecessary and painful labor.

Computers may even be able to "mind-read" certain patients who otherwise cannot communicate. Some people in comas or who suffer from a motor-neuron disease are aware of their surroundings but are unable to even blink an eye. The condition is called "locked-in-syndrome."

A team of Australian doctors has developed a so-called electro-cap which can interpret such patients' brainwaves. The cap, topped with an array of electrodes, collects brain-waves which are transmitted and analyzed by an artificial intelligence-based computer system. A simple thought like "yes" or "no" can be picked out of the "background noise." Using a series of prompting questions, the computer will be able to tell what's on the patient's mind.

Those are just a few examples.

I intended in this chapter to only give a broad overview of medical technology developments, because the real medical technology of the 21st century could be biotechnology, which will be taken up in the next chapter.

SOURCES

If you want to keep up on investment developments in medical technology, you may want to try:

Medical Technology Stock Letter
P.O. Box 40460
Berkeley, California 94704
510-843-1857

Sturza's Medical Investment Letter
424 West End Avenue
New York, New York 10024
212-873-7200

Other sources of information on medical technology/business are:

The BBI Newsletter
Biomedical Business International
1524 Brookhollow Drive
Santa Ana, California 92705
714-755-5757

FDC Reports - The Gray Sheet
FDC Reports, Inc.
5550 Friendship Boulevard
Chevy Chase, Maryland 20815
301-657-9830

Health Business
Faulkner & Gray's
Health Care Information Center
Washington, D.C.
202-828-4148

Health Systems Review
Federation of American Health Systems
1405 North Pierce Street
Little Rock, Arkansas 72207
501-661-9555

Journal of the American Medical Association
American Medical Association
535 North Dearborn Street
Chicago, Illinois 60610
312-280-7233

Because of the uncertainty surrounding the future of health care in the U.S., and the potential dynamic nature of the medical technology industry, you may want to leave investing in the field to the professionals. There are many stock mutual funds that invest in the broad category of health care, which includes medical technology companies. Some are listed below. Call for a prospectus.

Fidelity Select Medical Delivery
(800-544-6666)

Financial Strategic Health Sciences
(800-525-8085)

G.T. Global Health Care
(800-824-1580)

Putnam Health Sciences
(800-225-1581)

Vanguard Specialized Health Care
(800-662-7447)

There are a vast number of publicly-held medical device companies, and I am not going to list all of them here. The ones I will briefly mention are just representative of the industry, or of developing trends, or are involved in some of the technologies mentioned in the body of the chapter. They are not recommendations. If you want more information, call the company for an annual and/or 10-K report, or call a broker. Again, you may want to consider a mutual fund if you intend to invest in the medical technology field.

Some of the leading medical technology/device/instrument/supply companies are:

Abbott Laboratories (NYSE - ABT)
708-937-6100

Advanced Technology Labs (OTC - ATLI)
206-682-4500

Allergan, Inc. (NYSE - AGN)
714-752-4500

C.R. Bard (NYSE - BCR)
908-277-8000

Bausch & Lomb (NYSE - BOL)
716-338-6000

Baxter International (NYSE - BAX)
708-948-2000

Becton Dickinson (NYSE - BDX)
201-848-6800

Bergen Brunswig (ASE - BBC)
714-385-4000

Cordis Corp. (OTC - CORD)
305-824-2000

Datascope Corp. (OTC - DSCP)
201-265-8800

Diasonics Inc. (NYSE - DIA)
408-432-9000

   Diasonics is expected to break up into three publicly-traded companies in the summer of 1993 — OEC Medical Systems, Diasonics Ultrasound, and Focal Surgery.

Johnson & Johnson (NYSE - JNJ)
908-524-0400

Medtronic Inc. (NYSE - MDT)
612-574-4000

   Medtronic is one of the leading producers of implantable defibrillators.

Owens & Minor (NYSE - OMI)
804-747-9794

St. Jude Medical (OTC - STJM)
612-483-2000

SciMed Life Systems, Inc (OTC - SMLS)
612-420-0700

Manufactures disposable medical devices, including catheters and angioplasty balloon catheters.

Stryker Corp (OTC - STRY)
616-385-2600

U.S. Surgical Corp. (NYES - USS)
203-845-1000

Some other lesser known companies in the medical technology field are listed below. Medical laser companies are listed separately at the end. Again, these are not recommendations, nor is the absence from the list meant to be a reproach. These firms are merely representative of a dynamic industry.

ADAC Laboratories (OTC - ADAC)
408-945-2990

Makes computerized medical diagnostic imaging and information systems used for cardiology, nuclear medicine, oncology, and radiology.

ATS Medical, Inc. (OTC - ATSI)
612-553-7736

Small company that makes mechanical heart valves.

ABIOMED, Inc. (OTC - ABMD)
508-777-5100

Makes cardiac and dental diagnostic equipment. Also manufactures artificial hearts and surgical lasers.

Acuson Corp. (NYSE - ACN)
415-969-9112

Makes diagnostic ultrasound imaging systems.

Advanced Interventional Systems, Inc. (OTC - LAIS)
714-586-1342

Manufactures catheters and excimer laser angioplasty systems for the treatment of arterosclerosis in coronary arteries.

Advanced Magnetics, Inc. (ASE - AVM)
617-497-2070

R&D of contrast agents for magnetic resonance imaging and products for clinical use based on proprietary magnetic technology.

Advanced NMR systems, Inc. (OTC - ANMR)
508-657-8876

R&D on nuclear magnetic resonance imaging tomography systems for detection and diagnosis. Manufactures immunoassay diagnostic test kits.

Aequitron Medical, Inc. (OTC - AQTN)
612-557-9200

Manufactures various medical electronic products including computerized devices that process information from heart monitoring equipment.

American Medical Electronics, Inc. (OTC - AMEI)
214-918-8300

Makes proprietary products which generate electromagnetic pulses to enhance the healing of bone fractures and spinal fusions.

Applied Immune Sciences, Inc. (OTC - AISX)
415-326-7302

Immune system R&D. Proprietary products can isolate cells or proteins from blood and eliminate, change, or increase their number and then reinject them back into the bloodstream. Products can be used in AIDS and cancer treatment.

Ballard Medical Products (OTC - BMED)
801-572-6800

Makes disposable products primarily for providing critical-care patients with mechanical ventilation.

Biomagentic Technologies, Inc. (OTC - BTIX)
619-453-6300

Manufactures a magnetic source imaging (MSI) scanning device which produces a 3-D image of organs, and images the body's electrical activity by detecting faint magnetic fields.

Biomerica Inc. (OTC - BMRA)
714-645-2111

Develops and manufactures advanced medical diagnostic products, including some for home use.

Biomet, Inc. (OTC - BMET)
219-267-6639

Makes surgical implants and orthopedic support devices, including hip and knee joint replacements. Also develops proprietary electromagnetic bone healing devices.

Birtcher Medical Systems (OTC - BIRT)
714-753-9400

Produces various electrosurgery equipment and related items for conventional and endoscopic surgery.

Boston Scientific Corp. (NYSE - BSX)
617-923-1720

Develops and manufactures various medical devices worldwide. Primarily used by doctors to perform less invasive medical procedures.

Cabot Medical Corp. (OTC - CBOT)
215-752-8300

Makes medical devices primarily for improving female reproductive health care. Specializes in less-invasive surgical and diagnostic products, including laparoscopes.

Cancer Treatment Holdings, Inc. (ASE - CTH.EC)
305-321-9555

Develops, organizes, manages, and owns interests in outpatient radiation therapy treatment centers.

CardioPulymonics, Inc. (OTC - CRDS)
801-350-3600

R&D on cardiac-related and other medical products, including artificial lung technology.

ChemTrak Inc. (OTC - CMTR)
408-773-8156

Makes various efficient, disposable patented diagnostic test kits for the retail, consumer, and doctor's office markets.

Circon Corp. (OTC - CCON)
805-967-0404

Makes endoscopes and electrosurgery systems for diagnosis and less-invasive surgery. Products include ultra-miniature color video systems.

CliniCom, Inc. (OTC - CLIN)
303-443-9660

Manufactures computerized bedside information systems which keep track of hospital patients' care.

Criticare Systems, Inc. (OTC - CXIM)
414-797-8282

Makes diagnostic and therapeutic instruments and non-invasive sensors for patient monitoring in hospitals and alternate health care sites.

Cryomedical Sciences, Inc. (OTC - CMSI)
301-417-7070

Development stage company specializing in cryosurgical instruments which use low temperatures to destroy cancerous tissue.

Cygnus Therapeutic Systems (OTC - CYGN)
415-369-4300

Makes transdermal (patches) drug delivery systems.

Danek Group (OTC - DNKG)
901-396-2695

Makes and develops spinal implant devices used in the surgical treatment of spinal diseases and deformities. It's developing a porous biodegradable polymer that enhances and encourages tissue and bone growth.

Dimensional Medicine, Inc. (OTC - DMED)
612-938-8280

Makes computerized systems primarily used to process information and images for radiology departments. Manufactures image processing workstations which increase the productivity of CAT and MRI scans.

EDITEK, Inc. (ASE - EDI.EC)
919-226-6311

EDITEK makes on-site diagnostic and screening tests using patented technology. Also markets biomedical products.

EMPI, Inc. (OTC - EMPI)
612-636-6600

Primarily makes biomedical devices and computer-based diagnostic systems. Products include electrical nerve stimulation units to reduce pain. Also makes a non-invasive drug delivery system, and medical monitoring electrodes.

Endosonics Corp. (OTC - ESON)
510-734-0464

Makes ultrasonic imaging systems.

Everest Medical Corp. (OTC - EVMD)
612-473-6262

Small company that makes various endoscopic and laparoscopic products.

Gish Biomedical, Inc. (OTC - GISH)
714-261-1330

Manufactures various medical products, including specialty equipment used in open heart surgery. Makes left ventricle valves, arterial filters, and monitoring equipment.

Health Images, Inc. (OTC - HIMG)
404-587-5084

Operates outpatient MRI clinics.

Heart Technology (OTC - HRTT)
206-869-6160

Makes high-speed rotating blade to help treat arteriosclerosis.

Imatron, Inc. (OTC - IMAT)
415-583-9964

Makes high-speed computerized tomography scanners used in radiology and cardiology.

Imex Medical Systems, Inc. (OTC - IMEX)
303-431-9400

Makes ultrasound monitoring equipment.

International Remote Imaging Systems, Inc. (ASE - IRI.EC)
AKA: IRIS
818-709-1244

Makes cost-saving clinical laboratory computer workstations for automating chemistry profiling and microscopic visualization in urinalysis, hematology, and cytology using its patented, high-speed imaging technology.

Interspec, Inc. (OTC - ISPC)
215-540-9190

Makes ultrasound imaging diagnostic systems, and is engaged in R&D on advanced ultrasound technology.

Intramed Laboratories, Inc. (OTC - ITML)
619-455-5000

Small company that makes endoscopes.

Invacare Corp. (OTC - IVCR)
216-329-6000

Makes medical products used for home health care.

i-STAT (OTC - STAT)
609-243-9300

R&D on in-vitro diagnostic systems using miniaturized sensors.

Lifeline Systems, Inc. (OTC - LIFE)
617-923-4141

Makes personal electronic signaling systems that provide 24-hour emergency response service for medically at-risk individuals.

LifeQuest Medical, Inc. (OTC - LQMD)
210-366-2100

Develops vascular devices, including one that facilitates cancer and AIDS treatment by using a patient's bone marrow to access the vascular system for long-term infusion of drugs and fluids.

Lunar Corp. (OTC - LUNR)
608-274-2663

Manufactures equipment that measures bone density.

Maxum Health Corp. (ASE - MXH)
214-716-6200

Provides advanced diagnostic imaging services to rural areas or smaller cities.

MedChem Products, Inc. (NYSE - MCH)
617-938-9328

Makes fiber collagen product used to stop bleeding during endoscopic and other surgical procedures.

Medical Dynamics, Inc. (OTC - MEDY)
303-790-2990

Small company that makes blood flow monitors and surgical video camera systems used in endoscopic surgery.

Medical Graphics Corp. (OTC - MGCC)
612-484-4874

Makes computerized diagnostic systems for the early detection and treatment of heart and lung disease.

Medical Imaging Centers (OTC - MIKA)
619-560-0110

Sells high-tech diagnostic equipment to doctors and hospitals and helps them manage staff and billing.

Medicus Systems (OTC - MECS)
708-570-7500

Develops management computer software for the health care industry.

MEDphone Corp. (ASE - MPO.EC)
201-843-6644

Company makes and markets medical products that provide remote communication, diagnosis, and treatment over the telephone.

Medrad, Inc. (OTC - MEDR)
412-967-9700

Manufactures medical image enhancing products.

Micro Healthsystems, Inc. (OTC - MCHS)
201-731-9252

Develops management and financial systems software and hardware used in the health care industry.

Mitek Surgical Products, Inc. (OTC - MYTK)
617-551-8500

This small company makes minimally invasive surgical implants which make it easier for soft tissue-like ligaments and tendons to reattach to bone.

Molecular Biosystems, Inc. (NYSE - MB)
619-452-0681

Develops proprietary diagnostic contrast agents which enhance ultrasound imaging. Also makes diagnostic probe kits which allow for the in-vitro detection of certain infectious viruses and bacteria.

Nellcor Inc. (OTC - NELL)
510-887-5858

Makes electronic instruments and related sensors for patient monitoring.

New Image Industries, Inc. (OTC - NIIS)
818-346-4985

Makes computer imaging systems and imaging processing software that provide before and after pictures used by doctors and dentists. Also manufactures intraoral cameras.

Ophthalmic Imaging System (OTC - OISI)
916-646-2020

Small company that makes digital imaging systems used by ophthalmologists.

Organogenesis, Inc. (ASE - ORG)
617-575-0775

R&D in the field of tissue engineering. Company makes living tissue and organ equivalents.

Pyxis Corp. (OTC - PYXS)
619-625-3300

Pyxis went public in 1992. It's a leading maker of computer controlled systems that essentially automate the distribution of drugs and supplies in hospitals. The systems electronically capture and process every use of a medication, and allow direct billing of drugs to patients. They're reputed to be a major cost-saver for hospitals.

Quidel Corp. (OTC - QDEL)
619-552-1100

Makes various rapid diagnostic test kits, some of which are available for home use.

Respironics, Inc. (OTC - RESP)
412-733-0200

Makes ventilators and respirators for hospitals and home health care.

Rotech Medical (OTC - ROTC)
407-841-2115

Provides out-patient health care services and products, including oxygen and intravenous equipment.

Shared Medical Systems Corp. (OTC - SMED)
215-296-6300

Manufactures computer-based clinical, financial, and administrative information systems and provides related services for hospitals, clinics, doctors' groups, and health care corporations.

Spacelabs Medical, Inc. (OTC - SLMD)
206-882-3700

Makes patient monitoring devices and clinical information systems.

Supra Medical Corp. (ASE - SUP.EC)
215-459-4655

Develops and sells proprietary medical products for institutional and home health care.

Telios Pharmaceuticals, Inc. (OTC - TLIO)
619-452-6180

Makes wound healing treatment and tissue regeneration products.

Thermo Cardiosystems Inc. (ASE-TCA)
617-932-8668

R&D of ventricular assist devices.

Tokos Medical Corp. (OTC - TKOS)
714-474-1616

Provides home health care services for pregnant women and women with other complicated obstetrical and gynecological conditions. Manufactures a uterine activity monitoring device which can be used at home.

Utah Medical Products, Inc. (OTC - UTMD)
801-566-1200

Makes and sells a range of disposable medical products for the monitoring of patient vital signs.

Ventritex, Inc. (OTC - VNTX)
408-738-4883

Makes implantable defibrillators and related products.

Vision-Sciences Inc. (OTC - VSCI)
508-650-9971

Makes proprietary, disposable products designed to eliminate risk of infection from endoscopes.

Xytronyx, Inc. (ASE - XYX)
619-546-1114

Small company that's involved in the R&D of health care products, including a diagnostic test for periodontal disease, and a test to detect a form of pneumonia associated with AIDS. Also makes an ultraviolet warning badge that changes color to alert wearers of possible sunburn.

Zila Inc. (OTC - ZILA)
602-266-6700

Makes non-prescription medical products, including an oral cancer diagnostic aide.

Zoll Medical Corp. (OTC - ZOLL)
617-933-9150

Makes temporary, external pacemakers and defibrillators used in hospitals to treat some forms of cardiac arrest.

The following companies are engaged in the medical laser field:

American Dental Laser (OTC - ADLI)
313-649-0000

Candela Laser Corp. (OTC - CLZR)
508-358-7637

Coherent, Inc. (OTC - COHR)
415-493-2111

Excel Technology, Inc. (OTC - XLTC)
516-563-7067

Ion Laser Technology, Inc. (ASE - ILT.EC)
801-262-5555

JMAR Industries (OTC - JMAR)
206-869-6160

Laser Industries Ltd (ASE - LAS)
Israel-based firm
(972-3) 493241

Laser Medical Technology (OTC - LMET)
714-361-1606

Laser Photonics, Inc. (OTC - LAZR)
407-281-4103

Laserscope, Inc. (OTC - LSCP)
408-943-0636

LaserSight (OTC-LASE)
407-382-2772

Phoenix Laser Systems, Inc. (ASE - PXS)
415-373-2563

Spectra Science (OTC - SPSC)
AKA GV Medical, Inc.
612-559-4000

Spectranetics Corp. (OTC - SPNC)
719-633-8333

Summit Technology, Inc. (OTC - BEAM)
617-890-1234

Leading designer and manufacturer of laser systems to correct common vision problems like nearsightedness, farsightedness and astigmatism. Awaiting government approval to begin sales in U.S.

Sunrise Technologies (OTC - SNRS)
415-623-9001

Surgical Laser Technologies, Inc. (OTC - SLTI)
215-650-3210

Trimedyne Inc. (OTC - TMED)
714-559-5300

VISX, Inc. (ASE - VSX)
408-732-9880

    Develops and makes laser systems to correct vision disorders.

CHAPTER 8

MEDICAL MARVELS (Part 2): BIOTECHNOLOGY/ GENETIC ENGINEERING

"Biotechnology... is viewed by several countries as a key to the marketplace of the 21st century."

—John H. Gibbons, White House science adviser[1]

" 'Of course, if InGen can make full-size dinosaurs, they can also make pygmy dinosaurs as household pets. What child won't want a little dinosaur as a pet? A little patented animal for their very own. InGen will sell millions of them. And InGen will engineer them so that these pet dinosaurs can only eat InGen pet food...'
'Jesus,' somebody said."

—Michael Crichton, "Jurassic Park"[2]

The Mayor of Cambridge, Massachusetts said he didn't want any seven-foot tall monsters crawling out of the sewers in his town.

His reaction was, perhaps, the earliest form of biomania.

Like some of his constituency, the good mayor feared a catastrophe could float, or ooze, or walk out on its own from nearby MIT and Harvard labs, where scientists were tinkering with the mysterious blueprint of life—DNA.

That was back in the mid-1970s, and although the U.S. Patent Office has since allowed patents on genetically engineered animals, to date no Dr. Moreau-like monstrosity has ever been spotted.

But what has crawled, if not leaped, from the gene-labs in just a few years has been a worldwide, multi-billion dollar industry.

In 1976, the first so-called *gene splicing* company, Genentech (gen-EN-tech, for Genetic Engineering Technology), was formed. Four years later, October 14, 1980, Genentech made a public offering of shares on Wall Street—investors could now put their money into something new, which sounded strange and exciting, perhaps even dangerous. It had the requisite sexiness.

What happened that day was another, different type of October surprise for Wall Street.

Amid frantic floor trader screaming and gesturing, in less than half an hour, Genentech's share price jumped from an opening 35 dollars to as much as 89 dollars. The frenzy, unusual even for Wall Street, continued throughout the day, with the shares, after some profit-taking, eventually closing out at 70 dollars—double the original offering price.

All that for a company that did not yet have even one product on the market. Like some new volatile life-form, "Biomania," Wall Street-style, was born.

Investors knew little about biotechnology. Brokers were probably just as ignorant—I recall an episode of the old "Taxi" TV series where Louie, the brash, street-wise cab dispatcher, was forced to temporarily take a job as a stock broker. Caught up in biomania, Louie's shouted sales pitch to one phone customer consisted of, "YOU KNOW, CLONING, THAT KIND OF STUFF!"

With little more information than that, investors were willing to buy. Some were rewarded big-time—*a $10,000 investment in biotech firm Amgen in early 1985 would have ballooned to about three-quarters of a million dollars by mid-1992.*

However, in early 1993, Amgen's, and many other biotech share prices, plunged. Biotech suffers from mood swings, it is the manic-depressive of Wall Street.

But despite bouts of investor disenchantment, teeth-gritting roller-coaster share prices over the years, and still very few products on the market, in the last five years alone biotech stock investors have poured more than $4 billion into a group of roughly two hundred companies that, as an aggregate, "Are not even close to turning a profit," according to Dr. Mark Dibner, vice-president of Information for North Carolina's Biotechnology Center.[3]

It is a paradox of biomania, a fitting double-edge for a business based on the double helix. But just what is all the fuss about, and is biotech worth investing in?

According to the Government's Office of Technology Assessment (OTA), biotechnology consists of those "techniques that use live organisms (or parts of organisms) to modify products, to improve plants or animals, or develop micro-organisms for specific uses."[4]

But that definition could apply to some millennia-old processes, like beer-brewing, or selective dog-breeding. Indeed, "biotechnology has been a vital part of human activity for many thousands of years. In all probability the first biotechnologists were Neolithic men and women who may well have preferred the taste of fermented cereals to raw grain."[5]

But biotech, in the modern sense, consists of "new and innovative techniques to modify or to manipulate biological organisms to produce useful products."[6] That translates into the buzz words – genetic engineering, gene splicing, recombinant DNA, and cloning.

Simply by fiddling with the cell, modern biotech has the *potential* to turn out safer, more potent products that can make you healthier, and diagnose, treat, or cure many diseases. Or it can improve and increase the food supply. Or it can help make the planet green; biotech products can be environment-friendly and/or help clean up dangerous or unsightly wastes. And yes, biotech has an aesthetic side. For example, it can create blue roses or plants that have a soft luminescence.

So, biotech could make you feel better, eat better, and it could essentially take out the garbage. The OTA says, "Biotechnology may prove to be the last great revolution in knowledge in the 20th century and a significant underlying technology for the 21st century, but its full impact has not yet been felt."[7]

But does all that translate into growth potential as a market and an investment?

The Commerce Department predicts sales of biotech-derived products will grow 15 percent to 20 percent annually through 1997.[8]

Further down the road, "For investing in the future, biotech is *It.* It could be much bigger than anyone expects," said James McCamant, editor of the *Medical Technology Stock Letter.*[9]

Without going too much into the intricate details of the science of the cell, the road from biotechnology to biomania started in the 1950s, when scientists Francis Crick, James Watson, Rosalind Franklin, and Maurice Wilkins discovered the spiral-staircase shape of the deoxyribonucleic acid (DNA) molecule – the now famous double helix.

Most cells carry chromosomes which are primarily made up of DNA. Genes are portions of DNA. Taken all together, chromosomes, DNA, and genes are essentially a biological I.D. code. The code determines what each species, and each individual, will look like. Every external and internal characteristic that can be passed on from parent to child is carried in the genes, from the color of your hair, to the number of twirls in a pig's tail, to your disposition to a certain disease. Genes and DNA hold the blueprint for what, in many ways, distinctly makes you, "you."

With a true and clear picture — the double helix — of that blueprint, and how it works, it ultimately became easier for scientists to "redesign" the picture.

Now, using enzymes, which are just naturally occurring catalysts, scientists can cut DNA at very specific points, and reconnect them. That's gene splicing. Gene splicing, genetic engineering, and recombinant DNA are all different words for essentially the same thing. Recombinant is just a fancier word for re-combined.

In 1972, scientists from Stanford University combined bits of DNA from a bacterium with bits of DNA from a virus. The result was the first ever manmade recombinant DNA molecule. About a year later, another gene splicing experiment was performed that apparently even sent shudders through the scientific community. Essentially, a new creature was created.

DNA from a toad was spliced onto a type of bacteria called E. coli. The result was called a chimera, from the Greek word for a monstrous beast — its tissue was made-up from two different species. More importantly, when the little bacterial chimera reproduced, its offspring carried the same bit of toad DNA. And so on. Scientists now had a method and a machine to make copies, or clones, of DNA.

Shortly after that, scientists, possibly fearing its potential, pushed for a worldwide, temporary ban on genetic engineering until they could come up with safety guidelines.

In 1977, a human gene was spliced into E. coli. The new bacterium was able to produce the human hormone somatostatin, which basically controls how fast we grow. Biotechnology had come up with a new way to make a scarce medical product that previously was very hard to manufacture.

The usual source of somatostatin was sheeps' brains. It would take half a million such brains to make as much somatostatin as two gallons of gene-spliced E. coli.

A year later, another human hormone, insulin, was genetically engineered. There are millions of diabetics who need daily injections of insulin to stay alive.

Genetically engineered products were about to move from the labs to the marketplace. And the market had the potential to be huge. Businessmen, and certainly some scientists, smelled big money.

The National Critical Technologies Panel says biotechnology demonstrates " ... perhaps more vividly than any other discipline, the synergy between scientific discovery and the commercialization of innovative and life-enhancing products."[10] In other words, the structure was in place for the genesis of biomania.

In the 1980s, an average of 75 biotech companies per year were formed. About one and a half billion dollars of venture capital poured into the industry during that same decade. And after years of little more than hype and promise, the pay-off may finally be coming.

Total revenues for the biotechnology industry are currently estimated at about $4 to $5 billion a year. But according to the Commerce Department, that figure will grow to $40 billion worldwide by the year 2000. Other estimates put it over $50 billion, some as high as $100 billion.[11]

With that type of promise, biomania periodically explodes on Wall Street. As one scientist so aptly put it, "Interferon (a natural protein and biotech product) is a substance you rub on stockbrokers."[12]

In 1991, biomania hit with a vengeance — biotech stock prices as a group more than doubled.

Financial or otherwise, the ability to alter genes can have staggering implications. If there is one emerging industry that probably most symbolizes the 21st century, with all its contradictory scenarios of potential utopias and dystopias, it is biotechnology.

To the extreme on one side, are those who see in biotech the "Creature from the Black Lagoon" scenario, or the "Demon mutant bacterium" scenario, or the "Hitler clones" and "Eugenics" scenarios. The paradise seekers see a hunger-free, disease-free world, where people live as youths for centuries, all because of genetic engineering.

I guess a case could be made that any and all scenarios may be possible. Biotech can be heady, serious stuff. But for the time being, and for the foreseeable future, the marketplace reality lies elsewhere.

Reprinted by permission: Tribune Media Services

I like to think part of that market reality is best captured by the following, actual headline:

'JAPAN TRIES TO CURB BELCHING COWS'[13]

The story goes on to say that Japan's government will start a research program to stop cows from belching methane — because methane is one of the gases that contributes to the greenhouse effect and global warming.

The cows' stomachs, it seems, contain micro-organisms that help the cows digest cellulose, and in the process produce methane.

The Japanese want to create a new genetically engineered micro-organism that produces less or no methane, and can be transferred into the cow's stomach.

Japan plans to spend 80 million yen a year (more than half a million dollars at then exchange rates) on the program.

The story pretty much has it all as far as biotech is concerned — the potential to ease a hazardous, worldwide problem, government and business involvement, and fairly large amounts of money come into the picture.

But more seriously, and not to belittle some genuine social and ethical concerns about it, biotechnology has already created something of a revolution in medicine and health care.

"Every disease we know about is either being attacked with genetics or is being illuminated through genetics," says David Baltimore, president of Rockefeller University.[14]

About three-quarters of all biotech companies specialize in human health care, and by the new millennium it's estimated that biotech products will account for 15 percent to 25 percent of all drug sales.

From the commonplace to the devastatingly unique, biotechnology has widespread possibilities in health care — from clearing up warts, to freeing the boy-in-the-bubble from his prison. And if there is a cure for cancer or AIDS, it probably lies in the genes.

In the 20 years or so that modern biotechnology has existed, biotech firms, using gene splicing and other techniques, have manufactured commercial quantities of substances which can check and treat many diseases, including vaccines against the flu and hepatitis, human insulin for diabetics, human growth hormone to combat dwarfism, drugs that battle cancer, and biopharmaceuticals to bust-up blood clots and treat anemia.

In addition to therapies, biotech is creating new ways, probes, to detect or diagnose many diseases, including hepatitis, cystic fibrosis, and various kinds of cancer, as well as those diseases that are sexually-transmitted.

Many biotech companies use the *recombinant DNA* technology to fight diseases. The trick here generally is to gene splice naturally occurring proteins, like interferon, which are part of the body's own immune system — therefore, fewer unpleasant side effects.

Other firms are involved in an unrelated technique to make *monoclonal antibodies.* These are essentially produced from a hybrid — part disease-fighting white blood cells, part tumor cells, which divide to create a cell culture that turns out identical antibodies. Because they're cloned from a single cell, they're called monoclonal. Monoclonal antibodies are designed to recognize and/or attack a specific disease-causing agent.

There are other areas of biomedical research, including *antisense technology,* which tries to trip-up disease-causing genes with molecules that can block certain messages to them. Using these and other methods, biotech firms are developing drugs to speed-up wound healing, and are finding ways to treat or detect many diseases and disorders, including AIDS and cancer, anxiety, rheumatoid arthritis, psoriasis, Lyme disease, and various disorders of the central nervous and cardiovascular systems.

Using *gene therapy,* scientists hope to someday treat or cure the more than 3,500 diseases that are inherited, such as sickle cell anemia, or Alzheimer's, and are essentially caused by a mutant or malfunctioning gene. With gene therapy, "good" genes are injected into the patient. In 1990, the first human trial of gene therapy was performed on a four year old girl who suffered from ADA (adenosine deaminase, or the "bubble-boy syndrome," which disables the immune system). Her condition improved significantly. About 25 human gene therapy trials are currently being performed or awaiting permission to go ahead.

The size of the pharmaceutical market is roughly $200 billion annually. Biotech has barely scratched its surface — as of this writing, only 16 biotech therapeutics or vaccines (representing just 11 companies) have been approved for the marketplace. But many more are waiting for approval, and over 100 are in various stages of clinical trials. And it's estimated that some 500 biopharmaceutical compounds are in pre-clinical stages.

Although Wall Street predicts there will not be any more high-profile drug approvals until late 1993 to 1994, "Biotech is a revolution in how drugs are developed, and it will eventually dominate the drug industry. Biotech products could impact virtually every illness mankind has," says McCamant.[15]

"Biotechnology is likely to be the principal scientific driving force for the discovery of new drugs as we enter the 21st century, and the impact of biotechnology on the discovery of new therapeutic entities is difficult to underestimate," according to one pharmaceutical company executive.[16]

Less spectacular, but perhaps more fun-sounding, is the impact biotech will have on agriculture and related industries — known as the ag-bio sector, or in some cases, "pharming."

Genetic engineers joke of half-breed giraffes/cows that can be milked by you, but graze on your neighbor's lawn, or of crossing pigeons with parrots so a bird can deliver spoken messages.

But will pigs fly?

Probably not, and as a native New Yorker who's had enough problems with strafing pigeons, I fervently hope not. But the reality of ag-bio still makes for some fascinating possibilities ranging from, if not flying pigs, then so-called "perfect" pigs, super tomatoes, blue roses, and cows that are lean, mean, milking machines.

And ag-bio may have the potential to help alleviate hunger in the world.

But to an even lesser degree than the health field, very few biotech products are on the market right now — just a few pesticides and genetically engineered animal vaccines. But a number of new products are on the verge of cracking through — *ag-bio has been called the new frontier for biotech. Worldwide sales for ag-bio products are estimated at less than $100 million a year. But some analysts see that growing to more than $1 billion early in the new millennium. Other estimates put the market for gene spliced plants at $20 billion by the year 2000.*

With biotech, scientists can essentially speed-up the conventional selective cross-breeding process, and quickly create new traits in plants that otherwise would have taken years. Also, gene splicing can introduce completely new traits from one plant to another (transgenic plants).

"I suspect that virtually all of our current policy thinking about agriculture is very near in time to be totally irrelevant. *Major crops such as corn and wheat could see thousandfold increases in yield through genetic manipulation,"* says Terry Sharrer, Smithsonian Institution curator of agriculture.[17]

Crops that are more disease, drought, and insect resistant will be developed. The ultimate upshot — higher crop yields, better quality and more nutritious crops, and lower production costs.

Genetically engineered cotton that kills bugs has already been created. Almost half of the insecticides used in the U.S. try to kill-off cotton pests. The gene-altered cotton gives off a protein that is fatal to moth larvae — the larvae die while feasting. But such crops face a regulatory maze. The Environmental Protection Agency, the Agriculture Department, and the Food and Drug Administration would all have to approve the seeds before they can go on sale.

While trying to reduce a plant's dependence on pesticides, biotech has also developed alternatives to chemical pesticides. *Biopesticides,* using microbes, are not dangerous to humans, wildlife, or crops, and are less polluting — they essentially biodegrade, or break down and die quickly in the environment.

Biopesticides have grabbed only a fraction of a potentially large market — over 600 chemical pesticides have been approved by the EPA.

Despite the problems biotech companies can face trying to push ag-bio products through the EPA and various other government agencies, some restrictions in the ag-bio sector are loosening. In 1992, the FDA made what could be a monumental ruling for ag-bio, saying that genetically modified foods present no greater safety concerns than regular foods, and consequently would be regulated the same way — no special rules or labeling required. That could allow ag-bio companies to avoid costly field and safety tests.

As of this writing, a "super" tomato awaits approval from the FDA. The genetically engineered tomato, made by Calgene, Inc., has a much longer shelf life — it's more resistant to rotting. If the FDA gives the go ahead for the "Flavr Savr" tomato as a food, it could trigger much more investment interest in the ag-bio sector. The "Flavr Savr" has been estimated to have a market potential as high as $500 million, which is greater than most cancer-treating drugs. As of this writing, FDA approval was expected in mid to late 1993.

As for the blue rose, rumored to have once existed during the Age of Chivalry, an Australian company, Calgene Pacific Proprietary Ltd., claims it will be able to make one by essentially transferring genes from a blue petunia to a rose. Right now it's still in the experimental stage; no genetically engineered true-blue rose has been created yet. But if it works out, the market could be relatively large — a billion roses a year are bought in the United States alone. I know I pay at least a buck fifty per long-stemmed rose, so you go figure the potential pay-off.

Also on the ag-bio agenda, the development of various genetically engineered animal hormones that will lead to leaner hogs and beef. And cows that will be able to produce more milk. The cow hormone BST (bovine somatotropin) can pump up milk production by 30 to 40 percent. It's been genetically developed by four U.S. companies, and is also currently waiting FDA approval. Again, huge markets could be affected — the beef and dairy industries are each worth billions of dollars every year.

An alternative to injecting genetically-engineered growth hormones into livestock is injecting the growth hormone genes themselves directly into the animals (transgenic animals). Some companies hope to create a transgenic "perfect" pig. No swine this — it grows faster but doesn't eat as much, has leaner meat with less cholesterol, and has an increased ability to reproduce. Pork is also a multi-billion dollar industry. The same type of gene technology is being used to improve the nutritional quality of fish and shrimp.

In various stages of development by gene-teams are a series of other potential ag-bio products. Among them: sweeter tasting carrots, peas, and tomatoes, pest-resistant corn, herbicide-tolerant tomatoes, cotton, and soybeans, and canola plants that can produce cosmetics, detergents, food ingredients, and industrial lubricants.

Additionally, a genetically engineered tomato has been created that makes a protein found in arctic fish — the protein slows down freezing, and should inhibit the formation of ice crystals in various frozen foods.

There is also a Twilight Zone between the ag-bio and drug sectors. In it we find biotechnologists who are creating transgenic sheep, goats, and pigs that can produce human pharmaceuticals in their milk. Also, companies are using plant tissue cell cultures to manufacture commercial quantities of a scarce compound found in the Pacific yew tree which has shown some promise in treating ovarian cancer.

Finally, put this in your pipe and smoke it — tobacco plants have reportedly been genetically engineered that can produce human monoclonal antibodies in their leaves.

Biotech also has the potential to help clean up the planet.

The most obvious example was in 1989, after the now infamous Exxon Valdez oil spill off Alaska — *naturally-occurring, non-genetically engineered* micro-organisms helped degrade the crude oil. Using biotech for, in essence, garbage disposal, is called *bioremediation*. Bioremediation can be used in several situations, including the clean-up of industrial wastes, PCBs, and wastewater sites.

Right now, all commercial bioremediation projects use naturally occurring organisms. Some genetic engineering research for bioremediation is going on, but the government concludes that the commercial use of gene spliced micro-organisms for waste clean-up is unlikely anytime soon because of a slew of scientific, regulatory, and economic problems. Because the bioremediation products that exist now do not have a high profit margin, venture capital only comes in at a trickle to this particular area.

So far, according to the OTA, "research and product development in the environmental sectors are minuscule compared to more commercially lucrative sectors influenced by biotechnology, and international activity to date is limited."[18] However, some estimates put the bioremediation market at $200 million by the start of the 21st century.

Biotech also has widespread possibilities in the huge chemical industry. In theory, any chemical change can be brought about by a genetically engineered bacterium. But instead of using pressurized vessels and electricity, as chemical companies use now, the bacterium would do its job in a warm liquid, using sugar or sunlight for energy. For example, fuel could be produced from waste products instead of from crude oil, several plastics could be made, and alcohol could be made from wood pulp. However, for the time being, and for the most part, it does not make economic sense to use genetic engineering to produce bulk chemicals.

But biotech does play a current, although limited, role in chemical synthesis. Production of some amino acids used as food additives (monosodium glutamate is an amino acid) and animal feed supplements can be increased with biotech. Also, genetic engineering can help pump up the output of certain industrial enzymes, or catalysts, used to speed chemical processes in various business sectors, including the beer, meat, and cheese industries. That means gene splicing can cut these industries' production costs.

This use of biotech does not find its way into the media glare, but as it becomes more economical, it could ultimately affect more people than the biopharmaceutical or ag-bio sectors.

There are many other possibilities for biotech in various experimental stages, which could ultimately impact several industries. Biotech's potential, and reality, is generating world-wide enthusiasm, and research.

"As commercial biotechnology expands in size and scope, its effect on the international economy is likely to increase. Biotechnology is likely to be seen as a national asset by more nations—both as a way to develop a high-technology base and to increase market share in several international sectors," concludes the Office of Technology Assessment.[19]

The U.S. Commerce Department identifies biotech as one of its critical technologies—critical to the national economic prosperity and to national security. In the United States, annual government biotech R&D spending, across many federal agencies, is over $4 billion. Total federal and private biotech R&D spending exceeds $50 billion a year.

The U.S. Government, through the National Institutes of Health and the Energy Department, is supporting the genetic equivalent of a Mars Mission.

The Human Genome Project will attempt to make a slow climb up and down DNA's spiral staircase and locate every gene, and identify its function. Scientists will search for the precise spot in the cell for specific genetic instructions, like predisposition to heart disease, or eye color, or intelligence. Some 2,000 genes have already been mapped, but there are about 100,000 genes in each cell. To complete the project, which actually involves tracking trillions of parts of genes, it's estimated it will take 15 years and a total of $3 billion. But

Calvin and Hobbes © 1992, Watterson. Reprinted with permission of Universal Press Syndicate. All rights reserved.

the payoff might be huge—the project could ultimately result in treatments for many debilitating and killer diseases.

With projects like this, the U.S. is certainly the world leader in biotech. But it will face increasing international competition, especially from Japan.

In 1981, Japan proclaimed biotechnology a key technology for future industries, and set as a goal worldwide primacy in biotech by the year 2000.

Japan's Ministry of International Trade and Industry has targeted biotech under its Research and Development Project on Basic Technologies for Future Industries. Those projects, which include new materials and superconductivity, usually last for six to 10 years, and have annual budgets of $2 million to $15 million. Several other Japanese government departments, and corporations, are sponsoring and funding biotech programs.

The Japanese appear to be focusing on non-healthcare areas, including food products and waste management, and devoting a lot of research to one intriguing sounding area—*biosensors.*

Biosensors are essentially sophisticated monitoring devices which, like the Six Million Dollar Man, are part biology, part electronics. The biotech layer of the sensor can consist of, for example, enzymes or antibodies which can react or bind with a chemical. That reaction triggers an electronic signal. Biosensors could be used to detect everything from narcotics, to toxic chemicals in the water supply, to cholesterol in the body.

However, Japan, unlike the U.S., does not have a solid research base, and is trying to gain access to biotech training in other countries.

Many European nations have strong biotech programs in place, or are developing them. Also, several programs under the European Community (EC) framework are being supported to encourage cross-border biotech research. As a base for developing biotech, Europe already has strong, mature pharmaceutical and agricultural industries.

Canada, Pacific Rim countries like Australia, Taiwan, South Korea, Thailand, Malaysia, and Singapore, and more developed Latin American countries are also encouraging and supporting a local biotech industry.

"Governments, on the whole, do not have comparable national policies to promote the semiconductor or electronics industry, foods, autos, etc. Yet, they are putting thrust behind biotechnology because they see it as fundamentally important to their economic growth," said Ernst & Young analysts G. Steven Burrill and Kenneth B. Lee, Jr.[20]

So, to update — biotech has generated a few products, and a lot of promise. But what about profits, and profit potential?

So far, the bottom line has not been good.

According to the latest available figures, about 80 percent of all publicly-held biotech companies are losing money. Since its inception, the industry as a whole has never turned a profit. The biotech industry loses about 3 billion dollars annually. Publicly-held biotech companies as a group lose more than half a billion.

The problem is basically very simple — many, if not most, biotech companies just don't have anything to sell. Yet. Either they're engaged in R&D on a product or a technology, and/or they're waiting for regulatory approval for a product. Most firms currently make their way on cash from reserves, R&D contracts, interest income, or stock issues. As a rule, a biotech company is still several years away from turning a profit and a positive cash flow.

The good news is, as previously mentioned, there are many more biotech products in the pipeline. To repeat, several biopharmaceuticals are waiting for FDA approval, and "Biotech has two to three times the success rate of the drug industry in getting approvals," said R. Brandon Fradd, biotech analyst with Montgomery Securities.[21]

About 150 biotech healthcare products are in various stages of human clinical trials. Hundreds more are in lower stages of development, some of which target cancer, AIDS, migraine headaches, anxiety, schizophrenia, Alzheimer's, and Parkinson's.

But the regulatory process can take as long as 10 years. And according to some estimates, it will cost a total of $5 billion to $15 billion to bring the 100 or so drugs undergoing clinical trials to market.

Obviously, biotech firms will have to continue to raise large sums of cash to stay in business. The average biotech company thinks it will need a total of $32 million in financing over the next 10 years.

The question for the investor is how many biotech companies will survive the next stages? And will they be able to transform themselves from essentially a lab into a business that can fight for market share and turn a profit? By some analysts' estimates, only one in five biotech firms will survive.

Biotech companies, although generally flush with cash, usually have very high burn rates, meaning they have little or no cash flow — they spend more cash than they generate. Some companies spend as much as 70 percent of their revenues on R&D. At current, average burn rates, most biotech companies have just about three years of cash left.

While raising additional capital will probably continue to come primarily through the equity markets, to prevent corporate burn-out in the 1990s many companies will have to give up on total independence.

Expect to see more consolidation and more strategic alliances within the biotech industry. That's standard when companies face high costs and increasing competition for a market or cash. Mergers, joint ventures, licensing, and marketing agreements will help diffuse financial risks.

"Strategic alliances will be the most reliable, and perhaps sensible, source of needed capital ... the only way for some firms to prevent takeover, bankruptcy, or liquidation as they reach the most expensive stages of development."[22]

More than 60 percent of biotech firms are already engaged in some sort of strategic alliance. Increasingly, these alliances are biotech firm-to biotech firm as opposed to a link up with an established pharmaceutical company.

Also expect more buyouts or takeovers. Nearly half of biotech firms expect to acquire another company within the next five years, and about a third think they'll be bought. A buyout can, of course, push up a share price.

For newer, and some more established companies, venture capital will also be a needed cash source. The venture capital community is still very interested in biotech. According to one survey, about half of all venture capital firms would prefer investing in genetic engineering than anything else.

Another survey showed divided opinion among venture capitalists as to whether interest in biotech was increasing or stable, versus decreasing.

The more pessimistic venture capitalists feel the big money that could be made in biotech has already been made — "A sense of realism is coming in, the euphoria is over," says one.[23]

But that's not necessarily a bad thing. If you listen closely, the optimists are essentially saying the same type of thing:

"Biotechnology is a mature industry now. There's proof that the technology works."[24]

Or, "Some (venture capital) firms are uneasy about the long time frames and capital intensity, but you can be selective. *If you are patient, returns can be good, even superb.*"[25]

And, "... *it's still exciting because there's a steady flow of new technologies as well as diseases than can be treated by pharmaceuticals.* And the big drug companies are increasingly willing to buy promising technologies."[26]

It sounds as through venture capitalists feel the drug sector of biotech has entered a new phase — it's becoming a mature, emerging industry. And that's a conclusion the companies themselves seem to have reached. Simply, biotech firms are realizing they'll have to find their business legs now that products are hitting, or are ready to hit the market. Their priorities are changing, and they're taking appropriate steps.

In the last five years, R&D spending as a percentage of total biotech expenditures has shrunk (dropping from 53 percent to 30 percent). At the same time, biotech firms are spending more to build sales and marketing infrastructures. "They have focused goals and many biotech companies are hiring experienced execs from other industries," according to Fradd, of Montgomery Securities.[27]

"The overriding message delivered by (Biotech) chief executive officers in their shareholder letters is that companies are shifting their focus from a pure science, R&D approach, to financial performance and the business reality of profit-making," says Ernst & Young's Burrill and Lee.[28]

The combination of more products in the pipeline, with more attention to the bottom line, should be good news for potential investors. But not for speculators.

The days of the fast buck, the rapid 100 percent, 200 percent, and even greater gains in stock prices may be over. But a period of steady sales and profits may be taking hold. Once biotech companies start generating sales, profits should follow — especially since management is becoming more hard-nosed about the bottom line. The conventional wisdom on Wall Street is that share prices should follow profits.

Amgen and Genentech have shown it's not far-fetched. Those two have already turned annual profits of millions of dollars. In 1991, Amgen became a member of the Standard and Poor's 500 index — that essentially means it's a large and influential company on Wall Street, joining others like AT&T.

Analysts predict growing sales of such top companies should lead the overall industry into a period of rapidly rising sales, resulting in many more profitable companies.

According to the Commerce Department, the biotech industry is primed for future growth, essentially because aging baby boomers will not go gently into the great goodnight. Demographers predict that in another 30 years, the number of Americans over the age of 50 will nearly double to more than 120 million. There will be an increasing demand for advanced drugs and medical services from aging populations in many industrialized countries. Additionally, that same group, and their children, are also more conscious of the health of the planet. Consequently, they'll demand more environmentally-safe industrial and agricultural products and processes.

"The future of biotechnology suggests a successful blend of science and business . . . . (that) support the development of healthy companies, more commercially available products, and solid returns on investment. The result will be a strong and growing industry, positively impacting our quality of life and environment for a better tomorrow. The biotech industry is ... moving from promise to reality," said Burrill and Lee.[29]

All of which is not to say that investing in biotech will be a cake walk. In addition to the usual investor question marks applicable to any industry or company, there are regulatory, legal, ethical, and social concerns to be wary of—but they should not make you overly cautious.

Biotech is perhaps already the most heavily regulated of industries. But in 1991, the President's Council on Competitiveness urged streamlined regulatory procedures. Also, an advisory committee to the FDA has recommended faster approval of drugs. (However, as of this writing, it was reported that the Clinton Administration wanted to slow down the pace of easing rules for genetically engineered plants and foods.)

But it's always possible a drug a company is pinning its future on may not be approved—and that could be devastating for a company's stock. To give you an example, in 1987 an FDA committee recommended the agency not approve a Genentech drug. Like a shot, Genentech's stock lost 25 percent of its value—in two days a 14 point skid. In 1993, Synergen's flagship drug reportedly performed poorly in clinical trials, and that sent the company's stock price down more than $28, or 68 percent in one day.

Also, a promising drug may be tied up in, or lose, a patent fight. Again, the potential razing of a company. And the question of gene-ownership will probably only become more complicated. Because not only can genes be patented, but now property rights are being claimed over pieces of genes. The government's National Institutes of Health has already put in patent applications for more than 2000 gene fragments. How all this will affect the industry is unclear at this point.

And sooner or later, biotech will have to come to grips with the prevailing, and long needed, desire to bring down the cost of health care in the United States. For example, Genentech's "Activase," which dissolves blood clots and is used to treat heart attack victims, can cost more than $2,000 for just one dose.

Then there is the public perception of biotech—in some people, the "Andromeda Strain" fear is triggered when they hear the words genetic engineering. However, it seems biotech may have actually become more generally accepted

"Thank God, that must be the clone ranger!"

Reprinted courtesy OMNI magazine, © 1984

over the years as its potential to ease human suffering and cleanse the environment is recognized. According to some surveys, a clear majority of consumers have a favorable opinion of biotech. But those are just surveys. And there are vocal consumer and environmental groups that think federal biotech regulations are too lax, and intend to fight for tougher restrictions. And all it would take, God forbid, is one biotech-equivalent of Bhopal or Three Mile Island to turn the industry topsy-turvey.

That is unlikely. There has never been one, not one, modern biotech accident. Labs take multiple safeguards. And genetically engineered bacteria are actually a step back from the millennia-old survival-of-the-fittest evolutionary process. Gene-spliced bacteria may have some unique lab-created properties, but they're not as tough as their natural relatives.

Finally, there are the broader moral and ethical implications that every investor will have to confront. To think that much of what we are is merely a code on a chemical strand that a cut-and-paste job could change is disconcerting at best. The potential of genetic screening for jobs or insurance is disturbing. The possibility of ordering children to specifications can titillate or outrage. You've heard the other words that provoke—playing God, man to Superman, eugenics, cloning. Will you want to put your money in an industry that, rightly or wrongly, is the basis for generating such thoughts and possibilities? It's a tough decision anyone interested in investing in biotech will have to make. Regardless, the fact is the technology will progress.

According to Arthur Levinson, Genentech's V-P of Research, "We've only seen the tip of the iceberg in terms of biotechnology's potential. I expect there to be major breakthroughs in the next 10 to 20 years that relate to aging, cancer, inflammation, drug delivery, gene therapy, nervous disorders, memory—breakthroughs that at this point we can't fully comprehend. The potential for biotechnology is tremendous and I don't see this changing in any of our lifetimes."[30]

SOURCES

If you want to keep up on the latest scientific and business developments and breakthroughs in biotech, you can try one of the following publications or associations:

AgBiotech Stock Letter and *Medical Technology Stock Letter*
P.O. Box 40460
Berkeley, California 94704

Association of Biotechnology Companies
1666 Connecticut Avenue NW
Washington, D.C. 20009
202-234-3330

BioPharm
Aster Publishing Corp.
859 Willamette Street
P.O. Box 10460
Eugene, Oregon 97440-2460
503-343-1200

BIO/TECHNOLOGY
Nature Publishing
65 Bleeker Street
New York, New York 10012
800-524-0328

BioVenture View
300 West 23rd Avenue
San Mateo, California 94403
415-574-7128

Genetic Engineering News
Mary Ann Liebert, Inc. - Publishers
1651 Third Avenue
New York, New York 10130-0060
212-722-3708

Industrial Biotechnology Association
(Reportedly merging with Association of Biotechnology Companies)
1625 K Street NW
Washington, D.C. 20005
202-857-0244

Pharmaceutical Manufacturers Association
1100 15th Street NW
Washington, D.C. 20005
202-835-3400

Sturza's Medical Investment Letter
424 West End Avenue
New York, New York 10024
212-873-7200

If you decide to invest in biotech, you may want to go the mutual fund route because of rapidly changing scientific and corporate developments. Two funds that invest heavily in biotech companies are (call for a prospectus):

Fidelity Biotech Portfolio
82 Devonshire Street
Boston, Massachusetts 02109
617-570-7000   800-544-8888

Oppenheimer Global Bio-Tech Fund
2 World Trade Center
New York, New York 10048
212-323-0200   800-525-7048

If you decide to go it alone, please call for an annual and/or 10-K report from the companies you're interested in. Things to look for: number of products on the market, number of products in the pipeline, possible competition, management experience in the science, and in running a business.

Some of the more established publicly-held companies on the following list, with products already on the market or about a year away are: Amgen, Biogen, Centocor, Chiron, Genentech, Genetics Institute, Genzyme, Immunex, Medimmune, and Xoma.

Some of the companies with products in clinical trials which could be about two to three years away from the market are: Advanced Tissue Sciences, Alteon, Applied Immune Sciences, Cytogen, Gensia Pharmaceuticals, IDEC Pharmaceuticals, Interneuron, ImmunoGen, Immune Response Corp, Scios Nova, and Synergen.

The ag-bio companies include: Agridyne, Biosys, Biotechnica, Calgene, Celgene, Crop Genetics, DNA Plant Technology, DeKalb Gene, DNX Corp, Ecogen, EcoScience, Embrex, Environmental Diagnostic, Escagenetics, InnoVet, Mycogen, Synbiotics, Syntro, and TSI Corp.

The following list does not include large non-biotech publicly-held companies, including drug or chemical companies, that also have units engaged in biotech R&D.

Because of the large number of listed biotech companies, I've included only some basic information on them. Any information, financial or otherwise, if not specified, applies to the early 1990s. Again, if you want more, call for an annual report. Any list of publicly-held biotech companies is, of course, subject to quick change because of new entries via IPOs, and exits due to mergers, buyouts, and just the inability to stay in business for whatever reason. If I've missed any biotech firms to begin with, I apologize.

Unless otherwise indicated, companies trade on NASDAQ.

Companies marked by an asterisk either have a biotech (in the modern sense of the word) product on the market, or are close to bringing one to market.

Advanced Biotherapy Concepts, Inc. (ADVB)
802 Rollins Ave.
Rockville, Maryland 20852
301-468-3269 Fax: 301-770-4833

Established 1985
5 employees
No sales yet
R&D on treatments for autoimmune diseases and AIDS.

Advanced Tissue Sciences, Inc. (ATIS)
10933 North Torrey Pines Road
La Jolla, California 92037
619-450-5730

Established 1978
50+ employees
Annual sales - $1 million+
R&D on technologies relating to the replication in culture of bone marrow cells, skin cells, and cells of other organs.

Agridyne Technologies, Inc. (AGRI)
417 Wakara Way
Salt Lake City, Utah 84108
801-583-3500

Established 1986
50+ employees
Annual sales - $3 million
R&D on environmentally-compatible insecticides and plant growth and enhancement products made from naturally occurring plant compounds.

Alliance Pharmaceutical Corp. (ALLP)
Road #1
PO Box 567
Otisville, New York, 10963
914-386-2891 Fax: 914-389-4941

Established 1983
80 employees
Annual sales - $1 million
R&D of medical and pharmaceutical products, including imaging agents to detect diseases and oxygen carriers that can be used as a temporary blood substitute. Also engaged in research of animal growth factors.

Alkermes (ALKS)
64 Sidney Street
Cambridge, Massachusetts 02139
617-494-0171

Established 1987
30+ employees
Annual sales - $200,000+
R&D of therapies and diagnostics for diseases of the central nervous system.

Alpha 1 Biomedicals, Inc. (ALBM)
Two Democracy Center
6903 Rockledge Drive
Bethesda, Maryland 20817
301-564-4400 Fax: 301-564-4424

Established 1982
15 employees
Annual sales - $30,000
Viral Technologies, Inc. subsidiary is a researcher and developer of an AIDS vaccine.

Alteon, Inc. (ALTN)
165 Ludlow Avenue
Northvale, New Jersey 07647
201-784-1010

Established 1986
30+ employees
Annual sales - $5 million

R&D on novel therapies and diagnostics for complications of diabetes and aging, focusing on ways to inhibit and/or reverse cell damage caused by glucose in the circulatory system.

Amgen, Inc. (AMGN)
1840 Dehavilland Drive
Thousand Oaks, California 91320
805-499-5725 Fax: 805-498-1242

Established 1980
1,000+ employees
Annual sales - $381 million

Produces and develops wide range of genetically engineered health care products.

Amylin Pharmaceuticals, Inc. (AMLN)
9373 Towne Centre Drive
San Diego, California 92121
619-552-2200

Established 1987
70+ employees
Annual sales - $100,000+

R&D on products to treat and diagnose diabetes and metabolic disorders, centering on amylin, which is a newly-discovered hormone that may regulate glucose metabolism.

Aphton Corp. (APHT)
26 Harter Avenue
Woodland, California 95776
916-666-2195

Established 1981
About 20 employees
Annual sales - $250,000+

Develops products to harness the immune system and induce antibodies to fight cancer, AIDS, and gastrointestinal diseases.

Applied Biosystems, Inc. (ABIO)
850 Lincoln Centre Drive
Foster City, California 94404
415-570-6667 Fax: 415-572-2743

Established 1981
1,000+ employees

Annual sales - $158 million

Makes systems used to purify, analyze, and synthesize biological molecules like DNA, RNA, and proteins.

Applied Immune Sciences, Inc. (ANSX)
200 Constitution Drive
Menlo Park, California 94025
415-326-7302

Established 1983
80+ employees
Annual sales - $500,000+

Developing therapies by manipulating cells and proteins of the immune system outside the body. Products are designed to improve effectiveness of bone marrow transplantation, and are used to fight cancer and AIDS. Also researching gene therapy and autoimmune diseases.

Athena NeuroScience, Inc. (ATHN)
800F Gateway Boulevard
South San Francisco, California 94080
415-877-0900

Established 1986
80 employees
Annual sales - About $5 million

R&D on pharmaceuticals to fight Alzheimer's, epilepsy, and multiple sclerosis.

Automedix Sciences, Inc. (AMED)
1815 Carnegie Avenue
Santa Ana, California 92705
714-263-8655

Established 1978
Fewer than 10 employees
No sales

R&D on a device that contains an enzyme which can remove from the blood of cancer patients an amino acid essential to the survival of cells. The cancer cells are unable to remain active without nutrient amino acid.

**Biogen, Inc. (BGEN)*
14 Cambridge Center
Cambridge, Massachusetts 02142
617-864-8900 Fax: 617-491-1228

Established 1978
300+ employees
Annual sales - $69 million
Develops gene spliced human pharmaceuticals.

Bioelectronics Corp.
13324 Farmington Road
Livonia, Michigan 48150
313-422-2211

Established 1982
10 employees
Annual sales - $1 million
Makes patented electronic equipment used by the biotech industry to alter cells.

Biomerica, Inc. (BMRA)
1533 Monrovia Avenue
Newport Beach, California 92663
714-645-2111

Established 1971
About 20 employees
Annual sales - $10 million+
Develops and markets diagnostic kits and other products for the health care industry.

Biosys (BIOS)
1057 East Meadow Circle
Palo Alto, California 94303

Established 1987
50 employees
Annual sales - $1 million+
R&D of bioinsecticides.

*BioTechnica International, Inc. (BIOT)
7300 West 110th Street
Overland Park, Kansas 66210
913-661-0611 Fax: 913-661-9273

Established 1987
200 employees
Annual sales - $17 million
Specializes in the genetic engineering of corn and soybean seeds.

Bio-Technology General Corp. (BTGC)
1250 Broadway
New York, New York 10001
212-239-0450 Fax: 212-239-0502

Established 1980

100+ employees

Produces cosmetics, pharmaceuticals, and animal health care products.

BioWhittaker, Inc. (NYSE - BWI)
8830 Biggs Ford Road
Walkersville, Maryland 21793
301-898-7025 Fax: 301-845-8338

Established 1991 to succeed 1947 corp.

400+ employees

Annual sales - $40 million+

Produces living cell cultures used for biotech research, human diagnostics, and biogenetic engineering. Provides viral research services.

Burst Agritech, Inc. (BRZT)
222 West Gregory Boulevard
Kansas City, Missouri 64114
816-444-2177

Established 1981

About 10 employees

Annual sales - $500,000

Produces agricultural chemicals, including some that can enhance a plant's growth and fruit bearing potential.

*Calgene, Inc. (CGNE)
1920 Fifth Street
Davis, California 95616
916-753-6313

Established 1980

200+ employees

Annual sales - $27 million

Involved in agricultural research, including genetic engineering of crops. Created the "Flavr Savr" tomato, which has a longer shelf-life (as of this writing waiting for FDA approval).

Caltag Laboratories, Inc. (CTAG)
436 Rozzi Pl.
South San Francisco, California 94080
415-873-6106 Fax: 415-873-2113

Established 1985

10+ employees

Annual sales - $1 million

Produces monoclonal antibodies. (Monoclonal antibodies only attack a specific disease-causing agent. They are produced from a single hybrid cell — a combination of disease fighting white blood cells with tumor cells that divide. The result is a cell that can produce large amounts of identical antibodies.)

*Cambridge Biotech Corp. (CBCX)
365 Plantation Street
Worcester, Massachusetts 01605
508-797-5777 Fax: 508-791-0224

Established 1981

About 300 employees

Annual sales - $20+ million

Primarily makes products for preventing, treating, and detecting human and animal infectious diseases.

Cambridge NeuroScience, Inc. (CNSI)
One Kendall Square
Cambridge, Massachusetts 02139
617-225-0600

Established 1985

About 50 employees

Annual sales - $1 million

R&D of products to treat neurological and psychiatric disorders, including strokes and schizophrenia.

Celgene Corp. (CELG)
7 Powder Horn Drive
Warren, New Jersey 07059
908-271-1001

Established 1986

About 50 employees

Annual sales - about $2 million

Involved in biocatalysis. Manipulates microorganisms or enzymes to facilitate chemical reactions that are otherwise hard or impossible, and are used to produce pharmaceuticals, agricultural chemicals, and systems to detoxify industrial waste.

CEL-SCI Corp. (CELI)
601 Wythe Street
Alexandria, Virginia 22314
703-549-5293 Fax: 703-549-6269

Established 1983
Less than 10 employees
No sales yet.
Engaged in R&D, including an AIDS vaccine, and immune boosting hormones for cancer.

Celtrix Pharmaceuticals, Inc. (CTRX)
3055 Patrick Henry Drive
Santa Clara, California 95052
408-988-2500 Fax: 408-450-4700

Established 1984
70 employees
Annual sales - $300,000+
R&D in various therapeutic products.

Centocor, Inc. (CNTO)
200 Great Valley Parkway
Malvern, Pennsylvania 19355
215-651-6000 Fax: 215-651-6100

Established 1979
1,000+ employees
Annual sales - $40 million+
Primarily engaged in the manufacture of monoclonal antibody diagnostics and therapeutics.

Cephalon, Inc. (CEPH)
145 Brandywine Parkway
West Chester, Pennsylvania 19380
215-344-0200

Established 1987
50+ employees
Annual sales - $5 million

R&D of therapies for neuro-degenerative diseases, like ALS (Lou Gehrig's disease) and Alzheimer's, utilizing small molecules that can cross the blood-brain barrier.

Chiron Corp. (CHIR)
4560 Horton Street
Emeryville, California 94608
510-655-8730 Fax: 510-655-9910
>   Established 1981
>   1,000+ employees
>   Annual sales - $100 million+

Produces and develops various biotech therapies, vaccines, and diagnostics.

Cistron Biotechnology, Inc. (CIST)
10 Bloomfield Avenue
PO Box 2004
Pine Brook, New Jersey 07058
201-575-1700 Fax: 201-575-4854
>   Established 1983
>   About 10 employees
>   Annual sales - $1 million
>   Produces recombinant DNA protein and monoclonal antibodies.

Clinical Technologies Assoc. Inc., (CTAI)
5 Westchester Plaza
Elmsford, New York 10523
914-347-2220
>   Established 1986
>   25+ employees
>   Annual sales - $1 million+

Develops biopharmaceuticals and oral drug delivery systems using microspheres.

Collaborative Research, Inc. (CRIC)
2 Oak Park
Bedford, Massachusetts 01730
617-275-0004 Fax: 617-275-0043
>   Established 1961
>   100 employees

Annual sales - $100 million
Makes biotech drugs and researches biochemicals.

Collagen Corp. (CGEN)
1850 Embarcadero Road
Palo Alto, California 94303
415-856-0200 Fax: 415-856-1430

Established 1975
300+ employees
Annual sales - $60 million+
Makes collagen products used to repair and replace damaged human tissues.

COR Therapeutics (CORR)
256 East Grand Avenue
South San Francisco, California 94080
415-244-6800

Established 1988
50 employees
Annual sales - $2 million
R&D of new biopharmaceuticals for the treatment and prevention of cardiovascular diseases, including anticlotting drugs.

Corvas International, Inc (CVAS)
3030 Science Park Road
San Diego, California 92121
619-455-9800

Established 1987
50+ employees
Annual sales - $300,000+
R&D of biopharmaceutical therapies for cardiovascular diseases like thrombosis.

Crop Genetics International Corp (CROP)
7170 Standard Drive
Hanover, Maryland 21076
301-796-4633

Established 1987
90 employees
Annual sales - Almost $2 million

Develops crop protection systems designed to provide pest control superior to chemical pesticides. Develops plant vaccine systems with genetically engineered microorganisms which produce biotoxins that protect the plant.

Curative Technology, Inc. (CURE)
14 Research Way
East Setauket, New York 11733
516-689-7000

Established 1984
100+ employees
Annual sales - $9 million
R&D of therapies and wound healing using naturally occurring human growth factors.

Cyanotech Corporation (CYANC)
PO Box 4384
Kailua Kona, Hawaii 96745
808-326-1353

Established 1983
40+ employees
Annual sales - $1.5 million+
Produces microorganisms and proteins derived from algae.

Cytel Corp (CLTY)
3525 John Hopkins Ct.
San Diego, California 92121
619-552-3000 Fax: 619-552-8801

Established 1987
100+ employees
Annual sales - $7 million
Actively pursuing R&D in biotech, and is developing a treatment for Hepatitis B.

CYTOGEN Corp. (CYTO)
600 College Road East
Princeton, New Jersey 08540
609-987-8200 Fax: 609-452-2975

Established 1980
100+ employees
Annual sales - $10 million

Performs R&D in biochemical systems and monoclonal antibodies for detecting and treating cancers, cardiovascular, and other diseases.

DeKalb Genetics Corp. (SEEDB)
3100 Sycamore Road
DeKalb, Illinois 60115
815-758-3461

Established 1912
2,000+ employees
Annual sales - $275 million

Develops and improves products for three agricultural segments — seeds, hybrid swine breeding stock, and egg-laying poultry breeding stock.

Diagnon, Inc.
9600 Medical Center Drive
Rockville, Maryland 20850
301-251-2801

Established 1981
About 100 employees
Annual sales - $5 million

Biotech research under various federal government contracts.

Disease Detection International, Inc. (DDII)
2 Thomas
Irvine, California 92718
714-457-1787 Fax: 714-457-1790

Established 1985
20 employees
Annual sales - $500,000

Makes diagnostic kits to detect the presence of parasitic diseases in humans and livestock.

DNA Plant Technology Corp (DNAP)
2611 Branch Pike
Cinnaminson, New Jersey 08077
609-829-0110 Fax: 609-829-5087

Established 1981
100+ employees
Annual sales - $10 million

Develops ag-bio products including vegetables, crops, and tropical plants, and products for the detection and/or control of plant diseases, environmental contaminants, and pests.

DNX, Inc. (DNXX)
303B College Road East
Princeton, New Jersey 08540
609-520-0300 Fax: 609-520-9864

Established 1984
100+ employees
Annual sales - $1 million+

Conducts research on growth hormone for livestock, and provides transgenic mice for pharmaceutical research.

Ecogen, Inc. (EECN)
2005 Cabot Boulevard West
Langhorne, Pennsylvania 19047
215-757-1590

Established 1983
90 employees
Annual sales - $6 million+
R&D of biopesticides.

Ecoscience Corp. (ECSC)
3 Biotech Park
One Innovation Drive
Worcester, Massachusetts 01605
508-754-0300

Established 1988
30+ employees
Annual sales - $200,000+
R&D of biopesticides.

Embrex, Inc. (EMBX)
1035 Swabia Court
Morrisville, North Carolina 27560
919-941-5185

Established 1985
35 employees
Annual sales - About $50,000

Develops bioengineering based products to increase the productivity of the poultry industry. Manufactures an injection system to inoculate eggs.

Emisphere Technology (EMIS)
5 Westchester Plaza
Elmsford, New York 10523
914-347-2220

Established 1986
25+ employees
Annual sales - $1 million+

Develops biopharmaceuticals and oral drug delivery systems using microspheres that don't break down from stomach acid or enzymes. They can replace injected drugs that are poorly absorbed from the gastrointestinal system.

Enzo Biochem, Inc. (ENZO)
40 Oak Drive
Syosset, New York 11791
516-496-8080

Established 1976
30 employees
Annual sales - $5 million

Makes DNA probes to detect tumors, and DNA test kits to probe for viruses and bacteria.

Enzon, Inc. (ENZN)
40 Cragswood Road
South Plainfield, New Jersey 07080
908-668-1800 Fax: 908-668-1811

Established 1981
100+ employees
Annual sales - $2 million

Develops enzymes and proteins used for the treatment of various physical conditions, and produces enzymes used in the chemical and pharmaceutical industries.

Epitope, Inc. (EPTO)
8505 Southwest Creekside Pl.
Beaverton, Oregon 97005
503-641-6115 Fax: 503-643-2781

Established 1979
100+ employees

Annual sales - $3 million

Produces human diagnostic monoclonal antibodies, and tests for the AIDS virus. Its subsidiary Agritope, Inc. performs genetic R&D on plants.

ESCAgenetics Corp (ASE - ESN)
830 Branston Road
San Carlos, California 94070
415-595-5335 Fax: 415-595-4332

Established 1978

50+ employees

Annual sales - $2 million+

Develops plant-derived products used by food processors to enhance flavor or appearance of foods. Also does biotech R&D for food processors.

Exovir, Inc.
111 Great Neck Road
Great Neck, New York 11021
516-466-2110

Established 1987

Fewer than 10 employees

Annual sales - $250,000+

R&D of biological and synthetic materials for use in the treatment of human diseases, including a topical preparation of interferon for herpes simplex.

GENElabs Technologies, Inc. (GNLB)
505 Penobscot Drive
Redwood City, California 94063
415-369-9500 Fax: 415-368-0709

Established 1984

100+ employees

Annual sales - $11 million

R&D on various biopharmaceutical products, including monoclonal antibodies.

*Genentech, Inc. (NYSE - GNE)
460 Point San Bruno Boulevard
South San Francisco, California 94080
415-266-1000 Fax: 415-588-3255

Established 1976

2,000+ employees

Annual sales - $500 million+

Produces and develops various human healthcare products through gene splicing.

Genetic Engineering, Inc. (GEEN)
136th Avenue and North Washington Street
PO Box 33554
Denver, Colorado 80233
303-457-1311

Fewer than 10 employees
No sales.

Genetic R&D on poultry and swine semen and pesticides. Products will be used for animal health care and genetic improvements.

*Genetics Institute, Inc. (GENI)
87 Cambridge Park Drive
Cambridge, Massachusetts 02140
617-876-1170 Fax: 617-876-1504

Established 1981
600 employees
Annual sales - $40 million

Produces and develops various genetically-engineered human health care products.

Genetic Therapy, Inc. (GTII)
19 Firstfield Road
Gaithersburg, Maryland 20878
301-590-2626

Established 1986
About 50 employees
Annual sales - $150,000+
R&D of delivery systems for human gene therapy.

Gensia Pharmaceuticals, Inc. (GNSA)
11025 Rosells Street
San Diego, California 92121
619-546-8300

Established 1986
250+ employees
Annual sales - $8 million+

R&D of novel pharmaceutical products to treat and diagnose cardiovascular diseases.

Genta Corp (GNTA)
3550 General Atomics Court
San Diego, California 92121
619-455-2700 Fax: 619-455-2712
>Established 1989
>About 50 employees
>Annual sales - $2 million

R&D of pharmaceutical products to treat cancer and viral diseases. The company focuses on oligonucleotides, which block or regulate the production of disease-related proteins by controlling certain actions of RNA or DNA.

Genzyme Corp. (GENZ)
1 Kendall Square
Cambridge, Massachusetts 02139
617-252-7500
>Established 1981
>600+ employees
>Annual sales - $50 million+

Produces enzymes for treatment and diagnostic kits, and makes synthetic fatty acids.

Gilead Sciences, Inc. (GILD)
346 Lakeside Drive
Foster City, California 94404
415-574-3000
>Established 1987
>50+ employees
>Annual sales - $1 million+

R&D of new pharmaceuticals based on nucleotides, which are molecules that can be chemically modified to inhibit the production or activity of disease-causing proteins. Company is targeting AIDS.

Glycomed, Inc. (GLYC)
860 Atlantic Avenue
Alameda, California 94501
510-523-5555
>Established 1987
>50+ employees

Annual sales - $3 million+

Develops pharmaceuticals based on the biological activities of complex carbohydrate molecules to yield treatments for cardiovascular, inflammatory diseases, and tissue repair.

Hycor Biomedical, Inc. (HYBD)
7272 Chapman Avenue
Garden Grove, California 92641
714-895-9554

Established 1981
250 employees
Annual sales - $17 million

Through its Ventrex Division makes medical test kits, monoclonal and polyclonal antibodies, purified proteins, and viral antigens.

ICOS Corp. (ICOS)
22021 20th Avenue S.E.
Bothell, Washington 98021
206-485-1900

Established 1989
About 100 employees
Annual sales (grant revenues) - $800,000+

Biopharmaceuticals company engaged in the R&D of medications for chronic inflammatory diseases like arthritis, as well as multiple sclerosis and asthma.

IDEC Pharmaceutical Corp. (IDPH)
11099 North Torrey Pines Road
La Jolla, California 92037
619-458-0600 Fax: 619-546-9274

Established 1985
100 employees
Annual sales - $6 million
R&D in monoclonal antibodies for human health care.

IDEXX Laboratories Corp. (IDXX)
100 Fore Street
Portland, Maine 04101
207-774-4334 Fax: 207-774-0726

Established 1983
200 employees

Annual sales - $17 million

Makes biodetection products to monitor the health of animal and poultry flocks, and detect animal diseases. Also involved in monoclonal antibodies and DNA probes for human healthcare and other uses.

Igene Biotechnology, Inc. (IGNE)
9110 Red Branch Road
Columbia, Maryland 21045
410-997-2599 Fax: 410-730-0540

Established 1982
Fewer than 10 employees
Annual sales - About $1 million

Produces yeast cell culture technologies, enzymes, and makes natural pigments and pesticides used by the food industry.

Imclone Systems, Inc. (IMCL)
180 Varick Street
New York, New York 10014
212-645-1405

Established 1984
50+ employees
Annual sales - $5 million

R&D on therapies for treating cancers, inflammatory diseases, and disorders of the blood-making system.

Imreg, Inc. (IMRGA)
144 Elk Place
New Orleans, Louisiana 70112
504-523-2875 Fax: 504-523-6201

Established 1981
30 employees
No sales

R&D on biological substances shown to affect the human immune system. Products under development include an AIDS treatment. Company also develops diagnostic tests for immune functions and cancer.

ImmunCell Corp. (ICCC)
966 Riverside Street
Portland, Maine 04103
207-878-2770 Fax: 207-878-2117

Established 1982

20+ employees
Annual sales - $3 million
Produces various antibody-based therapies for human and animal health-
care.

ImmuLogic Pharmaceutical Corp. (IMUL)
1 Kendall Square
Cambridge, Massachusetts 02139
617-494-0060 Fax: 617-577-8686

Established 1987
100+ employees
Development stage
R&D in immunology and genetic engineering to develop various therapies for human healthcare.

The Immune Response Corp. (IMNR)
5935 Darwin Ct.
Carlsbad, California 92008
619-431-7080 Fax: 619-431-8636

Established 1986
About 50 employees
Annual sales - $4 million
R&D in therapies for AIDS and various other diseases.

Immunex Corp. (IMNX)
51 University Street
Seattle, Washington 98101
206-587-0430 Fax: 206-587-0606

Established 1981
500+ employees
Annual sales - $34 million
Produces and researches anti-cancer therapies and treatments for immune
system disorders.

ImmunoGen, Inc. (IMGN)
60 Hamilton Street
Cambridge, Massachusetts 02139
617-661-9312 Fax: 617-661-9334

Established 1981
100+ employees
No sales

R&D in antibody-based treatments for cancer.

Immunomedics, Inc. (IMMU)
150 Mount Bethel Road
Warren, New Jersey 07060
908-647-5400 Fax: 908-647-5888

Established 1982

50+ employees

Annual sales - $4 million

Develops products to detect, diagnose, and treat cancer and other diseases.

InnoVet, Inc.
141 NW 20th Street
Boca Raton, Florida 33431
407-394-0621

Established 1986

Fewer than 10 employees

Annual sales - $500,000+

R&D on animal healthcare products and consumer products, including pet stain and odor remover.

Interneuron Pharmaceuticals, Inc. (IPIC)
One Ledgemont Center
99 Hayden Avenue
Lexington, Massachusetts 02173
617-861-8444

Established 1990

About 20 employees

Annual sales - $100,000

R&D on pharmaceutical products which mimic or stimulate neurotransmitters and neurohormones, leading to therapies for sleep disturbances, appetite, memory, and mood.

ISIS Pharmaceuticals, Inc. (ISIP)
Carlsbad Research Center
2280 Faraday Avenue
Carlsbad, California 92008
619-931-9200

Established 1991

About 100 employees

Annual sales - About $2 million

R&D on new drugs using oligonucleotides and antisense molecules that can block messages from DNA which can cause disease.

Lifecore Biomedical, Inc. (LCBM)
3515 Lynan Boulevard
Chaska, Minnesota 55318
612-368-4300 Fax: 612-368-3411

Established 1968
100 employees
Annual sales - $5 million
Produces biochemicals.

Life Sciences, Inc. (LFSCS)
2900 72nd Street North
Saint Petersburg, Florida 33710
813-345-9371 Fax: 813-347-2957

Established 1962
25 employees
Annual sales - $1 million

Produces interferon for cancer treatment. Makes enzymes used in genetic engineering research. Breeds pathogen-free mice for research. Also provides biohazardous waste disposal services.

The Liposome Co., Inc. (LIPO)
One Research Way
Princeton Forrestal Center
Princeton, New Jersey 08540
609-452-7060 Fax: 609-452-1890

Established 1981
50+ employees
Annual sales - $7 million

R&D on liposomes, developing products to treat meningitis and breast cancer.

Liposome Technology, Inc. (LTIZ)
1050 Hamilton Court
Menlo Park, California 94025
415-323-9011 Fax: 415-323-9106

Established 1981
50+ employees

Annual sales - $2 million

Produces liposomes and other lipid-based products to treat life-threatening diseases. Liposomes are microscopic spheres used to encapsulate and transport drugs to specific parts of the body.

Magainin Pharmaceuticals, Inc. (MAGN)
5110 Campus Drive
Plymouth Meeting, Pennsylvania 19462
215-941-4020

Established 1987

20+ employees

Annual sales - $200,000+

Company discovered, and synthesized new peptides (magainin) that can kill diseased cells. Used to treat cancer and infectious diseases and promote wound healing.

Medarex, Inc. (MEDX)
22 Chambers Street
Princeton, New Jersey 08542
609-921-7121 Fax: 609-921-7450

Established 1987

20+ employees

Annual sales - about $400,000

Develops monoclonal antibody treatments for leukemia and AIDS victims.

MedImmune, Inc. (MEDI)
35 West Watkins Mill Road
Gaithersburg, Maryland 20878
301-417-0770 Fax: 301-417-6289

Established 1988

50+ employees

Annual sales - $5 million

Produces various biopharmaceuticals, including vaccines and therapies for infectious diseases and cancer.

Meridian Diagnostic, Inc. (KITS)
3471 River Hills Drive
Cincinnati, Ohio 45244
513-271-3700 Fax: 513-271-0124

Established 1977

100 employees
Annual sales - $8 million
Produces test kits to detect and diagnose various diseases.

Molecular Biosystems, Inc. (MOBI)
10030 Barnes Canyon Road
San Diego, California 92121
619-452-0681 Fax: 619-452-6187

Established 1980
100 employees
Annual sales - $7 million
Develops DNA probes to detect various infectious diseases.

Mycogen Corp. (MYCO)
5451 Oberlin Drive
San Diego, California 92121
619-453-8030

Established 1987
250+ employees
Annual sales - $18 million+
R&D biopesticides and bioherbicides.

Neogen Corp. (NEOG)
620 Lesher Place
Lansing, Michigan 48912
517-372-9200

Established 1981
100+ employees
Annual sales - $5 million
Makes products used to monitor or control agricultural residues, like chemicals or natural toxins, that can affect the food or environment.

NeoRx Corp. (NERX)
410 West Harrison Street
Seattle, Washington 98119
206-298-9442

Established 1984
50+ employees
No sales
R&D of monoclonal antibody-based products used to detect and treat various types of cancer.

Neozyme Corp. (NEOZ)
One Kendall Square
Cambridge, Massachusetts 02139
617-252-7500

Established 1990

Annual investment income $2 million+

Company formed to accelerate the R&D of Genzyme Corp.

Neurogen Corp. (NRGN)
35 Northeast Industrial Road
Branford, Connecticut 06405
203-488-8201

Established 1987

30+ employees

Annual interest income - $300,000+

R&D of treatments for psychiatric and neurological disorders using various applications including molecular biology, biochemistry, and cell biology.

New Brunswick Scientific Co., Inc. (NBSC)
44 Talmadge Road
Edison, New Jersey 08818
908-287-1200 Fax: 908-287-5566

Established 1973

300+ employees

Annual sales - $29 million

Makes high-tech equipment used by the biotech industry for R&D of various products including drugs, enzymes, and biochemicals.

North American Vaccine, Inc. (AMVX)
12040 Indian Creek Court
Beltsville, Maryland 20705
301-470-6100 Fax: 301-470-6198

Established 1987

30+ employees

Annual sales - $3 million

R&D of various vaccines, including those that prevent childhood infectious diseases.

Oncogene Science, Inc. (ONCS)
350 Community Drive
Manhassat, New York, 11030
516-365-9300 Fax: 516-365-9328

Established 1983
50+ employees
Annual sales - $6 million

Produces monoclonal antibodies, and probes for human genes that may be associated with cancer.

Oncor, Inc. (ONCR)
209 Perry Parkway
Gaithersburg, Maryland 20877
301-963-3500 Fax: 301-926-6129

Established 1983
50+ employees
Annual sales - $2 million

Makes DNA/RNA probes for the detection of cancer, HIV-1, and genetic disorders.

Osteotech, Inc. (OSTE)
1151-E Shrewsbury Avenue
Shrewsbury, New Jersey 07702
908-542-2800 Fax: 908-542-2906

Established 1986
50+ employees
Annual sales - $8 million

Has developed a process to graft genetically different tissues to each other.

Pioneer Hi-Bred International, Inc. (PHYB)
700 Capital Square
400 Locust Street
Des Moines, Iowa 50309
515-245-3500

Established 1926
4,000+ employees
Annual sales - $1 billion+

Produces and breeds various hybrid seeds. Its Microbial Genetics Division produces plant disease control systems and veterinary inoculants.

Protein Design Labs, Inc. (PDLI)
2375 Garcia Avenue
Mountain View, California 94043
415-903-3700

Established 1986
About 50 employees
Annual sales - $4 million+

Involved in the computer-based design of antibodies and other proteins to treat viral, infectious, and autoimmune diseases.

Quest Biotechnology, Inc. (QBIO)
320 Fisher Building
Detroit, Michigan 48202
313-873-0200

Established 1986
About 10 employees
Annual sales - $200,000+

Company formed to acquire, develop, and sell biotech and human health-care products and processes, and to buy companies which own such products and processes.

Regeneron Pharmaceuticals, Inc. (REGN)
777 Old Saw Mill River Road
Tarrytown, New York 10591
914-347-7000

Established 1988
150+ employees
Annual sales - $7 million+

R&D of biotech-based compounds to treat neuro-degenerative diseases and injuries. Develops drugs based on natural human proteins it discovered which are required for nerve cells to grow and sustain themselves.

Repligen Corp. (RGEN)
1 Kendall Square
Cambridge, Massachusetts 02139
617-225-6000 Fax: 617-494-1786

Established 1981
100+ employees
Annual sales - $10 million

Produces recombinant proteins, involved in R&D of various health care products, including an AIDS vaccine, and cancer treatments. Performs other biotech research through its Repligen Sandoz Research Corp. unit.

Ribi ImmunoChem Research, Inc. (RIBI)
PO Box 1409
Hamilton, Montana 59840
406-363-6214 Fax: 406-363-6129

Established 1981
50+ employees
Annual sales - $1 million

Produces immunotherapeutic agents to treat cancer and infectious diseases. Its "Ribigen" product is a veterinary anti-tumor agent.

SciGenics, Inc. (SCGN)
87 Cambridge Park Drive
Cambridge, Massachusetts 02140
617-876-1170

Established 1991
Interest income - $1,000

Performs research on how protein factors influence embryonic cell development to form adult tissues.

*Scios-Nova, Inc. (SCIO)
2450 Bayshore Parkway
Mountain View, California 94043
415-966-1550 Fax: 415-968-2438

Established 1981
100+ employees
Annual sales - $12 million

Develops treatments for diseases and genetic disorders using recombinant DNA technology.

Sepracor, Inc. (SEPR)
33 Locke Drive
Marlborough, Massachusetts 01752
508-481-6700 Fax: 508-481-7683

Established 1984
100+ employees
Annual sales - $7 million

Markets products and processes for the synthesis, separation, and purification of compounds, including biopharmaceuticals.

Somatix Therapy Corporation (SOMA)
850 Marina Village Parkway
Alameda, California 94501
510-748-3000 Fax: 510-769-8533

Established 1979
50+ employees
Annual sales - $6 million
Researches therapeutic proteins and gene therapy to develop treatments for various diseases, including hemophilia and diabetes.

Somatogen, Inc. (SMTG)
5797 Central Avenue
Boulder, Colorado 80301
303-440-9988

Established 1989
75 employees
Annual sales - $1.5 million+
Uses its recombinant technique to develop a human blood substitute.

Sphinx Pharmaceuticals Corp. (SPHX)
Two University Place
Durham, North Carolina 27717
919-489-0909

Established 1990
About 100 employees
Annual sales - $200,000
Researches the role of cell membrane lipids in regulating cellular processes to develop pharmaceutical products for the treatment of diseases involving inflammation.

Synbiotics Corp. (SBIO)
11011 Via Frontera Drive
San Diego, California 92127
619-451-3771

Established 1982
100+ employees
Annual sales - $7 million

Develops biomedical products, including detection kits and monoclonal antibodies, for use in human and animal healthcare.

Synergen, Inc. (SYGN)
1885 33rd Street
Boulder, Colorado 80301
303-938-6200

Established 1982
200+ employees
Annual sales - $14 million
Develops protein-based pharmaceuticals, using recombinant DNA and other techniques, to treat inflammatory diseases, slow or nonhealing wounds, and neurological disorders.

SYNTHETECH, Inc. (NZYM)
1290 Industrial Way
Albany, Oregon 97321
503-967-6575 Fax: 503-967-9424

Established 1980
10+ employees
Annual sales - $2 million
R&D services for bio-organic and organic synthesis. Emphasizes synthesis of peptide building blocks, using a combination of organic chemicals and biocatalysis, which can lead to the cost-effective production of pharmaceuticals, chemicals, and flavors.

Syntro Corp. (SYNT)
9669 Lackman Road
Lenexa, Kansas 66219
913-888-8876

Established 1981
50 employees
Annual sales - $3 million
R&D on animal vaccines, and some human healthcare products. Developed DNA vaccine for swine pseudo-rabies.

Systemix, Inc. (STMX)
3400 West Bayshore Road
Palo Alto, California 94303
415-856-4901

Established 1988

75+ employees

Annual sales - $1.5 million+

Researches cells, processes to develop products to treat diseases of the bone marrow, blood, and immune system.

TAGO, Inc. (TAGO)
887 Mitten Road
Burlingame, California 94010
415-692-4015 Fax: 415-692-9004

Established 1979

Fewer than 50 employees

Annual sales - $2 million

Produces monoclonal and polyclonal antibodies for diagnosis of human diseases.

T Cell Sciences, Inc. (TCEL)
38 Sidney Street
Cambridge, Massachusetts 02139
617-621-1400 Fax: 617-864-0854

Established 1983

50 employees

Annual sales - $10 million

Produces monoclonal antibodies for diagnosis and therapies, DNA probes, proteins vital to proper immune function, human diagnostic recombinant DNA, diagnostic kits to test for various diseases, including AIDS and cancer, and agents used to suppress the immune system in organ transplants.

Techniclone International Corp. (TCLN)
14282 Franklin Avenue
Tustin, California 92680
714-838-0500 Fax: 714-838-9433

Established 1981

25+ employees

Annual sales - Less than $500,000

Produces monoclonal antibodies for diagnosis and treatment. R&D on biological agents to detect AIDS and cancer.

Telios Pharm Inc. (TLIC)
4757 Nexus Centre Drive
San Diego, California 92121
619-622-2600

Established 1987
100+ employees
Annual sales - $6.5 million+

Research on the cellular area to develop products for the treatment of severe and chronic dermal wounds, ophthalmic wounds, and cardiovascular diseases.

TSI Corp. (TSIN)
Innovation Drive
Worcester, Massachusetts 01605
508-755-0550

Established 1986
400+ employees
Annual sales - $16 million+

A life sciences concern. Develops new products by genetic engineering to efficiently test new drugs, improve productivity of food animals, and cut the cost of making biopharmaceuticals. Develops more reliable transgenic animals, used as models to predict human clinical reactions.

Unigene Laboratories, Inc. (UGNE)
110 Little Falls Road
Fairfield, New Jersey 07004
201-882-0860 Fax: 201-227-6088

Established 1980
25+ employees

Develops therapies and diagnostic products for human health care using bacterial culture, enzymes, and genetic engineering.

Univax Biologics, Inc. (UNVX)
12280 Wilkins Avenue
Rockville, Maryland 20852
301-770-3099

Established 1988
About 50 employees
Annual sales - $1 million+

R&D of intravenous antibody preparations designed to deliver specific antibodies directly into the bloodstream. Develops proprietary vaccines and immunotherapeutic products for serious infectious diseases.

VimRx Pharmaceuticals, Inc. (VMRX)
1177 High Ridge Road
Stamford, Connecticut 06905
203-321-2115

Established 1986
Fewer than 10 employees
Annual sales - $100,000+

Develops therapies from plant compounds to treat viral diseases, including AIDS.

Vega Biotechnologies, Inc. (VEGA)
1250 East Aero Park Boulevard
Tucson, Arizona 85734
602-746-1401 Fax: 602-889-4139

Established 1979
About 20 employees
Annual sales - $5 million

Makes equipment for the synthesis of strings of amino acids (proteins) called peptides used for research in immunology and the development of biochemicals. Also makes DNA synthesizers.

Vertex Pharmaceuticals, Inc. (VRTX)
40 Allston Street & 625 Putnam Avenue
Cambridge, Massachusetts 02139

Established 1989
50+ employees
Annual sales - $4 million

Involved in rational drug design. Produces small molecule compounds designed at the atomic level which interact with proteins leading to orally administered drugs for antiviral therapies.

Vestar, Inc. (VSTR)
650 Cliffside Drive
San Dimas, California 91773
714-394-4000 Fax: 714-592-8530

Established 1981
50+ employees
Annual sales - $3 million

Makes liposome-based drugs used to diagnose and treat cancer and AIDS.

Viragen, Inc. (VRGN)
2343 West 76th Street
Hialeah, Florida 33016
305-557-6000

Established 1980
Fewer than five employees
Annual sales - $100,000+
R&D on interferon for anti-viral therapeutics and anti-cancer agents.

*Xoma Corp. (XOMA)
2910 7th Street
Berkeley, California 94710
510-644-1170 Fax: 510-644-0539

Established 1981
300+ employees
Annual sales - About $15 million
Develops products to treat infectious diseases and immune system disorders using monoclonal antibody and gene splicing techniques.

CHAPTER 9

MILLENNIUM MISCELLANY

"Have you feared the future would be nothing to you?
Is today nothing? Is the beginningless past nothing?
If the future is nothing they are just as surely nothing... "

—Walt Whitman, "To Think of Time"

"Some men see things as they are and ask, 'Why?'
Others dream things that never were, and ask 'Why not?'"

—Robert F. Kennedy

"The silent hours steal on ... "

—William Shakespeare, "Richard III"

The future contains infinite possibilities. The following topics cannot be as clearly defined as emerging markets—there may be a lack of information, too few companies are involved in them right now, or, at this point, they're more a concept than anything else.

Their potential as an investment may not be as solid as some of the other subjects. But I just felt I couldn't write a book about the 21st century without at least mentioning them. They are presented in no particular order.

HIGH DEFINITION TELEVISION (HDTV)

Let's say you're a sports fan. You click on your HDTV to catch the ballgame. With a vividness that doesn't exist now, you see the beads of sweat and the grimaces of exertion. Like you're right at the stadium, you'll hear the grunts of competition, the crack of the bat, and perhaps even the whining of the modern-era athlete. You'll experience, on a much higher level, the thrill of victory, the agony of defeat.

Wide-screen TV with the rich, bright, crystal clarity of a movie, and sound as crisp as a compact disc's. That's essentially what HDTV is all about. It's really nothing that mind-boggling — just a much better TV picture, but it's a TV for the millennium generation. You may be wondering, what's the point? Considering the current state of TV programming, it might make more sense to try for a less clear picture.

But as Richard Wiley, chairman of the Federal Advisory Committee on HDTV once said, "This is not just about pretty pictures."

HDTV will hasten the inevitable merger of television and computers. Instead of the so-called analog electromagnetic TV signals used now, the HDTV signals will eventually be transmitted in digital pulses, which means they're sent out in the zero-one or on-off code that a computer understands. HDTV signals are easier to transmit through cable than through the air. Consequently, HDTV will probably give a further push to the development of the information superhighway, multi-media, and interactive or two-way TV.

"HDTV developments are driving the state-of-the-art in several information and communication technologies more rapidly than are developments in computers or telecommunications," according to the Office of Technology Assessments.[1] Research in HDTV will spark advances in various fields, including defense. The Pentagon is backing many HDTV projects, to the tune of more than $10 million a year.

HDTV will also mark the comeback of the United States to the TV industry.

In 1993, American groups that had been competing to develop the accepted U.S. standard of HDTV decided to collaborate instead, and will work on one system. That alliance could mean the U.S. will leapfrog Japan and Europe, who have had a head start on HDTV. U.S. HDTV sets could now be available by 1995, and the 1996 Olympics is a definite broadcast target date.

The HDTV sets will be wide-screen (otherwise their high picture quality is somewhat pointless), and are expected to initially cost $1,000 to $2,000 *more* than current large models. (Early Japanese HDTVs sell in Tokyo for about $8,000.) Prices will come down. If you still don't see the need for an HDTV, or can't afford one, don't worry. Broadcasters will be obligated to continue transmitting regular (analog) signals for the old sets well into the 21st century. But in the way black-and-white gave way to color TV, HDTV will eventually supplant today's televisions, which some think will be phased out by 2008.

The market potential for HDTV is big. The Commerce Department estimates global annual sales for the broader area of digital imaging to hit $5

Reprinted courtesy *OMNI* magazine, © 1981

billion by the year 2000.[2] *Other estimates put annual HDTV sales as high as*
$40 billion, and still other predictions say HDTV will be worth hundreds of
billions of dollars in the 21st century for its indirect impact on other electronics
markets.

SOURCES

For more on developments in HDTV:

HDTV Newsletter
Advanced Television Publishing
753 East Fall Creek Road
Alsea, Oregon 97324
503-487-4186

Publicly-held U.S. firms involved in developing HDTV are:

American Telephone and Telegraph Co. (NYSE - T)
212-605-5500

Compression Labs (OTC - CLIX)
408-435-3000

General Electric (NYSE - GE)
203-373-2211

 Developing HDTV through its NBC unit.

General Instrument Corp. (NYSE - GIC)
312-541-5000

Motorola, Inc. (NYSE - MOT)
708-397-5000

 Motorola will make some of the chips needed for HDTV.

Philips NV (NYSE - PHG)

 This Dutch company's U.S. unit, NA Philips, is also developing HDTV with other American companies.

Texas Instruments, Inc. (NYSE - TXN)
214-995-3773

 TI is developing silicon imaging chips that could make HDTV sets smaller and cheaper.

Zenith Electronics Corp. (NYSE - ZE)
708-391-7000

NANOTECHNOLOGY

i

Take a good look at the above i. Now look at the dot over it.

 There are functioning devices already being made that are about the size of the dot of the i. Machines so small you might accidently breathe one in. Pretty unbelievable.

 But for what nanotechnology ultimately envisions, those dot-size devices are, well, small-time.

 Nanotechnology comes from the Greek "nanos" or dwarf. A nanometer is about one billionth of a meter. Nanotechnology is "Honey, I shrunk the machines." Visionaries of nanotechnology hope someday to build micromachines or robots that are as small as molecules. But they wouldn't just putter around in Lilliput.

 Nanomachines would be driven by an internal microcomputer, and their proponents say they could be used for an infinite number of amazing things, like patrolling the body to destroy invading viruses, or performing surgery on cancer, or clearing clogged arteries, or repairing damaged cells which would mean extended lifespans. They could be cut loose in the environment to grapple with pollution. Or they could be given raw material and be programmed to build just about anything atom-by-atom. Eventually, the nanomachines will build more of themselves.

If it sounds like science fiction, it isn't.

The Pentagon's Advanced Research Projects Agency and the National Science Foundation support research in nanotechnology and micromachinery by several U.S. universities.

In mid-1993, scientists at Yale, the University of South Carolina, along with Los Alamos National Laboratory, produced molecules that can assemble themselves into nano-tiny wires. Also that year, IBM accidently found a way to form carbon tubes one billionth of a meter in diameter, with walls an atom thick.

Japan has a 10-year, $200 million R&D effort up and going in nanotechnology.

The future of nanotechnology could evolve from manufacturing techniques used in microcircuits and microsensors. It's called the top-down approach to nanotech.

For example, Analog Devices Inc. (NYSE - ADE, 617-329-4700) makes a mini-sensor (an accelerometer) used in cars to measure speed and impact which are used for safety air bags. Private company IC Sensors (Milpitas, California 408-432-1800) makes a similar device. Privately-held Lucas NovaSensor (Fremont, California 415-490-9100) makes a speck-sized sensor that keeps track of blood pressure inside the heart during operations.

From 1993 to the year 2000, the market for micromachines and microsensors is expected to grow about eight-fold to an $8 million industry.[3]

The other approach to nanotechnology is the bottom-up approach, which basically involves trying to manipulate atoms with sophisticated devices like the so-called scanning tunneling microscope. Using one of those babies, IBM was able to move atoms around to form its corporate logo.

Other major companies involved in some form of nanotechnology and micromachinery R&D include AT&T, DuPont, Ford, Hewlett-Packard, Honeywell, Monsanto, Motorola, Texas Instruments, Upjohn, Westinghouse, and Xerox.

Because nanotechnologists dream of building self-replicating, unobtrusive, computer-controlled machines that could build anything from the atoms on up, we're talking about a potentially revolutionary technology that could change the basis of a society. I want to stress that these types of molecule-sized machines are strictly a vision right now, and some scientists think they may never be possible because of certain effects on matter at the atomic level.

In any case, you can keep up with developments in nanotechnology by contacting:

The Foresight Institute
Box 61058
Palo Alto, California 94306
415-324-2490

SPACE COMMERCE

You already know about space garbage. Now something possibly even more distressing is invading the final frontier.

Space advertisements.

A company called Space Marketing, Inc. in Roswell, Georgia arranged for Arnold Schwarzenegger's name and the title of his 1993 movie, "Last Action Hero," to be painted in blazing red, yellow, and orange on a 60-foot rocket bound for space in the spring of 1993 — just before the movie's summer release.

Columbia Pictures paid half a million dollars for the ad which, really, no one will see (sort of like the movie). The rocket's payload, a science satellite, will also carry the movie's logo. More than two dozen companies were reportedly vying for the ad space.

The companies involved in the launch were Westinghouse Electric (NYSE - WX), Space Industries Inc. of League City, Texas, and EER Systems Corp. of Vienna, Virginia.

Space Marketing is also planning, in 1996, to help launch a mile wide satellite made of thin plastic that could reflect sunlight off aluminized letters down to Earth. The satellite, possibly the first of many, would appear to be larger than the size of the half-moon. The letters would be legible to the naked eye. The company, however, says not to worry, the satellite would only be visible for 10 minutes over any one spot on the Earth, and could not be seen at all at night.

To its credit, the "orbiting billboard," so named by its opponents, will also carry devices to study the Earth's atmosphere, and it would cost the government nothing. The satellite would be bankrolled by commercial sponsors who could use its symbol in their marketing plans.

But it seems the grand visions for space commerce, the construction projects, the shining cities and space ports on the Moon and Mars, the orbiting hotels, the new space-manufactured materials and pharmaceuticals, the asteroid mining, the solar powered satellites that could beam clean energy from space to earth, all the dreams for space, for the time being, have partly given way to the tackiness of the late 20th century.

Due in part to the Challenger disaster, and the lurching, seemingly directionless U.S. space program, space commerce became an iffy issue during the 1980s and 1990s. The U.S. went to the Moon and then forgot about it. But many entrepreneurs still believe that many billionaires of the 21st century will make their fortunes from space.

There are some hopeful signs for their dreams.

- Total U.S. space commerce revenues (including commercial satellites, commercial space launches, satellite services, materials research and processing in space, and satellite remote sensing) rose from about $2.7 billion in 1989 to $4.9 billion in 1993. The demand for launches of satellites for communications and remote sensing (and Global Positioning Systems for vehicle tracking) will probably continue to be strong.[4]

- NASA commercial space officials have said the agency would expand industry-led projects, possibly setting up consortiums with businesses.

- The Clinton Administration's 1994 spending plan included increases in space commercial programs and space research and technology. (Final budget still being debated in Congress at this time.)

- NASA has 17 Centers for the Commercial Development of Space which more than 200 companies have taken advantage of to do commercial space research.

- Florida has established a privately operated spaceport which launched its first payload in 1992. Hawaii also wants to build a commercial spaceport. Alaska has a launch facility that it's pitching to private companies.

- There will be increasing international cooperation in space, especially between Russia and the U.S. Europe, Japan, and China all have developing space commerce programs.

- New rockets, alternatives to the shuttle, are being designed by NASA and the private sector that will be able to get more payloads up in space at a lower cost. For example, McDonnell Douglas is testing the wingless, reusable 'Delta Clipper.' The Clipper's designers hope the ship will be able to lift off every few days, as opposed to the shuttle's four weeks, and will cost $10 million per launch compared to the shuttle's $500 million. One other interesting difference from the shuttle — the Clipper lands (and takes off) vertically, like some of those rocket ships you've seen in science fiction movies.

- A scaled-down version of a permanent U.S. spacelab will probably be orbiting sometime in the '90s. The 1990s.

- On a more esoteric note, at a 1993 shipping conference, the Greek billionaire George Livanos said that in the future, cargo ships will be replaced by rockets.

But perhaps most importantly, space invariably generates a lot of enthusiasm and interest in young people. It is that wave that will certainly carry us to the stars. Businesses and support services will follow, creating the fortunes of the future.

There are many groups that support space exploration, development, and commerce. Among them are:

National Space Society
922 Pennsylvania Avenue, S.E.
Washington, D.C. 20003
202-543-1900

Space Studies Institute
Box 82
Princeton, New Jersey 08542
609-921-0377

United States Space Foundation
2860 South Circle Drive
Colorado Springs, Colorado 80906
719-576-8000

"... Hello, NASA? .... I have a crate for the next moon shuttle ..."

Reprinted courtesy OMNI magazine, © 1989

To keep up on developments in space:

Aviation Week & Space Technology
McGraw-Hill, Inc.
1221 Avenue of the Americas
New York, New York 10020
212-512-2000

Space News
The Times Journal Co.
6883 Commercial Drive
Springfield, Virginia 22159

Among some of the obvious beneficiaries of expanding space commercialization would be many huge publicly-held companies, including: Allied Signal, Boeing, GE, GenCorp, General Dynamics, GM-Hughes (NYSE - GMH), Grumman, Hercules, Lockheed, Loral, LTV, Martin Marietta, McDonnel Douglas, Northrop, Rockwell International, Thiokol, TRW, and United Technologies.

One lesser known publicly-held company that is actively involved in space commerce is:

Orbital Sciences Corp (OTC - ORBI)
21700 Atlantic Boulevard
Dulles, Virginia 20166
703-406-5000

Orbital developed its own rocket which is launched from under the wing of a plane, and delivers space payloads. The company turned a profit in 1991 and 1992 after a few years of losses.

SUPERCOMPUTERS

The Death Stars and dreadnoughts of computers. But just like the comic book Superman had a rough go of it in the 1992–1993 period, so did supercomputers.

As their name implies, supercomputers are faster and more powerful. They can perform incredibly complex operations at incredibly high speeds that other computers just couldn't handle. Supercomputers can perform billions of operations per second. The Pentagon expects that to jump to trillions by 1996, and quadrillions by 2006.

Many scientists and industries increasingly rely on supercomputers. For example, supercomputers can help oil companies decipher seismic data and determine where the next big strike will be. Airplane manufacturers use them to design better jet frames or engines. Supercomputers help pharmaceutical and biotech companies design drugs. They perform economic modeling for Wall Street. They can sift through complex climatological and geological data and help predict weather and earthquakes.

There are essentially two kinds of supercomputers. The type that's been around since the 1970s is called a *vector supercomputer.* The new kid on the block is the *parallel supercomputer or massively parallel processor (MPP).* To oversimplify the difference, a vector model uses a few processors to do a problem one step at a time. An MPP combines hundreds and sometimes thousands of processors and essentially farms out different parts of the problem to them.

MPPs are apparently becoming the supercomputers of choice because they can be faster and cheaper. But they have one major problem — proven software, or programming, for parallel supercomputers is difficult to come by. It's sort of like owning a great sports car without knowing how to drive a stick shift.

Total U.S. supercomputer sales were about $2 billion in 1992, up 5 percent. However, parallel supercomputer revenues rose about 30 percent. But all-in-all, it was the worst year ever for supercomputer sales, which had been gaining more than 25 percent annually for a decade.

Part of the problem was that companies were waiting for the shakeout in the supercomputer industry to see which model — vector or parallel — would become the dominant system. Another problem was the ongoing, worldwide economic slowdown. During uncertain times, businesses are less likely to spend a lot of money. Supercomputers can cost anywhere from $500,000 to $30 million. Another potential hang-up is the scaling back of the military, which is a major customer for supercomputers.

However, many business and government analysts believe supercomputers are critical to America's ability to compete in the 21st century global economy, and they expect sales to pick up again. By some estimates, U.S. supercomputer sales will grow about 15 percent annually from 1993 to 1996.

The Commerce Department reports annual supercomputer sales could hit $50 billion to $100 billion early in the 21st century.[5]

Under the High-Performance Computing and Communications Initiative, the U.S. Government will organize the acquisition, use, and development of supercomputers for the public sector. The government is expected to spend $800 million in 1993 to advance supercomputers. Most of the money will go towards software research.

Progress in supercomputer technology will also be driven by research in materials, photonics, superconductivity, and artificial intelligence. As the Commerce Department sees it, *"In terms of capability, today's supercomputer is tomorrow's desktop workstation and the following day's classroom tool."*[6]

The U.S. publicly-held players in the supercomputer field are:

Convex Computer Corp. (NYSE - CNX)
214-497-4000

Cray Computer (OTC - CRAY)
719-579-6464
Spun-off from Cray Research.

Cray Research, Inc. (NYSE - CYR)
612-683-7100

Hewlett-Packard Co. (NYSE - HWP)
415-857-1501

IBM (NYSE - IBM)
914-765-1900

Intel Corp. (OTC - INTC)
408-765-8080

Kendall Square Research (OTC - KSRC)
617-895-9400

Silicon Graphics, Inc. (NYSE - SGI)
415-960-1980

Sun Microsystems, Inc. (OTC - SUNW)
415-960-1300

SOLAR ENERGY OR PHOTOVOLTAICS

Solar energy doesn't pollute, doesn't contribute to global warming, and for all practical purposes comes from an infinite supply source. So what's the problem?

With photovoltaics, sunlight is converted to electricity. Essentially what happens is that photons, or particles of light, strike a semiconductor material such as silicon and knock loose electrons, creating a flow of electrons, which is electricity.

The problem is the process isn't as efficient yet as it needs to be to become widely used. For the time being, at best, about 30 percent of the sunlight can be converted to electricity. A more realistic conversion rate for the mass production level is much lower (but your solar-powered calculator only needs about 3 percent efficiency). When you factor in high production costs and maintenance costs of solar cells and/or panels, it's just not worth it in most cases.

But solar cell efficiency consistently improved through the 1980s, and researchers are working with new techniques, materials, and manufacturing processes that could enhance cost-effectiveness, and make photovoltaics a major contributor to America's 21st century energy grid.

From 1986 to 1989 the number of U.S. photovoltaic (pv) shipments doubled as they were used more frequently in consumer products, lighting, and telecommunications. By some estimates, the number of solar cells, modules, and systems shipped in the U.S. could increase six-fold through the 1990s as pv becomes more widely used by electric utilities.

"Continued double-digit annual increases in U.S. domestic and export (pv) sales are projected for the period 1995–99," predicts the Commerce Department, suggesting annual U.S. pv system sales could hit more than $600 million at the beginning of the 21st century.[8]

"The Department of Energy estimates that solar energy systems could be a multibillion dollar market for U.S. firms," according to the National Critical Technologies Panel.[9]

To keep up on the solar energy field:

EPRI Journal
Electric Power Research Institute, Inc.
P.O. Box 10412
Palo Alto, California 94303
415-855-2000

Photovoltaic News
Photovoltaic Energy Systems, Inc.
P.O. Box 290
Casanova, Virginia 22017
703-788-9626

Solar Energy Industries Association
777 N. Capital St., N.E.
Washington, D.C. 22202
202-408-0660

There are not may pure-plays in photovoltaics, but some of the companies that are actively involved are:

Alpha Solarco, Inc. (OTC - ASCO)
11534 Gondola Drive
Cincinnati, Ohio 45241
513-771-1690

Develops photovoltaic and thermal solar products. Alpha is closely affiliated with *Solectric Corp.*, same address as above, which is engaged in the development of a solar electric energy system. Solectric's stock also reportedly trades over the counter.

Alpha's annual sales in 1992 were approaching $2 million and it was profitable.

Photocomm, Inc. (OTC - PCOM)
7681 East Gray Road
Scottsdale, Arizona 85260
602-948-8003

Company was formed in 1988 and employs more than 50.

Photocomm develops, makes, and sells photovoltaic components, and power systems and related products used in telecommunications, water pumping, irrigation, and lighting.

Annual sales are about $11 million.

Solar Electric Engineering, Inc.
116 4th Street
Santa Rosa, California 95401
707-542-1990

Company manufactures solar powered cars.

Its annual revenues, according to most recently available figures, are about $1 million.

Solar Electric's stock reportedly trades very lightly over the counter.

Spire Corp. (OTC - SPIR)
One Patriot's Park
Bedford, Massachusetts 01730
617-275-6000

Company primarily manufactures semiconductor structures and material surfaces using proprietary methods. Spire also makes equipment used in photovoltaic systems, and engages in R&D on materials for use in photovoltaics. About 20 percent of its overall business is reportedly devoted to solar power.

Spire's annual sales are in the $15 million to $20 million range.

(Also see Energy Conversion Devices, Inc. below.)

ELECTRIC CARS

Electric cars were actually being built in the early 1900s. Before they died out in popularity, London had some 10,000 electric cars on the streets in 1910. But it will probably take until 2010 for electric cars to make a reasonable dent in the U.S. market.

The simple fact is not too many consumers want one right now. Despite offering "green," clean, quiet transportation, according to a 1993 J.D. Power and Associates survey, only 6 percent of American drivers said they were definitely willing to buy an electric car.[10] Part of the problem is, as the technology stands today, electric cars can't really satisfy America's need for speed. Most electric autos tool along at *top* speeds in the 60–80 mph range.

Also, they can only go a maximum of about 150 miles before they need a recharging. However, studies show that on an average day, most drivers don't take the car out for more than 30 miles.

Among the other complaints—they're too small, and too expensive. An electric car can cost three times as much as a fossil-fuel equivalent.

The hang-up is battery technology. The batteries cost too much, are too heavy, don't generate enough power for their weight, and each recharging, of which there are many, takes a long time (usually eight to 12 hours).

However, there are some 200 projects around the world to develop the better battery, battery charger, and electric car.

The Big Three—Ford, GM, and Chrysler—along with the U.S. Department of Energy have formed the U.S. Advanced Battery Consortium. It's not that they necessarily want to build an electric car, but they may be forced to because of certain environmental and legal requirements.

California has, in effect, mandated that electric cars be sold there. By law, starting in 1998, two percent of vehicles on the market in California must be "zero emission." That, at this point, essentially translates into electric cars. By 2001, 5 percent of vehicles on the California market must be electric, rising to 10 percent in 2003.

California is usually the nation's trendsetter, and other states have already passed, or are expected to pass similar legislation.

(In 1992, Sacramento, California and Tampa, Florida opened public parking lots where electric vehicles can recharge their batteries with solar-generated electricity.)

CALSTART, a California consortium, is developing a prototype electric car that will incorporate some of the latest in defense and aerospace high-tech. Among the consortium members are GM-Hughes, Intel, Lockheed, and Southern California Edison. The group foresees a potential market of half a million electric cars in California sometime early in the 21st century.

However, according to some people, despite the legal push, the Big Three aren't really serious about building an electric car, and may subtly try to kill the market by pricing electric cars too high. In other words, they can obey the California law by putting a certain amount of electric cars on the market, but if they cost too much and no one buys them, the market dies. (In 1993, GM, for the time being, killed plans to mass produce a two-seater electric car.)

Apparently, one of the reasons the Big Three reportedly aren't too crazy about electric cars is because a high-tech model would not have many parts that wear out and need replacing. Electric cars have less than one-tenth the moving parts of conventional autos. Big Three critics say the only reason Ford, Chrysler, and GM formed the Advanced Battery Consortium is because it's a good way to get government money. If all this is true, the slack may be picked up by Japanese and European auto manufacturers and the 21st century electric car equivalents of Henry Ford and Ransom Olds.

A Swedish company, Clean Air Transport, is investing $40 million to develop an electric car, and it hopes to build 30,000 models a year. It may do assembly work at a California site. In Denmark, there's CityCom, which has already sold 6,000 three-wheeled electric cars. In the Netherlands, the intriguingly-named Maharishi Technology Corp. wants to build electric autos.

In America, there are many privately-held companies devoted to developing, manufacturing, or selling electric cars, or components, or kit plans. Some of the electric cars are converted from regular models. Among the companies:

California Electric Cars, Seaside, California

Clean Air North America, Laguna Hills, California

Clean Air Revival, San Francisco, California

Clean Air Transit, Santa Barbara, California

Clean Air Transport, Los Angeles, California

Cushman, Lincoln, Nebraska

Dolphin Vehicles, Sunnyvale, California

Doran Motor Co., Sparks, Nevada

Dreisbach Electromotive, Santa Barbara

Electric Auto Crafters, Batavia, Illinois

Electric Vehicle Marketing Corp., Dallas, Texas

Electric Vehicles of America, Maynard, Massachusetts

Electric Vehicles Corp., Los Angeles, California

Electro Automotive, Felton, California

Eyeball Engineering, Fontana, California

The Hybrid Electric Vehicle Project, Stanford, California

KTA Services, Orange, California

Kaylor Energy Products, Boulder Creek, California

Nordskog Electric Vehicles, Redlands, California

Performance Speedway (sells), Jacksonville, Florida

Renaissance Cars, Jessup, Maryland and Melbourne, Florida

Solar Car Corp., also in Melbourne

Solar Components Corp., Manchester, New Hampshire

Solectria Corp., Arlington, Massachusetts

Specialty Vehicle Manufacturing Corp., Downey, California

Taylor Dunn, Anaheim, California

Suntools, Fort Bragg, California

Triple 'O' Seven Corp., Everson, Washington

Also, Solar Electric Engineering, mentioned above under photovoltaics, is reportedly planning to produce an electric van in conjunction with publicly-held Consulier Engineering, Inc. (OTC - CSLR) of Riviera Beach, Florida, 407-842-2492.

Anyone who tells you the use of solar power, nuclear power, wind power, or the like will break America of its crude oil habit is naive. Crude oil, per se, is pretty much useless. Oil becomes useful by way of being refined into by-products, the main ones being heating oil, gasoline, and other transportation fuels. So, unless somebody can show me a car that effectively runs on pluto-nium, uranium, or windmills, America will still need a lot of oil.

Electric cars alone won't necessarily help the oil or pollution problem, because charging up all those batteries would just force utilities to use more fossil fuels. In fact, some claim that with current technologies, total emissions are higher with electric cars than with conventional ones. So it will take a widespread, cross-industry alternative energy approach to reduce America's reliance on oil.

For more on electric autos:

Alternative Transportation News
Earthmind
P.O. Box 743
Mariposa, California 95338
408-336-5026

Battery & EV Technology News
Business Communications Company, Inc.
25 Van Zant Street
Norwalk, Connecticut 06855
203-853-4266

CALSTART
3601 Empire Avenue
Burbank, California 91505
818-565-5600

Center for the Biology of Natural Systems
Queens College
Flushing, New York 11367
718-670-4189

Electric Auto Association
2710 St. Giles Lane
Mountain View, California 94040
1-800-537-2882

Electric Vehicle Association of the Americas
20823 Stevens Creek Boulevard
Cupertino, California 95014
408-253-5262

Electric Vehicle Industry Association
P.O. Box 59
Maynard, Massachusetts 01754
508-897-6740

EV Insider
Earth Options Institute
6030 McKinley Street
Sebastopol, California 95472
707-829-4545

Electric Vehicle News
1911 North Ft. Myer Drive
Arlington, Virginia 22209
703-276-9094

Electric Vehicle Progress
Alexander Research & Communications, Inc.
215 Park Avenue South
New York, New York 10003
212-228-0246

I couldn't find any pure-play electric car manufacturers. In the U.S., they're all private (see above), or divisions of the larger car companies. (But see Consulier Engineering above.)

I will give mention to:

Energy Conversion Devices (OTC - ENER)
1675 West Maple Road
Troy, Michigan 48084
313-280-4808

Company develops "amorphous" materials for various industrial uses, primarily in the energy and information industries. Its energy products include *solar cells* which attempt to maximize light absorption and efficiency. It also engages in superconductivity research.

Through its Ovonic Battery Company subsidiary, it is developing a battery that could be used for electric vehicles.

In 1992, Ovonic was awarded an $18.5 million contract from the U.S. Advanced Battery Consortium to develop its nontoxic battery, which could allow a small electric car to go 300 miles before needing just a 15-minute recharge. Also, Ovonic's technology could accelerate that car from a standing start to 60 mph in eight seconds or less, and would allow the EV to achieve a maximum speed of 100 mph.

Energy Conversion Devices, which employs about 150, had annual sales for 1992 of about $15 million.

INTELLIGENT VEHICLE-HIGHWAY SYSTEMS (IVHS)

Women make the claim that men never ask for directions when they get lost driving. That purported difference between the sexes may become a quaint 21st century anecdote, because in the future it might be impossible to get lost on the road.

Stop worrying about gridlock and start thinking about the pleasures of symbiotic streets — smart cars, smart highways. IVHS will essentially allow drivers, cars, and highways to interact electronically. The Batmobile won't have much on the smart car of the 21st century. Imagine sometime in the near future you're driving around strange territory looking for a specific location. You give your car a voice command, tell it where you want it to go. On a dashboard screen, a "you-are-there" type of digital-electronic map is displayed, showing the location of the car, your destination, and the various best routes to it. As you drive along, the position of the car changes on the map. The car can talk you through the drive, telling you when to turn until you reach your desired spot. The same car will be equipped with various safety devices — smart back-seat drivers — like radar-type equipment that can warn you of impending haz-ards or if a collision is imminent, or computerized systems that can override a slow-reacting driver and take control of the car if an emergency situation arises. In time, if you want, you'll be able to sit back and enjoy the ride, because safe, self-driving cars will be possible.

The asphalt below won't be the same either. Just as cars will be aware of their surroundings, roads will be aware of traffic. The highways of the future will be set up with cameras, sensors, monitors, radio transmitters, and infrared beams which, when used along with satellite monitoring, will keep track of traffic and relay the information either to your car, or to some sort of central traffic control, where road traffic would be diverted to optimum alternate routes, the way an air-traffic controller does now with planes. It's possible that on busy freeways, groups of cars will be "platooned" — controlled to travel at equal speeds, equidistant from one another.

The upshot of all this — fewer injuries and deaths, less pollution, less grid-lock, less time and money wasted.

It's estimated that the loss of productivity from traffic tie-ups costs the U.S. about $100 billion annually, and deaths from traffic accidents add another $130 billion every year. If nothing is done about traffic congestion, it's been estimated vehicle delay hours will increase 350 percent from 1985 to 2000.

For the fiscal years 1992–1997, the U.S. Government approved more than $600 million for the development of IVHS, which is really an amalgamation of technologies that include satellite sensing and navigation, electronics, telecom-munications, sensors, and computers.

Reprinted courtesy *OMNI* magazine, © 1993.

IVHS programs are already being developed and tested on roads in New York State; Orlando, Florida; Chicago; Richmond, California; and, of course, Los Angeles. Dozens of other U.S. IVHS test projects are being set up. Europe and Japan are also developing and experimenting with IVHS.

It's estimated that more than $200 billion will be invested in IVHS deployment to 2012, with most of that spent by private industry and transportation consumers.[11]

Privately-held companies like San Diego, California's *IVHS Technologies* and its subsidiary *Vorad Safety Systems* develop radar systems for cars that Greyhound is installing on its buses. *Etak Inc.* (owned by Rupert Murdoch's News Corp. — NYSE - NWS) of Menlo, California makes digital maps for navigation systems. Germany's Siemens and Robert Bosch GmbH, and Holland's Philips are at the forefront in developing an aspect of Continental-style IVHS. In Japan, Pioneer Electronic Corp. and Nissan are leaders.

Large, publicly-held U.S. companies that are actively involved in some form of IVHS R&D are: AT&T (testing on a New Jersey turnpike an acoustic-detection system that can distinguish a car from a truck from other vehicles), Chrysler, Eaton (NYSE - ETN), E-Systems (NYSE - ESY), Ford, GM-Hughes, Lockheed, Motorola, Pacific Telesis (NYSE - PAC), Rockwell, TRW, and Westinghouse.

Amtech Corp. (OTC - AMTC)
17301 Preston Rd.
Dallas, Texas 75252
214-733-6600

Amtech is a smaller company that makes various hardware and software products and electronic auto I.D. tags that could be useful in IVHS.

To stay on top of IVHS, contact:

IVHS America
1776 Massachusetts Ave., N.W.
Washington, D.C. 20036
202-857-1202

PERSONAL COMMUNICATIONS SERVICES OR SYSTEMS (PCS)

It's not quite the Dick Tracy two-way picture wrist-radio, but with PCS — something like advanced mobile phone service, but cheaper — it seems we're inevitably headed that way.

PCS's basic piece of equipment will most likely be a pocket-size, cordless phone that will cost less than conventional cellular phones and will reportedly allow those who can't afford those expensive mobile phones to essentially have the same type of service. But the big difference, and the big drawing card for PCS, is that each PCS user will have a personal phone number, independent of location. In other words, a telephone number is associated with a person rather than a place.

If someone needs to contact you, it doesn't matter what area code you're in, you'll still have the same phone number. Even if you're in the outer reaches of the rain forests, all the person trying to reach you has to do is dial "your" number and they'll get you, no matter where you are. PCS means direct one-to-one communication regardless of geography. In time, other services besides voice will be added, like data, faxing, and perhaps video.

The initial main customers for PCS will probably be sales reps, tourists, traveling executives, and the on-the-go self-employed. But *an industry group expects 40 million PCS subscribers by 2002. And "A.D. Little predicts 50–60 million PCS subscribers generating revenues of $35–40 billion beyond current levels in the United States by 2010, and an equal number of subscribers in the rest of the world."*[12]

The Federal Communications Commission has granted experimental licenses for PCS and is in the process of determining where to allocate radio frequency bandwidth for PCS in the already-crowded communications spectrum. Congress wants to establish auctions to determine which companies become players in PCS.

"Ultimately, PCS is expected to have a profound impact not only on the future telecommunications network, but also the U.S. manufacturing base, employment, and society," says the Commerce Department.[13]

PCS consumer products could make their first appearance in 1994.

On a related note, in early 1993, six U.S., Japanese, and European companies formed the General Magic consortium to develop hand-held devices that are hybrids of telephones and computers. The group wants to create new personal communications products and, in effect, set the standards for them. Consortium members are AT&T, Apple, Matsushita, Motorola, Philips, and Sony.

Also, companies like Apple, AT&T, Compaq, Franklin Electronic Publishers (OTC - FPUB), GE, Hewlett Packard, IBM, Microsoft, Motorola, and privately-held EO Inc. (Mountain View, California) are developing so-called hand-held personal intelligent communicators or personal digital assistants. PDAs are essentially a combination of phone, computer, electronic notepad and organizer, diary, and fax.

With a PDA you'd be able to send and receive electronic mail, messages, or faxes, and make phone calls. Any information you'd want to store or send could be jotted down on an electronic screen with a stylus in your own handwriting—the units would contain handwriting-recognition software.

(In mid-1993, the AT&T-EO 440 went on sale—the first electronic, pen-based computer. About the size of a hardcover book, the 440 can fax, send electronic mail, and can be used as a cellular phone. The cheaper version goes for about $2,000, the more expensive model for $4,000. Also in the summer of 1993, Apple's *Newton* became available, and initial sales were brisk.)

The market for PDAs is seen hitting more than $7 billion by 1997.

As stated earlier, Congress wants to enact legislation to establish auctions for PCS. So it's difficult to determine which publicly-held companies will be among the leaders, but they could include:

Allen Group (NYSE - ALN)

ALLTEL (NYSE - AT)

Andrew Corp. (OTC - ANDW)

Arch Communications (OTC - APGR)

Associated Communications (OTC - ACCMA)

AT&T

Audiovox (ASE - VOX)

The Bell Regional Companies

Cellular, Inc. (OTC - CELS)

Cellular Communications (OTC - COMMA)

Centennial Cellular (OTC - CYCL)

Century Telephone (NYSE - CTL)

Cincinnati Bell (NYSE - CSN)

Comcast (OTC - CMCSK)

Contel Cellular (OTC - CCXLA)

Ericsson (OTC - ERICY)

Fleet Call (OTC - CALL)

GE

GTE

Lin Broadcasting (OTC - LINB)

Lincoln Telecommunications (OTC - LETC)

McCaw Cellular (OTC - MCAWA)

MCI Communications (OTC - MCIC)

Mobile Telecommunications Technologies Corp. (OTC - MTEL)

Motorola

Northern Telecom Ltd (NYSE - NT)

Page America (ASE - PGG)

PageNet (OTC - PAGE)

ProNet (OTC - PNET)

Rochester Telephone (NYSE - RTC)

Rogers Cantel Mobile Communications (OTC - RCMIF)

QUALCOMM (OTC - QCOM)

Southern New England Telephone (NYSE - SNG)

Sprint (NYSE - FON)

Tele-Communications, Inc. (OTC - TCOMA)

Telephone & Data Systems (ASE - TDS)

U.S. Cellular (ASE - USM)

Vanguard (OTC - VCELA)

Vodaphone (NYSE - VOD)

Considering the large number of possibilities, and that the PCS field still has to shake out, it would be a good idea to contact the Personal Communications Industry Association to keep up with PCS:

Telocator
1019 19th Street N.W.
Washington, D.C. 20036
202-467-4770
    or

The National PCS Consortium

For information contact:

Telmarc Telecommunications Inc.
265 Franklin Street
Boston, Massachusetts 02110
617-261-6335

INVESTING IN THE
TECHNOLOGIES OF TOMORROW

Some scientists blamed it on the Great Galactic Ghoul.

In the summer of 1993, NASA announced it had "Lost all communications contact with the Mars Observer." The U.S. spacecraft, in its final swoop toward the Red Planet after a journey of millions of miles, had mysteriously disappeared.

Some perfectly rational people accused NASA of a hoax, claiming the Observer, which would be able to take photos of the planet's surface that were 50 times clearer than any other, would reveal irrefutable evidence of alien structures and artifacts on Mars.

(David Letterman said the Observer disappeared because NASA didn't use 'The Club'.)

But it was certainly something else. Simply, the technology failed. Even with NASA's best minds working on it, single-minded scientists with a common goal, all that cutting edge technology against the vastness of time and space was nothing but a will o' the wisp.

Simultaneously, down on Wall Street, stocks were hitting new highs. The Dow, for the first time ever, breached 3600. But as these words are being written, investors are bracing for that dread time for the stock market, October, a month when so much money has disappeared with the finality of the Observer.

It's like that with technology, investments, and the future. No guarantees.

And yet . . .

About the same time the Observer vanished, Russia and the United States signed an accord which would essentially put an end to Cold War-type competition in space. The former rivals would explore the stars together. Despite many

Reprinted courtesy *OMNI* magazine, © 1979

setbacks to NASA, there seems to be an inevitability to the human race's move away from the lonely cradle of Earth, and an inevitability to the technological progress that evolution will generate.

Also, through the summer of 1993, it seemed there was almost a self-fulfilling inevitability to the progression of many of the technologies mentioned in this book. As one scientist said about the Information Superhighway, like some field of dreams, "If you build it, they will come."

It was as if every magazine, newspaper, and TV news show at some time did a piece on virtual reality, or photonics by way of interactive multimedia, or a gene being discovered that was associated with a disease. At the movies, box offices in the summer of 1993 exploded open with a cautionary tale about genetic engineering and killer dinosaurs, and closed with another 'promising' vision of the 21st century called "Fortress."

Perhaps at times through a glass darkly, partial outlines of early 21st century technology and society appear to be taking shape.

I remember seeing some words once by a Russian cosmonaut who said something along the lines that when we move beyond this planet and settle other worlds, we will have to come up with a new word, something like nostalgia, to describe that poignant sensation we'll feel when we miss Earth. As we hurtle into the 21st century, we may eventually need new words to describe what we feel for the 20th century. It may be akin to longing, it may be good riddance. I guess it's all relative, and depends on what unfolds in the coming century. Certainly, we will need new words to describe emerging technologies of the next millennium.

Where do we go from here? I don't know. But in the past few years, the Berlin Wall has crumbled, the Soviet Union's disintegrated, the Cold War ended, and, very recently, Israel and the Palestine Liberation Organization signed what was essentially a peace treaty. Perhaps the table is being set for something better. In any case, as an investor, you must be an optimist by nature. You are a time-traveler, and as you make the journey from one century to another, you have no reason to not be positive about your technology investments.

But reserve a part of yourself to deal with any Galactic Ghouls.

INTRODUCTION—MONEY, MADNESS, AND THE MILLENNIUM

1. Barry McGuire, "Eve of Destruction," (ABC) Dunhill Records, 1965

2. Muntzer account from Norman Cohn's *The Pursuit of the Millennium*, NY: Oxford University Press, 1970, pgs. 247–248

3. *New York Daily News*, November 24, 1991

4. Account from Charles Berlitz's *Doomsday 1999 A.D.*, Doubleday, 1981, pgs. 10–13

5. Quotes from Barbara Tuchman's *A Distant Mirror: The Calamitous 14th Century*, NY: Ballantine Books edition 1979, p. 25

6. Ibid., p. 122

7. Interview with author

8. Ibid.

9. *Omni Future Almanac*, World Almanac Publications, 1983, p. 279

10. Schneiderman, Leo, *The Psychology of Social Change*, Human Sciences Press, 1988

11. Cohn, op. cit. p. 122

12. *Omni* magazine, January 1990, p. 83

13. Paul Hoffman, editor in chief, *Discover* magazine, November 1988, p. 4

14. *Omni*, July 1984, p. 87

15. U.S. Department of Commerce, "Report of the National Critical Technologies Panel," March 1991, p. 1

16. *New York Times,* February 23, 1993, p. A1

17. U.S. Department of Commerce, "Emerging Technologies: A Survey of Technical and Economic Opportunities," 1990, p. 5

18. Ibid., forword

19. Marvin Cetron and Owen Davies from *The Futurist,* Sept./Oct. 1991 – Adapted from their *The Crystal Globe: The Haves and Have Nots of the New World Order,* St. Martin's Press, 1991

20. Pentagon quoted in the Department of Defense's (DoD) "Critical Technologies Plan," 1991, Ch. 1, p. 2

21. Kiplinger, Austin and Kiplinger, Knight, "America in the Global 90's," Kiplinger Washington Editors, 1989, p. 218

CHAPTER 1—SUPERCONDUCTIVITY

1. Alan Schriesheim, director–Argonne National Laboratory, quoted in Superconductor Applications Association release

2. Dr. Bill Graham, Chairman XSIRIUS, Inc. in interview with author

3. Eric Goldman, analyst with the Equity Group, in interview with author

4. Dr. Roger Poeppel, group director–Argonne National Laboratory, in interview with author

5. "What Do Venture Capitalists Think about Superconductivity?" Coopers & Lybrand, 1989, p. 8

6. From Council on Superconductivity for American Competitiveness report, "Superconductivity in the 90's: From Curiosity to Commerce"

7. Schriesheim in speech to the Achievement Awards for College Scientists, March 1988

8. In interview with author

9. MRI industry size from Department of Defense's "Critical Technologies Plan," Ch. 19, p. 3

10. From American Superconductor Corp.'s 1993 annual report, p. 4

11. Commerce, "Emerging" op. cit., p. 41

12. Defense, "Critical" op. cit. Chapter 19, p. 16–17

13. Interview with author

14. Strategic Analysis, Inc. report "Superconductivity: The Business Opportunity"

15. Interview with author

16. Coopers & Lybrand, op. cit., p. 3–4

17. Ibid., pgs. 4, 8

18. Defense, "Critical" op. cit., Chapter 19, p. 2

CHAPTER 2—VIRTUAL REALITY

1. Gibson, William, *Neuromancer,* Ace Books, 1984, p. 51

2. *CyberEdge Journal,* May/June 1993, p. 4

3. Interview with author

4. Courtesy Dr. John Latta, 4th Wave, Inc., Alexandria, Virginia 22306

5. Interview with author

6. Interview with author

7. Interview with author

8. Numbers from *The Wall Street Journal, Technology Supplement,* April 6, 1992

9. Quoted in *Wired,* July/August 1993, p. 100

10. Interview with author

11. Interview with author

CHAPTER 3—ROBOTS

1. "Doom" account from *Robotics,* Omni Publications, edited by Marvin Minsky, 1985, (*The Machine Servant,* Richard Wolkomir, p. 219–220)

2. Quoted in 'Managing Automation,' Thomas Publications, June 1992 special edition, 'Robots and Machine Vision Make a Comeback'

3. Commerce Department, "U.S. Industrial Outlook, 1993," p. 16–5

4. *Robotics,* Omni Publications, op. cit., ('Man Makes Man,' T.A. Heppenheimer), p. 31

5. Interview with author

6. *Robot Times,* Winter 1992, p. 4

7. Figures from Commerce, "Outlook," op. cit.

8. Ibid.

9. Figures courtesy Market Intelligence Research Corp./Frost & Sullivan, executive summary 'Resurgence of Robots in the U.S.,' December 1991

10. 'Managing Automation' op. cit.

11. *Robotics Today,* First quarter, 1992, p. 7

12. Commerce, "Critical" op. cit., p. 33

13. Ibid., p. 39

14. Commerce, "Emerging" op. cit., p. 35

15. Commerce, "Critical" op. cit., p. 35

16. OTA, "Making Things Better: Competing in Manufacturing"

17. "Technology: The Engine of Growth," Clinton/Gore team, p. 13

18. Clinton, Bill & Gore, Al, *Putting People First,* Times Books, 1992, p. 13

19. Defense, "Critical," op. cit., Section 3, p. 4

20. "Managing Automation," op. cit., p. 5

21. Commerce, "Emerging" op. cit., p. 40

22. Market Intelligence Research Corp./Frost & Sullivan, executive summary, "World Machine Vision System, Component and Software Markets," July 1992

23. Interview with author

24. Interview with author

25. *National Service Robot Association News,* Summer 1992, p. 2

26. Interview with author

27. Commerce, "Outlook" op. cit.

28. Interview with author

CHAPTER 4—ARTIFICIAL INTELLIGENCE

1. Engelberger, Joseph, *Robotics in Service,* MIT Press, 1989, p. 99

2. Interview with author

3. Commerce, "Emerging" op. cit. p. 32

4. Quoted from "74 Trends That Will Affect America's — and Your–Future," an abstract of their book *American Renaissance: Our Life at the Turn of the 21st Century,* Marvin Cetron & Owen Davies, St. Martin's Press, 1989

5. Commerce, "Outlook," p. 26–38

6. Figures courtesy H. Newquist, The Relayer Group, Scottsdale, Arizona

7. Interview with author

8. Ibid.

9. Figures courtesy Colin Johnson, Cognizer Co., Portland, Oregon

10. Interview with author

11. Interview with author

12. Courtesy the Relayer Group

13. Ibid.

14. Kurzweil, Raymond, *The Age of Intelligent Machines,* MIT Press, 1990, p. 21

CHAPTER 5—MIRACLE MATERIALS

1. Defense, "Critical" op. cit., p. 18–3

2. Commerce, "Critical" op. cit., p. 9

3. Suppliers of Advanced Composite Materials Association and the United States Advanced Ceramics Association — "Recommendations & Initiatives on Implementing President Clinton's National Technology Policy," March 1993, p. 1

4. "Advanced Materials & Processing: The Federal Program in Materials Science & Technology," preface

5. Ibid., p. 5

6. Commerce, "Emerging" op. cit., p. 30

7. Interview with author

8. Ibid.

9. Ibid.

10. Commerce "Critical," op. cit., p. 26

11. Defense, "Critical," op. cit., p. 18–3

12. Ibid., p. 18–5

13. Commerce, "Critical," op. cit., p. 26

14. Ibid., p. 25

15. SACMA & USACA, op. cit., pgs. 1 & 3.

CHAPTER 6—PHOTONICS, OPTOELECTRONICS, AND FIBER OPTICS

1. Quoted at the International Intermedia Conference, San Jose, California April 1993

2. Interview with author

3. Interview with author

4. Ibid.

5. Defense, "Critical" op. cit., p. 61

6. Ibid.

7. Commerce "Outlook" op. cit., p. 29–12

8. Corning 1992 annual report

9. Commerce "Outlook" op. cit., p. 29–12

10. From CNN report, 2/23/93

11. Wire service report, 4/13/93

12. Figures from Commerce, "Outlook" op. cit.

13. Interview with author

14. Interview with author

15. IBM press release 7/29/92

16. Defense, "Critical," op. cit., 6–1

17. Ibid.

18. Commerce, "Critical" op. cit., p. 60

19. Commerce, "Outlook" op cit.

20. Commerce, "Emerging" op cit.

21. Courtesy Frost & Sullivan/Market Intelligence, Mountain View, California, from executive summary report "World Fiber Optic Sensor Market," April 1993, p. 1

22. Quoted at International Intermedia Conference, San Jose, California, April 1993

CHAPTER 7—HIGH-TECH MEDICINE

1. Interview with author

2. Baxter 1992 annual report

3. Commerce, "Emerging" op. cit., p. 38

4. Interview with author

5. Interview with author

6. Battelle study from "Business & Health," January 1992

7. Commerce, "Critical" op. cit., p. 90

8. Commerce, "Outlook" op. cit., p. 44–2

9. Ibid., p. 44–4

10. *Wall Street Journal,* March 3, 1993, p. B8

11. Ultrasound figures from UMI/Data Courier abstract of an article that appeared in *Modern Healthcare,* April 6, 1992

12. Quoted form the July 19, 1993 issue of *Business Week,* (p. 51) by special permission. © 1993 by McGraw. Hill, Inc.

13. Figures reprinted by permission of Standard & Poor's (S&P), "Industry Surveys," August 20, 1992, Healthcare, p. 42

14. Estimate from *Business Week,* January 11, 1993

15. Figures reprinted by permission of Standard & Poor's, op. cit.

16. "The Laser Marketplace 1992," The International Society for Optical Engineering, 1992, p. 21

17. Figures reprinted by permission of Standard & Poor's, op. cit., p. 40

18. Figures from UMI/Data Courier abstract of an article that appeared in *Health Industry Today,* November 1992

CHAPTER 8—BIOTECHNOLOGY/GENETIC ENGINEERING

1. Quoted in Office of Technology Assessment (OTA) report, "Biotechnology in a Global Economy," Forword

2. Crichton, Michael, *Jurassic Park,* Ballantine Books, © 1990 by Michael Crichton. Reprinted by permission of Alfred A. Knopf, Inc., p. 67

3. Interview with author

4. OTA quoted in Commerce Department's "Report of the National Critical Technologies Panel," p. 85

5. OTA, "Global" op. cit., p. 97, from Industrial Biotechnology Association report, 'Biotechnology . . . in Perspective'

6. OTA, "Global" op cit.

7. Ibid.

8. Commerce, "Outlook" op cit., p. 43–8

9. Interview with author

10. Commerce, "Critical," op. cit., p. 83

11. Figures from Commerce, "Emerging" op. cit.

12. OTA, "Global" op. cit., p. 43, quoted from *Forbes* magazine, Sept. 1980

13. Reuters wire report, Aug. 19, 1992

14. Quoted in *U.S. News & World Report,* Nov. 4, 1991, p. 64

15. Interview with author

16. OTA, "Global" op. cit., p. 74, quoting M. Montague, research operations director, Monsanto Company, in a personal communication, Dec. 1990

17. OTA, "Global" op. cit., p. 97

18. Ibid., p. 129

19. Ibid., p. 32

20. Burrill, G. Steven and Lee, Kenneth B., *Biotech '92: Promise to Reality,* Ernst & Young, 1991, p. 9

21. Interview with author

22. OTA, "Global" op, cit., p. 50

23. "What Do Venture Capitalists Think About Biotechnology?," Coopers & Lybrand, 1990, p. 9

24. Ibid.

25. Ibid.

26. Ibid.

27. Interview with author

28. Burrill and Lee, op. cit., p. 9

29. Ibid., p. 10

30. Genentech 1991 annual report, p. 28

CHAPTER 9—MILLENNIUM MISCELLANY

1. OTA quoted in Commerce Department's "National Critical Technologies Panel Report," op. cit., p. 67

2. Commerce "Emerging" op. cit., p. 34

3. Figures from Battelle Europe study quoted in *Business Week,* April 26, 1993, p. 92

4. Figures from Commerce "Outlook," 1993, p. 27–1

5. Commerce, "Emerging" op. cit., p. 37

6. Commerce, "Critical" op. cit., p. 65

7. Commerce, "Outlook" op. cit., p. 18–5

8. Ibid., p. 18–7

9. Commerce, "Critical" p. 110

10. From CNN report, May 10, 1993

11. From "IVHS of America" brochure

12. Commerce, "Outlook" op. cit., p. 29–2

13. Ibid., p. 29–10

INDEX